HARLEY AND ME

HARLEY AND ME

Embracing Risk on the Road to a More Authentic Life

BERNADETTE MURPHY

COUNTERPOINT • BERKELEY, CALIFORNIA

Library of Congress Cataloging-in-Publication Data
Names: Murphy, Bernadette M. (Bernadette Mary), 1963-
Title: Harley and me : embracing risk on the road to a more authentic life /
Bernadette Murphy.
Description: Berkeley, CA : Counterpoint Press, 2016. | Includes
bibliographical references.
Identifiers: LCCN 2015046428 | ISBN 9781619025974 (hardback)
Subjects: LCSH: Murphy, Bernadette M. (Bernadette Mary),
1963–Travel–United States. | Middle-aged women–Travel–United States.
| Women motorcyclists–United States–Biography. | Middle-aged
women–United States–Biography. | Motorcycling–United
States–Psychological aspects. | Middle-aged women–Psychology. |
Risk-taking (Psychology) | Self-actualization (Psychology) | Authenticity
(Philosophy) | United States–Description and travel. | BISAC: BIOGRAPHY
& AUTOBIOGRAPHY / Personal Memoirs.
Classification: LCC CT275.M778 A3 2016 | DDC 305.244/2–dc23
LC record available at http://lccn.loc.gov/2015046428ISBN

Cover design by Gerilyn Attebery
Interior design by Neuwirth & Associates

Counterpoint
2560 Ninth Street, Suite 318
Berkeley, CA 94710
www.counterpointpress.com

Printed in the United States of America
Distributed by Publishers Group West

10 9 8 7 6 5 4 3 2 1

For Jarrod, Neil, and Hope.
Though parents are supposed to raise their children,
in this case, you three have raised me.

And for Emily Shokouh, my sister in crime.

CONTENTS

NOTE TO READER

The phrase *look, lean, roll* originates in a motorcycle safety class. When making a turn on a motorcycle, the whole process goes against every natural instinct. You don't turn the handlebars in the direction you want to go; rather you first look in the direction you wish to move, then lean your body mightily in that direction—even when you're sure that such a lean will cause you to fall over. Finally, you roll the throttle to give the bike more gas to recover from the turn. In the midst of the most difficult parts, it feels as if something is horribly wrong, yet leaning hard into the turn is the only way to go. If you try to be conservative and commit only halfway, you will fail to complete the turn. The riskier the turn feels, and the more you're certain you cannot possibly make it, the more you have to fully tilt into it.

Then turn on the gas.

The secret of life is to have a task, something you devote your entire life to, something you bring everything to, every minute of the day for your whole life. And the most important thing is—it must be something you cannot possibly do.

—HENRY MOORE

HARLEY AND ME

Only those who will risk going too far can possibly
find out how far one can go.

—T. S. ELIOT

The day is finally starting to soften with the onset of evening as a storm assembles to the southeast. The sun has been scorching my retinas all day and is just now starting to dim. I've been riding my motorcycle more than eight hours today, winding first through the stunning canyons of Utah, veering into Idaho for a bit, and now entering the spectacular open range of western Wyoming. My forearms are leaden; my shoulders sag. I vaguely remember the tasteless lunch I ate hours ago, but now I'm hungry. The air is hot, even hotter inside the road armor I'm wearing. I am saddlesore and this is only day two.

Rebecca and I are trekking by motorcycle from Los Angeles to Milwaukee and back, a sixteen-day, five-thousand-mile adventure, the first extended road trip for either of us. We originally met in the mommy realm, room parents together at the small, parochial grade school our kids attended. Now, our children are mostly grown and both of us have only recently left long-term marriages. Having fled the cocoon of the suburban world we'd long inhabited, we find ourselves at midlife, crossing the country on motorcycles, unsure of the road ahead but determined to move forward anyhow.

Before we left, we faced questions to our sanity and the opposition of loved ones. "You're packing heat?" asked Levi, one of the salesmen at Harley-Davidson of Glendale, more a statement than a question.

No, we aren't packing heat. We are packing Lärabars, ibuprofen, lip balm, and hair scrunchies. We're two women eager to see the country on motorcycles, aware that we don't know jack about what we're doing and that we might need to depend on others along the way. Still, we're tentatively confident we can navigate what lies ahead.

Day two seems interminable. How could it not yet be nighttime when we've been going and going for so long that we are well past all reserves of endurance we thought we possessed? For this early leg of the journey, we've joined up with a couple we know from home. Edna and George, both seasoned cross-country riders, take the lead. Their presence emboldened us to leave the main highway earlier today east of Salt Lake and take a more scenic but lightly traveled route to Jackson Hole. We filled our gas tanks thirty minutes ago in a tiny town, a cluster of thickset, adobe buildings that seemed to be holdovers from the late 1800s. Since then, we haven't encountered a soul.

We are still an hour and a half out of Jackson. My body gives off a pungent tang of sweat and my hands have lost feeling from grasping the clutch and brake levers all day. I dream of pulling off my stiff road pants, stripping the layers of salt-glazed shirts and underthings, then treating myself to the soothing comfort of a bath. That will be followed by a meal, a real sit-down meal not ordered from a takeout window. We will rest our tired bodies while crunching chips with salsa and waiting for our tamales to be served. Or spoon up spicy Thai goodness. Or chow down on veggie burgers and sweet potato fries. The type of food doesn't matter, only its promise.

The monotony of the road has become so hypnotic it takes me a moment to realize that Edna has pulled off to the shoulder. Rebecca slows behind her. George and I turn our bikes and head back to see what's up. A fringe of prairie June grass forms wispy boundaries on either shoulder of the empty highway. Crows call out and the wind sighs. The magnificent nowhere of Wyoming takes away my breath.

Getting off the motorcycle, little explosions of pain detonate in my hips and back. My joints feel fused by so many hours crouched on the frame of the bike. Twisting the full-faced helmet from my sweat-drenched head is an amazing relief, as is the abrupt lack of vibration and the now-silenced roar of the pipes. Riding all day and then stopping is like stepping off a boat and being instantly aware that the swell of the waves has ceased. I locate my supply of trail mix from the pack strapped to my sissy bar before I go over to investigate.

Rebecca edges next to me. Edna has a flat, she says. The front tire.

That doesn't sound so bad. A call to the Auto Club and we'll be on our way again. But George is already dialing his cell phone and unable to get service. Rebecca tries hers but the screen shows zero bars.

The situation begins to take on new clarity. Unlike a car, Rebecca explains, a motorcycle flat is not an easy roadside fix. We obviously aren't carrying spares, and a tow truck driver will not be carrying one either. Besides, changing a motorcycle tire is like surgery. If repairing a car flat is an outpatient procedure, with a motorcycle, we're talking organ transplant. There's no question: Edna's bike will have to be flatbedded to a town.

That is, if we can get a cell phone signal to call for help.

George carries a Harley road guide and asks Rebecca to look for the nearest dealer that can provide motorcycle service while he continues trying to connect with the Auto Club. Soon, she's shaking her head. There isn't a single Harley service department within a hundred-mile radius.

Rebecca, George, Edna, and I sit on the soft, raised shoulder, sharing trail mix. A fence runs parallel to the road, tilting and collapsing in places, breaking down from neglect. It's obvious no cattle have grazed this plain in ages. The motorcycle pipes and cylinder heads tick as they cool. Shadows from the cotton-white clouds mottle the landscape. Scanning the 360-degree-countryside, it's all sky and grasslands, everything vast beyond comprehension. Not a car or another soul in sight. I've been backpacking to remote peaks in the High Sierra out of reach of cell phone service and any human convenience. But that was by intent. This was not part of the plan.

We consider our options. Rebecca and I can ride until we get a cell phone signal. Or we can all stay together and hope one of our phones will pick up a signal soon. Meanwhile, the inky clouds to the southeast tumble in our direction; a curtain of rain pelts the low hills in the distance. We all carry rain suits but are not anxious to try them out.

As we debate possibilities, a loud crack splits the silence. It sounds more like the compact, ballistic report of a rifle than the rolling clap of thunder.

We look to George. Was that a gun?

"Could be hunting season," he speculates, eyebrows lifted. "Or maybe there's a shooting range nearby."

The sharp cracks come more frequently. Multiple shooters. Whoever they are, they seem to be moving closer.

We all go by certain assumptions that we live in a largely civil, law-abiding society. Still, it's hard not to flash back on the final scenes of *Easy Rider* with its denouement of casual, explosive violence against the free-spirited, live-and-let-live cross-country riders. But that was only a movie, right?

Right?

I glance at Rebecca for an assuring look that will confirm I'm overreacting. But her widened eyes and the taut set of her jaw tell me she's frightened, too.

It comes back to me how casually I dismissed Levi at the dealership and his earnest assumption that we were "packing heat." Did he understand something about the open road we've blithely dismissed?

I again turn to Rebecca. We had agreed we do this trip together. Now what?

The exhaustion has so drained my reserves that I no longer trust my judgment. I am hungry, sore, and running well past empty. Am I crazy to be here in the first place? Sitting on the side of a road in the middle of nowhere, we watch the storm on a direct path toward us, while each volley of gunshots gets closer and louder. How in the world did I get to this place? And why?

STARING INTO THE EYES OF THE BEAST

◎

> In life, it's rarely about getting a chance,
> but about taking one.
>
> —ANONYMOUS

For some, it starts with a smile from a gorgeous stranger across a room, eyes hooded and enticing, an attraction that cannot be denied. Think Anna Karenina or Madame Bovary. For others, a website for a mountain-climbing expedition keeps calling you back, baiting, tempting you, a thrum underneath daily life that won't go away. *This is crazy!* you think, but continue returning to the web page or the stranger's eyes, staring, daydreaming.

The desire for excitement is sometimes little more than a whisper. You can't explain it, but you've always wanted to swim with dolphins, or learn to speak Mandarin. Thelma and Louise started out on a simple road trip, a weekend getaway. Maybe you'll begin to awaken when you finally sign up for that oil painting class. Or take those singing lessons. Or buy those ballet slippers.

Or maybe, you just get so damn tired of being scared by life that you decide to stare down the beast and challenge it.

For me, the beast is a motorcycle.

• • •

"So, there's an opening for the Rider's Edge class that starts tomorrow night," my close friend and running partner Rebecca says one hot Wednesday in August.

I have only mentioned in passing my very slight interest in taking the motorcycle safety class Rebecca's dealership offers. It's a complete fluke she even remembers. Rebecca has recently taken over ownership of the Harley dealership her father founded thirty-five years earlier. On our regular runs, we discuss everything: our kids, stubborn issues involving parents or siblings, our troubled marriages, our careers, our dreams and desires. We have bonded by a need to experience life more fully, to step out of our roles as mothers, wives, and women to pursue a future for ourselves unburdened by stereotypes and preconceptions.

During one of our runs, I mention I'm doing research for a novel. Wouldn't it be fun to write a female character who rides a motorcycle? I can pump Rebecca for information about bikes. But if I also take the class, I'll be able to describe the experience with more authority.

I have no idea that saying yes to this course will completely upend my life.

The next evening, I find myself in the Harley-Davidson Rider's Edge class: three nights in the classroom and two full days in the saddle of an actual motorcycle. I figure I'll learn how to do this one quirky thing, have a funny little anecdote to share at cocktail parties, and have enough information to write my character. For one weekend, I will live a tiny bit on the edge. After that, I can pull back into my safe zone.

In the midst of the second Rider's Edge class, my cell phone vibrates. I ignore it. The group of eleven students and I are standing around a large sheet of paper taped to the wall with a stick-figure sketch of a motorcycle. We draw slips of paper from a helmet with words like *throttle, rear brake, speedometer,* and *clutch* on them, taking turns identifying where those components are located. I correctly identify the turn signal cancel switch and feel a little jolt of excite-ment—I'm starting to get it—when the phone vibrates again. I pull it from my back pocket to check who's calling so insistently.

It's my brother, Brendan. I excuse myself to step into the hallway and take the call.

"What's up?" I ask.

"Dad's worse," Brendan says, "and I can't take this much longer. I was here last night and I'll be here again tonight, but I'm at the end of my rope. We'll need someone to stay with him Saturday night and Sunday, too. Can you set up something?"

We've all been taking turns visiting and staying with Dad, who's in home hospice care. He's ninety, has bile duct cancer, and lives an hour away from any of us. My stepmother, Jean, eighty-two, has been getting no sleep. Since Dad needs to be physically lifted during the night to use the bathroom, the men from the family have been staying over with him, while my sister and I are out there regularly, helping however we can.

I make calls for the next ten minutes, standing in the hallway, missing class, arranging for family members to take turns staying the night with Dad.

I return to the class and try to pick up the lesson. I force myself to concentrate, but one question repeats: What the hell am I doing in a class to learn how to ride a motorcycle while my father is dying?

After class, I call my friend Kitty.

"This is insane, isn't it? I should just drop everything and get out to Dad's house."

"You've been out there every chance you can," she says. Maybe you need a distraction."

"Maybe . . ."

"There's no knowing how this will unfold," she continues. "When you get quiet inside, what do you feel you need to do?"

"I don't know. I haven't felt quiet inside lately."

"That's your first job, then. Let everything settle inside and see how you feel."

It won't be until later, when I immerse myself into the brain chemistry of risk taking and examine the changes that happen at midlife—in our brains, in our bodies, in our psyches—that any of this will start to make sense. At first, I will think I'm crazy. Because on the face of it, I have been making some pretty harebrained choices lately, acting as if I'm someone other than whom I know myself to be. Which is, simply put, a chickenshit.

I grew up in a household where chaos could erupt at any minute, turning all my plans head over heels before breakfast time. As an adult, I developed a serious obsession for routine and order. Everything had to be planned out in advance. Before any trip, my suitcase was ready at least a day ahead of time; I packed a house a week before the movers arrived. I had contingency plans for contingency plans. I hated to do things if I don't know I'd be good at them. I'm totally averse to meeting new people or venturing outside of what is comfortable. Heights, especially, freak me out. I am the woman who, as a young mother, became so terrified of exposed elevations that I crawled on hands and knees backward down the four hundred steps of Moro Rock in Sequoia National Park; I kept imagining my children, who had dashed ahead with their father, plunging down that one-thousand-foot rock face. I avoid any situation where I cannot be in complete control.

So what explains my forays into backpacking and mountain-climbing in the High Sierra that began few years ago? Though I still may be found cowering at the top of a twelve-thousand-foot pass, feeling the vertigo of all that distance between me and the ground, the desire to climb those heights somehow supersedes the stomach lurching that comes when I reach their summit. Somewhere along the line, the draw of adventure became stronger than my fear.

The same was true with running. I am asthmatic and spent most of my childhood incapacitated by bronchitis and pneumonia, restricted from PE and any activity that would make me breathe hard. But after I got in mountain-climbing shape a few years ago, I wanted to maintain my gains over the winter months, so I started slowly trotting around the local high school track. Run half a lap. Walk half a lap. Rebecca often ran with me. And I was the one who always said I hated running! After months of early-morning workouts, we entered our first 5K, a Turkey Trot on Thanksgiving, before we headed back home to prepare the family feast. Then we signed up for a 10K. A year later, we'd signed up for half marathons. Within two years, we had trained and completed the full 26.2 miles.

And now: a motorcycle class.

I am not a physically imposing person, slender with bird bones and Olive Oyl arms. And yet I find myself drawn to these challenges, all of which raise serious doubts about my abilities. Each requires a kind of risk: to move out of my comfort zone and experiment with activities that scare me.

Yet, as I master each step along the way—running my first mile without stopping, or carrying a forty-pound backpack for four days over elevation gains of several thousand feet—I feel a rush. Is it endorphins? Adrenaline? Self-esteem? Whatever it is, I am hooked.

This physical realm seems to be the only one where I can exert some control these days. After years of trying to manage my children, my spouse, my household, and my work, the old control-freak ways no longer work. When I give up trying to control the people and circumstances around me, though, I'm left facing myself, alone.

I sit quietly as Kitty suggests, and I see it: My life feels deadened. My children are nearly grown and need me less. My marriage has felt empty for years. I thought that when the kids got older, J and I might rekindle the closeness that had originally brought us together. I see now how unlikely that is. My skin feels bruised, chafed with the sadness of it all.

Oddly, these physical pursuits with their elements of risk seem to ease this discomfort. When I feel unsure of my ability to master a new scenario and yet persevere, new vigor and energy flow, a sense that my life might not be as predictable as I thought. I am still capable of surprising myself, of learning something new about my life. Because, let's face it: My life is not working out the way I had planned. But maybe there's a chapter about to open that I didn't know to anticipate. Maybe there's a different life to discover, making its way toward me.

I also feel a little foolish because, at my age, taking these risks makes absolutely no sense. It's utterly illogical. There is no reason for me to learn to ride a motorcycle, no reason to topple the entire structure of my adult life. Perhaps the fact my father is dying has something to do with it. That, on top of the need to escape the pain of a sad marriage. It's just a distraction; that's what it is.

Why do seemingly normal people like me do risky, difficult, sometimes impulsive things when there's no real payoff, no financial reward? Nothing tangible is at stake. No reason to put one's life on the line. No prize, not even a cookie.

According to evolutionary scientists, risk taking is part of everyone's DNA—some of us more than others. We take risks because biologically we're programmed to, because it benefits our species. Sociologists find that risk taking is a common trait across all cultures. One theory focuses on the most evolutionarily ancient part of our brain, known in lay terms as the reptilian brain—that portion of our neural system that controls survival and reproductive instincts. This is the part of the brain that impels us toward risk. That impulse is aided and abetted by brain chemicals, particularly endorphins, those feel-good, naturally produced opiates the brain releases in response to imminent physical danger.

If we look into our ancient history, the pattern is present from the get-go. Early risk takers were probably the nonconformists. Those likely to explore new trails might have found fresh resources for the tribe, or those who tried to do things differently may have invented original tools or weapons or eaten something no one had ever tried before, thereby discovering a new food source. Because these activities would benefit the whole tribe, those who succeeded with their risks were both lauded as heroes and flooded with pleasant brain chemicals, which produce a high often compared to sex. When we are in danger, certain biological changes occur. Whether that danger is produced by circumstances beyond our control or at own hand doesn't matter to our bodies; it's all risky business at the cellular level. The heart speeds up and breathing quickens as the threat looms. When danger passes, we experience deep feelings of release and relaxation. A sense of power, momentary invincibility, a catharsis of sorts.

It's a potent brew.

• • •

I follow Kitty's suggestion, sitting silently for twenty minutes. After, I feel revitalized. I've made a clear decision: Unless I feel a definite prompt to run out to Dad's house, or am asked to help, I am going to stick with the class.

By deciding to take the motorcycle class, I realize I'm after something more than an organic high. I want to remind myself that I am strong and capable. I've been taught that I should be afraid of big, muscular things like motorcycles. As a woman, I've been programmed to believe I'm too delicate emotionally and physically to handle a machine so demanding. Some part of me knows that's not true. I *can* do things that frighten me. In doing so, I hope to discover I am strong enough to survive the approaching loss of my father, the only real parent I've ever known.

• • •

I drive the fifteen minutes from my home in the suburban foothills into the city, looking for the Costco/Best Buy parking lot. Hidden behind these superstores is an even larger parking lot used by Glendale Harley as its training range. My fellow students gather near a large metal storage building with a rigged-up sunshade. Three lines of four motorcycles each are queued up and waiting. My heart hammers. I've spent the past two evenings doing the book-learning part necessary, but somehow I didn't think about this next step—actually getting on a motorcycle. I've got to ride one of those damn things.

I examine my fellow students. The three other women in the class are outfitted in Harley gear—leather jackets, black half helmets, tight-fitting sequined tank tops, and kick-ass boots. Our faces are going to be enclosed in helmets in ninety-degree weather, yet two of the women are wearing makeup. The guys are almost as decked out. Most wear boots and leather jackets. The youngest guy in the class—who has yet to touch the starter button on a bike—has just bought a designer leather jacket along with a $400 helmet already wired with Bluetooth. The corporate-looking guy from Santa Monica, who confessed last night that he was taking this class while his wife is out of town, is carrying a new modular flip-up helmet. If his wife finds out, he says, she's going to kill him. I wonder where he plans to hide his helmet.

And me?

In baggy men's Levi 501s, a stained T-shirt, gardening gloves, and hiking boots, I look more like a hired hand than a biker chick. At this moment, I'd love a pair of killer motorcycle boots.

I pick out a helmet and our instructors, Mario and Kathie, review the safety rules and then assign us each a bike. We will be riding Buell Blasts, yellow or black, 492-cc bikes manufactured by a division of Harley, the standard trainers for first-time riders in this course. The plastic bodywork pieces covering the bikes are made from Surlyn. It's a substance used on the outside of golf balls, which gives some idea of the kind of beating they are intended to take. The side-view mirrors have been removed and the taillights are cheap plastic expected to be replaced. They say there are only two kinds of bikers in the world: those who have put down a bike and those who are waiting to do so. (This is not comforting.) I am assigned a black motorcycle, number sixteen. Finally, we are told to mount our bikes.

I've ridden on the back of a motorcycle before. In my late teens, I dated a guy with a Honda Rebel and rode around L.A. and up and down Angeles Crest Highway, a twisty mountain road notorious for the number of motorcycle accidents there. The sheriff's department Life Flight helicopters practically run a shuttle between the winding crest and the trauma centers down on the flats. No helmet, no safety gear. Those were the days before California's mandatory helmet laws. I was young; I felt nothing bad could happen. I was lucky, but now I am too old to believe myself invincible.

But riding by myself? Not a passenger but the driver?

I swing my right leg over the saddle and sit. When instructed, I turn the handlebars to straighten the wheel. I lean the bike to an upright position and sweep away the kickstand with my left foot. I stand, straddling a machine that weighs 360 pounds and rock it gently side to side beneath me. I feel every ounce of the bike's weight and heft, a gravity I didn't expect that makes the hairs on the base of my neck bristle. I touch the starter button, and the engine fires. It seems to want to do whatever I might ask it to; friendly, even eager to please.

There is something mystical about the moment, as if I've been handed powers. I am sitting on this machine that can go—go fast—at my slightest touch. It is intoxicating. And terrifying.

• • •

In our evolutionary history, those who took risks and responded well to the chemicals released by their brains during the ensuring danger lived to take other risks and pass their risk-taking tendencies on to their offspring. And those who didn't succeed didn't. According to Charles Darwin's theory, we can surmise that the successful risk takers survived because they were the "fittest" of our species. The risk taking helped them and the entire species evolve.

Over millions of years the human body has grown so used to taking risk and being rewarded chemically and socially that people go out of their way to expose themselves to risk, though the degree to which we need or want risk varies within each individual.

Women, for instance, are more risk averse than men when risk is confined to a physical realm. This stance makes perfect sense from the perspective of the species' continuation. While men ventured forth, hunting and exploring, women stayed back with the children to care and nurture, insuring the species' survival. I wouldn't have left my children when they were young for anything. No motorcycle, no handsome man, no adventure could have pulled me away. This was not simply a matter of virtue. The chemicals a woman produces while child-rearing, oxytocin and estrogen, almost ensure her risk-averse response.

Cultural conditioning may also play a part in a woman's reluctance to expose herself to physical risk. I was recently challenged to name a book or movie in which a female character embarks on a road adventure without ending up raped or dead. This was harder than I would have thought. Think about it: Thelma and Louise drive off a cliff. There is no female Huck Finn, nor even Sal Paradise and Dean Moriarty (characters from Jack Kerouac's autobiographical novel *On the Road*). Women in road films are rarely driven by a pursuit of adventure—more likely they're in flight from abusive males.

It is in the films we consume and in the stories we read that the stage is set for the choices we believe are available to us. Yet seldom do we question the stories. A few film critics have seen the truth about the male bias in cinematic depictions of road narratives and nail it: "The women are essentially along for the ride, and are not part of what is constantly being redefined as an exclusive male enclave," writes Mark Williams in *Road Movies: The Complete Guide to Cinema on Wheels*. "Time after time, one can detach the females without endangering the structure of the main plot," writes Frederick Woods in the essay "Hot Guns and Cold Women."

The importance of female role models who take to the road, enter the male realm, or engage in other kinds of adventure cannot be understated. Not only do women need to know it's possible to pursue their dreams by watching others. It's just as important for the larger culture to witness her exploits. If a woman undertakes a road trip because she watched a film that encouraged her, or read a book that gave her nerve, great. But if the men she encounters on the road have not seen that film or read that book, they may not have in their consciousness the same idea: that it's okay for women to be on the road. That such a choice is not an invitation to abuse or danger. And that many women want to see the world and experience different ways of being just as much as men do.

But until women are depicted that way in the stories that form our cultural consciousness, very real perils will remain.

Vanessa Veselka, a writer and former hitchhiker, writes about this issue, arguing that true quest is about agency and the capacity to be driven past our limits in pursuit of something greater. "It's about desire that extends beyond what we may know about who we are. It's a test of mettle, a destiny. A man with a quest, internal or external, makes the choice at every stage about whether to endure the consequences or turn back, and that choice is imbued with heroism. Women, however, are restricted to a single tragic or fatal choice. We trace all of their failures, as well as the dangers that befall them, back to this foundational moment of sin or tragedy, instead of linking these encounters and moments in a narrative of exploration that allows for an outcome which can unite these individual choices in any heroic way."

The archetypal stories that drive us as a species—the hero's journey and its many incarnations—either leave women out of the picture, or ask us to mold our adventures onto a male prototype. Or worse, they scare us into inaction with their warnings of failure and violence. Male-driven stories subconsciously limit the options women think we can explore. Where are the heroines' journeys that are life enriching?

Surely, countless other women like me want to engage adventure. But we hesitate for lack of a role model, for lack of a story line that provides a positive outcome, or out of fear of being ostracized or harmed.

One positive role model comes shimmering into the foreground. I speak with Cheryl Strayed, author of *Wild: From Lost to Found on the Pacific Crest Trail*, a memoir about hiking 1,100 miles alone in her early twenties that was recently adapted into a film.

"It was hard," she says of days she spent alone on the trail, dirty, bruised, sometimes lost. "It was physically hard for me to move over that space. I traveled by foot with a big weight on my back. But," she pauses, "it was life changing . . . Once you have had that experience, you never forget that you're capable of giving yourself everything you need and surviving."

• • •

Back on the motorcycle range, we learn to walk our bikes in first gear across the asphalt, pushing them at the end of each lap to turn. And then, before we know it, we're riding. Just little jaunts, but we're moving and our feet are off the ground and on the pegs. My fear has been that I won't be strong enough to keep the bike upright. How will I maneuver a machine that is three times my body weight? But physical strength isn't the key. It's more about agility and coordination, nimbleness and vigilance. And a bit of courage.

When the morning break arrives, we're all jubilant. Everyone figured out how to ride; no one flunked out. Mario and Kathie call us into the shade and ask us to record our thoughts about riding a motorcycle for the first time. I write a sentence or two and then step behind the storage building to call Dad.

For the past two hours, it's been a relief not second-guessing whether I should have gone out there this morning. Attempting something new and scary focused me, crowding out all other thoughts. I talk with my stepmom and hear that Dad is much the same. Very weak. Hardly able to stand, much less walk. I speak to him and tell him I love him. I don't mention that I'm learning to ride a motorcycle this weekend, that I've chosen to do this rash and perilous thing rather than come visit.

And now my brief moment of triumph has been replaced by shame.

• • •

I believe on some level I am a legitimate risk taker. But I don't feel proud of that fact. People generally associate *risk taker* with irrationality and impulsiveness, terms I don't think apply to me, someone regarded by family and friends as cautious and reserved. So who are these risk takers? Am I really one of them?

Risk takers have brains and bodies adapted with an enhanced capacity for dopamine reuptake: Our brains respond more strongly to that chemical than other people's brains. We seek out risk because we experience a more intense and pleasurable response to dopamine than other people. Risk takers are speculated to carry what's called the risk gene, or D4DR, the fourth dopamine receptor gene on the eleventh chromosome, a gene mutation that functions primarily in the limbic portion of the brain. Although one study showed this gene is responsible for only 10 percent of human risk-taking behavior, I feel both indicted and explained by it. I know, without really knowing, that I have this gene.

Risk takes many forms. Surgeons, for example, report the same kind of adrenaline surge during an operation that skydivers and other extreme athletes experience. Musicians, too, are familiar with the flood of euphoric chemicals while performing though no one's life is on the line. Even day-to-day choices like quitting an unrewarding job can rejuvenate a life and instill a sense of excitement. These choices are metabolized in the body with the same rush as jumping out of a plane. Scientists on the cutting edge of discovery regularly risk professional ridicule and humiliation in pursuit of complex research problems. They understand the "exposure" of announcing a breakthrough finding today that may be rejected and possibly mocked tomorrow. Charles Darwin waited twenty years after he developed his theory of natural selection before he finally published *The Origin of Species.* He understood the controversial nature of his findings. The gamble of going public with the suggestion that humans descended from apes was enormous. In fact, in some settings, it still is today.

Undoubtedly the risk Darwin felt was greater than my experience coming out as a biker chick in suburban Los Angeles at age forty-eight. Still, my feeling of vulnerability and exposure may not be any less intimidating.

• • •

A month after I pass the motorcycle safety class, I receive my M1 endorsement from the DMV on my driver's license. A month after that, death arrives. After sitting by my father's bedside for a week, going home at night to grab a few hours' sleep, praying for his peaceful passing, feeling awe and frustration at how the body hangs on by its cracked and bloodied fingernails long after the spirit has begged for rest, I get the call at 5:00 AM.

I drive, numb, to his home in Thousand Oaks. I bathe his life-less body with the help of the hospice nurse, startled at how small and shrunken he has become, this man who in life both adored and terrified me, reduced now to a cooling, fleshy bag of bones. When the mortuary men put him on the gurney, I ask them to wait a few minutes while I touch his face, hold his hand, whisper my good-bye.

The next day, I walk into the Harley dealership and buy myself a two-year-old all-black Sportster Iron 883 motorcycle. An example of grief made manifest? Absolutely. It is also a fullhearted embrace of life.

- CHAPTER TWO -
IZZY, MY LOVE

One can choose to go back toward safety or forward toward
growth. Growth must be chosen again and again; fear
must be overcome again and again.
—ABRAHAM HAROLD MASLOW

That night, I lie in bed tormented over the $8,000 used Harley parked in my garage, taking up space that might otherwise be filled with my Honda Civic. What is *wrong* with me? I will call Rebecca tomorrow and beg her to take it back. I am not a biker. I am a mom. A suburban mom. This is grief talking. I am coming completely unhinged.

Given my family history, these are not thoughts I take lightly. My mother was severely bipolar. She spent most of my childhood hidden away in her bedroom, medicated into a stupor, or institutionalized and undergoing shock treatments. I have struggled my entire life to ensure I don't follow that path. I feel as if I'm treading dangerous waters.

Resisting the impulse to call Rebecca and return the bike, I do research instead. I make phone calls. Carl Lejuez, a psychologist at the University of Maryland and an expert on addiction, reassures me. He tells me that risk is a good thing.

And the downside? I ask.

It takes only one bad judgment in any kind of risky situation, he says, and "you're toast."

See: I *am* treading on thin ice.

He tells me to take heart. The fact is most people are overly protective and risk averse. The field of psychology mostly focuses on pathologizing risk, looking at all the ways risky behavior can create problems. Scientists don't tend to study what's useful about it. And that's a shame, because risk taking can be an enriching and important part of life.

He tells me about BART, the Balloon Analog Risk Task, a computer game used to assess a person's capacity for risk. The player in goggles sees a cartoon balloon on a computer screen and presses a button to inflate the balloon. As the balloon gets bigger, the player accumulates money or points. But when the balloon pops, the player loses everything. The player can cash out at any time before the pop. The idea is to see how big the player will inflate the balloon before it bursts.

Most people are not willing to take on a healthy degree of risk, he explains. They're not expanding the balloon far enough to find the balance between risk and benefit. They cash out far too soon. As a species, he says, we have become much too conservative. This trend is especially notable as we age.

"If you think about transitions in other parts of life," Lejuez explains, "there's always new things. You go to a new school, you get your first job, you have your first child. I'm not saying everyone does all those things, but in life, up to middle age, there's always another transition, there's always something to knock you off balance and keep you smart."

We usually grade someone's success at midlife by how well they've removed all these types of transitions. And that, he says, is unfortunate. You've now landed in a safe spot and you feel comfort. The very success and prosperity you strived for becomes a double-edged sword. Risk taking, though, forces you to have transitions, to not always know the answers. It forces you to wake up and think that maybe something will happen today that is totally unexpected. Because by middle age, we don't usually have those days anymore.

The day-in, day-out process of midlife, especially for those who crave novelty and sensation, will start to feel deadening. "At first you think: *Wow! This is success!* And then you wake up one day and think, *What the fuck just happened? I thought this was what I wanted and I'm actually feeling less alive than before,*" Lejuez says.

The benefits of risk taking are operative whether the risk is physical—rock-climbing, BASE jumping, hang gliding—or not. Financial, emotional, spiritual, and creative risk can all provide the same stimulation. As a species, we often focus on physical risk because it's so tied to our biological need to persevere and continue life. But emotional risk can be even more influential because it keeps us healthy and sharp. It can hurt more than physical risk, too, as anyone who's ever had a heart broken can attest.

"We get to a certain point in life when we don't make mistakes anymore. We don't have negative consequences. Negative consequences are seen as bad things. But think of all the growth we go through when we're younger and how good it feels when you grow through things."

Lejuez explains the "learned industriousness theory," a way of thinking about resilience and perseverance. When bad events happen to us and we persevere, eventually the bad event goes away. The hard work that led to getting through it is what gets rewarded and reinforced.

"At a biological level, some people learn that effort and hard work and trying something new actually starts to feel good, because in the past, those behaviors were associated with what got them through something hard." If you're trying new things and taking risks, all that effort is getting rewarded. "Not only when they work out, but especially when they don't and then you keep at it until you get them to work out. The exertion and hard work make you feel more alive, as if you've been given another chance to learn and grow at a time in your life when, if you don't want to learn and grow any more, you don't have to.

"There's a famous saying," Lejuez says. "Middle age is when our waists expand and our mind shrinks."

• • •

Until this point in my life, I never felt a great affinity for motorcycles, never harbored the desire to learn. In fact, when my middle son Neil bought a motorcycle as a college freshman, I was apoplectic, utterly opposed. I railed about the danger of accidents. But when I signed up for that five-day class and found myself sitting on an asphalt training range atop a 492-cc motorcycle, I experienced a kind of giddy delight I had never previously known. Ever.

Add to that the loss of my last surviving parent. Heartrending, but also liberating; all parental expectations were finally buried with my father. Then there's the existential awareness of being the next generation up to bat. No more buffer between me and death. This is it. What I make of my life is in my hands and mine alone. I do not want to die blaming others for what I haven't done. I do not want my final days stained with regrets.

By learning to ride this motorcycle, I am utterly bewitched, all but seduced into an affair with steel and leather and speed, an affair as surprising as if I had fallen for an unlikely man, James Dean with dreamy eyes, slicked-back hair, and an air of defiance.

That is part of the attraction: the fact I never knew I could feel this way.

The experience opened the door to so many life changes I'm glad I had no way to know what was coming. I might have turned back right then. My story of transformation, of skin shedding, is emblematic for many women.

Women in midlife now face a set of issues different than our mothers did, and unlike what our daughters will encounter after us. Our uncertainties are different, too, from those that men face at midlife. Men might question their career choices or take up a new sport; some will buy sports cars and have affairs. Others will turn to hobbies or activities that give them pleasure and distraction as they settle into a quieting season in life.

Our mothers might have chosen to take on volunteering at a hospital, returning to school, or reviving a neglected career once the nest emptied. My own mother didn't live long enough to face those choices, but I saw friends' mothers grapple with these options. Some were trapped in the rut of their own maternal role; they couldn't seem to envision a life apart from spouses and children. Even as a young child, I couldn't help but believe there was so much more for them to discover. But they aged and in some cases went to their graves with their inimitable, irreplaceable selves still suppressed under a thick layer of estrogen, trapped within societal norms and the need for acceptance.

But for those of us in midlife—both those who have raised children and those who haven't—we might be asking ourselves if we wish to continue on the same path now that our career has been established or the children have embarked on their own lives. Perhaps we're aching to try something new or maybe we're questioning marital choices we made early on—how did I end up here?—weighing the chances of creating a better relationship with someone new, versus working on the relationship we're in. Or simply striking out on our own.

Though the questions assume different guises, ultimately they are the same for all of us: mothers, daughters, friends, partners, women and men alike. Have we done with our lives what we'd hoped to? If not, what can we do about it in the time remaining? Now that the struggling stage of earlier adulthood has passed, how do we place ourselves on the path of authenticity? And how, exactly, do we take the calculated risks that will make us feel absolutely, richly, uniquely ourselves?

• • •

It's delightfully cool this January morning, five months after I bought the motorcycle. It has taken three months for me to hazard a quick jaunt for an exit or two on the freeway, and a few more months before I can comfortably ride anywhere alone. By now, though, I am starting to feel in command of this brawny machine.

This morning, fog snakes through the streets of our neighborhood. The top of Verdugo Peak half a mile to the south is a ghost image of itself, barely an outline. Mountain lions and bobcats have recently been sighted there. Last fall, a California black bear strolled across our front lawn.

Yet we are part of the urban landscape, too, officially in the city of Los Angeles with skyscrapers visible from this vantage point. I will have to keep my eyes peeled for the coyotes that prowl our streets at dawn and dusk for prey.

We live at the margin of wild and tame.

Into this fog-shrouded morning, I prepare to enter. First, jeans, the ones with the "snake bite" burns on the inner right ankle from getting too close to the tailpipe when I first test-rode this motorcycle and hadn't learned to place my feet wide on the pegs. Then tall, wicking socks designed for backpacking, followed by twelve-inch leather boots with slip-proof soles and a left toe reinforced for shifting. Just walking in the boots gives me attitude. I feel like Wonder Woman or maybe Batgirl. A T-shirt is next, followed by a jacket with body armor.

Dressed like this, helmet in hand, I no longer look like myself. For the hour or so I plan to ride this morning, I will shed that old identity to become only a body with a set of skills, a person in sync with a precision machine, eating up miles and feeling a very distinct version of joy, the closest I can imagine to what it feels like to fly.

I open the garage door and the morning's sleepy trance is broken by the overhead light: harsh, too much. As my eyes adjust, I see her, the object of my love. Izzy. A three-year-old Harley-Davidson 883 Sportster Iron with Thunderheader pipes and a Screamin' Eagle exhaust. Matte black rim to rim, the stock chrome pipes traded out for soot-black tubes. Sleek: a black leopard. No saddlebags or encumbering accessories. Her solo seat gives a clear message: On this journey, there's no room for anyone but me. She's one retro-looking badass bike.

I speak quietly, asking her to be gentle with me. I run my hand the length of her leather seat, thrilled each time I touch her, each time I remember she's mine.

When I pull on my full-face helmet, my breath circles audibly inside the hermetic bubble covering me. This is the moment when fear gathers itself and reminds me of what I'm doing. I slow my respiration, hearing each exhalation in the sealed space as I wrestle with my body's sympathetic nervous system, that part of the autonomic nervous system that regulates the body's unconscious actions. Every cell in my being is calling out the flee-or-fight command as it recognizes that I am about to take my life in my hands. My preprogrammed instinct for survival wants me to go back into the house, back to where things are safe. My amygdala, that almond-shaped mass of nuclei located deep within the temporal lobe that is part of the limbic system, joins the act. This is the part of the brain that manages many of our emotions and motivations, particularly those related to survival. My amygdala starts screaming for me to do something, anything, other than what I plan to do next.

As a result of this unconscious biological programming, my heart and breathing begin to race. I consciously work to slow them, knowing that I need only to get past the fear to find freedom. Pulling on my leather gloves, adrenaline forces a line of sweat down my side, inching along my rib cage despite the cool morning.

Riding a motorcycle has always been a pleasant experience. But preparing to ride is another thing. My insides rebel. I start coming up with reasons why I shouldn't do this, primary among them the fact that I wish to live. I say a prayer to the god of motorcyclists to watch over me. And I mount Izzy.

The fear doesn't leave; it keeps tickling the back of my skull, making my hands a mite unsteady, my heart a jackhammer. But I know it will quiet. A mile or two in, like the big bad boogieman that fear is, it will eventually slink back into its corner and wait for another chance to frighten me into a smaller, quieter life.

• • •

What happens when we step out of what's predictable? Can our lives be enlarged just as our careers are finally on a set path or the kids go off to college, when it feels as if there are no more surprises to come? I have to ask myself: What is happening in my brain, in my psyche, in my personality that compels me to seek out scary, risky experiences?

Certainly I'm learning a few things: First, that the motorcycling is not an end in itself, a risk for risk's sake, but rather a pathway to a more authentic life, an unearthing of my own power and fortitude. Second, when I try something new, my capacity to learn and grow leaps geometrically; I feel empowered and alive. No material possessions, no amount of money, can buy that; I have to create it. Third, it's important to let others see me when I'm learning and failing and struggling and scrambling. No one on this planet has it all together. Yet we spend so much time thinking others are somehow better off, understand deeper, have mastered life in a way we never will. When I let others see me try and fail and try and fail better, we all grow. I expand in that I more fully accept myself, and those who witness me are perhaps challenged to do the same. Together we recognize a prickly truth about the human condition.

Today, the risk I undertake is riding a motorcycle. For someone else, it might be exploring a museum for the first time, or reading outside the familiar realm, or sharing honestly with a friend on a deeper level. Learning to cook a new dish presents its own set of risks, as does signing up for a class at the local university, or taking singing lessons.

I toggle the engine kill-switch to its "on" position, waiting for the lights to tell me Izzy's ready. When I thumb the ignition button, she rumbles deep and throaty. Five hundred and fifty pounds of metal come alive, all but begging me to rev the engine and let her run.

Lifting the kickstand with my right foot, I press down on the shifting peg with the ball of my left foot and feel the satisfying *clunk* of first gear. I twist the throttle gently while letting out the clutch and roll at low revs away from the house, a courtesy to my family and neighbors who probably don't want to be awakened this early on a weekend morning. I nearly asked the dealership to trade out the loud custom pipes on this bike when I bought her, thinking I was more suited to something quieter, more ladylike. But then I was reminded that the exhaust noise is actually a safety feature that would make other motorists aware of me. And besides: "Well-behaved women seldom make history."

Within minutes of leaving the hillside subdivision, Izzy and I are carving along La Tuna Canyon Road, paralleling the rise and fall of the San Gabriel foothills. I am en route to Little T (Little Tujunga Canyon), described on Pashnit, a website of California biking routes, as the place God would ride if he had a motorcycle. Its oscillating "twisties" wind through canyons and over summits, presenting one stunning vista after another.

I pass a few other bikers who obviously share the same idea. They gesture to me with a low-down peace sign. Signaling our kinship, I sign back. Were my bike to break down, one of these folks would undoubtedly stop and help. Were I to pass a biker on the side of the road, I would be compelled to do the same by the bond that unites us.

Riding this morning, I feel genderless and ageless, more a point of consciousness than a person. Identity and all the ways it separates me from others flees in the face of swift movement, immense power, and the conviction I am somehow defying the bear-hug of gravity.

People who don't ride often seem to have trouble getting their head around the idea of a female biker. No, I say, this is not my son's bike. It's not my husband's or my boyfriend's, either.

They also seem mystified that I don't fit any ready stereotype. Motorcycling women in pop culture fall into two general categories: There's the sexy biker chick in skin-tight leather with lots of cleavage. If she isn't on the back of some guy's bike as a kind of accessory, she is nonetheless linked by sexual appeal to male bikers and the sensual aura she brings them. Then there are the Dykes on Bikes–type of women riders, those who subvert mainstream gender roles and who often approach motorcycling with a strong, machisma persona. I like to think I fit neither stereotype. Like most of my sister riders, I am less concerned with the shiny veneer of how I appear than with the twang of experience. Just to get on a bike is to break prescribed gender roles even in this postfeminist age. By taking it one step further, refusing to be constricted by the typecast of the sexy biker mama or the hard-ass butch rider, is to accept one's true sense of self.

I like my motorcycle simply because I like to ride. I like the feel of the wind in my face and the air slamming my chest. As the air temperature fluctuates, I feel more alive, more aware of my surroundings, shivering when I make my way through extended cloud cover, then marveling in the sudden delight of warmth when I hit a patch of sun. I lift my face shield so I can smell the chaparral and notice when it turns to eucalyptus and then to more urban odors. The shifting olfactory experience makes me feel as though I've never really smelled before now: grilled onions near In-N-Out Burger and then roasted peppers by El Pollo Loco. A split lemon in the road fills me with its tangy, pulpy scent. The noxious perfume of burned diesel emanates off to the left. And my favorite, petrichor, that pleasant smell that accompanies the first rain after a long period of warm, dry weather. I like how my helmet squeezes my face so that when I smile, my cheeks jam against the sides of my helmet, making me keenly aware that I am experiencing bliss. I like to shift gears and feel a sense of competence on this machine that so outweighs me. And more than anything, I love the feeling of fear that thrums in my rib cage, coupled with the sense of satisfaction when that fear finally curls up and retracts its claws.

Too much of my life has been eaten up by fear. Too many opportunities missed, worried about how it might look or whose feelings I might hurt or how difficult something might be. I am at that place in my life when a standoff looms: me or the fear. One of us is going to win out and the other will be vanquished, if only for an hour or a day, until the next standoff. But to bow to fear in this moment, I know, is to shrink my life, to contract its borders, to cry uncle.

I want to feel all too alive, to chance encountering the divine. To feel fast and vulnerable, powerful and exposed all at once. I want to truly live while I still have breath within me.

But I'm not always sure I'm able.

Winding through the canyon, I think about the fact that so many of the crises we face in life occur without our approval or consent— illness, death of a spouse, problems with children, divorce, job loss, foreclosure. We have little choice but to endure these hardships. There is scant satisfaction in making it through because we know we never would opt for those challenges had we been given a choice. There is relief at the end of the ordeal and lessons learned, though often little else.

When I voluntarily do things that scare me, though, when I choose to wrestle with the specter of fear, I gain the skills and self-knowledge that will steel me for the next obstacle, the next soul-numbing, bone-crushing time I must face. At least, that's what I hope.

As I ride, I ponder my two-decade marriage and the shell of a rela-tionship it has become. Will I have the strength I need to stand up for the full life I desire? I don't know yet. But I do know this: Nothing so strengthens my resolve as having a regular, intimate encounter with the fear that tries to stifle me, that tells me I am not smart enough, or young enough, or pretty enough, or strong enough.

When I make peace with my fears and take risks of my own voli-tion, I learn the most powerful bit of knowledge possible. Maybe I *do* have what it takes. Joy often hides in the very things I am afraid of. If I can move past my fears, I might see how much more joy there is.

We all wake up in different ways. For me, it's in staring down this fear. In his own case, Lejuez, the addiction specialist, tells me about the tattoo that helped him wake up. "I was thirty-five, which I think for something like this is rather old, when I got a fairly large tattoo on my back. I remember that same kind of feeling: It felt exciting and almost as if I'd lulled myself into some kind of sleep with my life, and that doing something like this tattoo unlocked something else."

Middle age is a good time to consider adding some risk to a life, he says. Many people at middle age feel badly about the part of their inner selves that's calling them to engage risk. What usually happens is that they ignore and suppress it. But the drive is like a steam cooker that doesn't have a release. "And then, all of a sudden, one day, some crazy shit comes out and they do something that puts their family in danger or that's totally reckless because they didn't heed that need early enough."

People often think of adventurers as the ones taking the biggest risks, but Lejuez doesn't think that's so. "Talk to a lot of adventure people and they're like, 'We're not risky at all. We like the adrenaline, but we check everything first. It's that lunatic who comes out here and who doesn't have a plan, who doesn't do it right—he's the one to be concerned with.'"

So the question comes down to this: How do I feed at an early stage the need for risk that's growing inside of me, and do so in a way that is safe and healthy and can bring all the benefits of facing my fears? How can I stop suppressing what's inside me and asking to be nurtured?

• • •

Riding my motorcycle this morning is a way of containing all the contradictions that make for a textured life. It is like the neighborhood where I live. Rugged mountain foothill and part of a big city, a place harboring both wild beasts and domesticated backyard pets. As a female biker, I get to embody numerous incongruities. Doing something that scares me in order to tap into my ever-present well of courage. Being a mother and wife who needs, every so often, to escape the responsibilities that threaten to overwhelm her. And finally, as a female biker who fits no stereotype, I get to be more fully, more completely myself than at any other time.

· CHAPTER THREE ·

DEATH IS CERTAIN, THE HOUR IS NOT

The trouble is, you think you have time.
—MISATTRIBUTED TO BUDDHA,
actual source unknown

Gaining a sense of command and comfort on Izzy was a slow process. She's like an exuberant Great Dane puppy, unaware of her own strength and size. Our partnership took training for us both.

This gradual courtship unfolded over the course of several months and was tempered by more than a few mishaps, during which I questioned my commitment. *Life would be so much easier if I simply quit now.* But then a flash of enjoyment would happen along to keep me trying. Still, the pleasures were vastly outnumbered by the frustrations. I often thought about selling her and putting the crazy-ass motorcycle scheme to bed. Just getting gas for the first time was an unexpected challenge. I had to call Rebecca and have her walk me through, step by step: Always buy premium. Retract the rubber sleeve on the nozzle so it doesn't shut off the gas when the tank is only half full. Carefully monitor the flow to avoid overfilling the tank and drenching the bike in a gasoline bath, something I did more than a few times.

For reasons I didn't fully understand, I wanted, I needed, to gain competence on the motorcycle. Some unconscious part of me must have understood the mess my personal life would soon become. I was going to need these boosts of self-confidence that kept blossoming each time I mastered a new skill. Gaining proficiency operating this formidable machine was shoring up my emotional strength.

At the close of the training class earlier this year, each of us had been asked to write a few motorcycling goals. "1. Learn to ride on the freeway." I wrote. "2. Take an overnight trip somewhere. 3. Ride at night." Then I threw in a fourth, one I was certain I wouldn't fulfill for at least a year. "4. Do the Love Ride."

The Love Ride is an annual fundraising ride sponsored for the past three decades by Glendale Harley-Davidson. The longest-running charity ride of its kind, it attracted fifteen thousand riders each year during its peak as well as a celebrity following. Performers included Lynyrd Skynyrd, Mick Fleetwood, ZZ Top, Jackson Browne, Bruce Springsteen, and Crosby, Stills, and Nash. I remember seeing the bikers riding in formation, filling the freeways of Los Angeles in a seemingly never-ending stretch, roaring in the morning air. Bikers pay an entry fee to ride en masse to a venue, listen to concerts, drink beer, and eat, with all proceeds going to support charities like the Muscular Dystrophy Association. And though rider participation has declined in recent years, it's still an impressive event.

A month after I'm licensed, Rebecca asks if I'd like to help at the Love Ride, working the morning registration table.

"Absolutely."

"And maybe we could ride together," she suggests. Although, as the daughter of a dealership founder who has grown up around the motorcycle culture and been licensed since she was in her twenties, Rebecca admits she's as intimidated as I am by the scale and machismo of the Love Ride.

"I'm not sure I can be ready in time," I stall.

"We can go after the main group leaves," she suggests. "We'll ride at an easy pace. We won't feel pressure to keep up with any of the crazy testosterone guys."

"Maybe," I hazard, realizing I'm starting to get comfortable with the idea.

I practice my freeway skills on the less traveled 210 in the foothills above Los Angeles. At first, I can only summon the nerve to ride one freeway exit to the next. As my confidence expands, I venture two consecutive exits. It's weird to be on a freeway and not inside a car. Having grown up in L.A., I'm accustomed to freeway travel, and yet I've never experienced it like this. I'm amazed and terrified. I can actually look down at my feet and see the little grooves scored into the concrete to disperse the rain.

Eventually I'm able to stay on the freeway for five miles at a time. The wind pounds against my upper body at sixty-five miles per hour and feels like a rogue ocean wave rising to swat me from my precarious platform. I'm certain my hands will be ripped from the handlebars. I hang on with sweating palms as if my life depends on it—because, actually, it does.

Since buying this motorcycle, I've thought about death more than any other time in my life.

In our culture, it's not something we spend a lot of time thinking about: our own eventual death, according to psychologist Robert Firestone, PhD. "All people maintain a belief that they will not die despite conscious awareness to the contrary." Most people spend their lifetimes without a great deal of self-awareness, rarely reflecting on their circumstances, addicted to a lifestyle of form and routine.

"Humans are a meaning-seeking species," he says. When the experience of death is limited or excluded from our thoughts, we deprive ourselves of our human heritage.

This perspective was furthered in a 2012 study by researchers at the University of Missouri. "When Death Is Good for Life: Considering the Positive Trajectories of Terror Management" asserts that "awareness of mortality can motivate people to enhance their physical health and prioritize growth-oriented goals." In other words, when we ponder our own eventual death, good things happen: We're more likely to live up to the positive standards and beliefs we have for own lives. We strive to build supportive relationships. We work toward creating peaceful, charitable communities. And we tend to foster what the researchers term "open-minded, growth-oriented behaviors." Awareness of death, it turns out, is a critical force motivating human behavior.

In this study, American test subjects were reminded of death or a control topic and then either imagined a local catastrophe or were reminded of the global threat of climate change. When the threat was local, people aggressively defended their homegrown groups, and when the threat was globalized, "subjects associated themselves with humanity as a whole and become more peaceful and cooperative," said Ken Vail, lead author of the study.

With real catastrophes, such as the terrorist attacks of 9/11 and the Oklahoma City bombing, he explains, the awareness of death brought some remarkable outcomes. "Both the news media and researchers tended to focus on the negative reaction to these acts of terrorism, such as violence and discrimination against Muslims. But studies also found that people expressed higher degrees of gratitude, hope, kindness, and leadership after 9/11," said Vail.

In another example, after the Oklahoma City bombing, divorce rates declined in surrounding counties. "After some stimuli escalates one's awareness of death, the positive reaction is to try and reaffirm that the world has positive effects as well."

Thinking about death on a daily basis is changing me. I am more aware of time ticking past, of the things I want to accomplish and the limited time frame in which to do so. It's not a morbid fascination or a squeezing of my days, but the opposite. An awareness that adds a kind of breathing room; I'm becoming clearer about my priorities.

That said, fear continues to dog me, but if I don't get too ambitious on any one day, I make incremental progress toward refining my motorcycling skills.

The Love Ride departs from Glendale early one Sunday morning in October. The wall-to-wall thundering column almost a mile long moves up the 5 freeway to Castaic Lake. A party will ensue with bands, booths selling motorcycle gear, exhibits of synchronized motorcycling, contests for the best tricked-out bikes, food, and a big biker soiree. I'm not interested in the party element; I simply want to say I did the ride. Jay Leno is the grand marshal and will lead the pack. Though Leno and other celebrities ride their bikes to the venue, word has it that a trailer transports the celeb's bikes back so the guys can relax and not worry about the return trip after a long day in the sun and probably more than a few beers. But like the ordinary Joe (and Jane) participants, if I decide to ride to the lake, I'll have to get myself back home. Rebecca suggests a plan. We'll both ride our bikes to registration in Glendale. If we feel up to it, we'll ride together to Castaic. If not, we'll take the shop truck to the lake.

The day before the event I set two goals: (1) To ride Izzy the eight miles from my house down to Glendale Harley, negotiating a freeway overpass that terrifies me. I will be following the same route tomorrow morning at 4:00 AM with only my headlamp to light the way. I need to be sure I can make it to the starting point. (2) To pre-ride the route to Castaic Lake to see if I have the stamina for the nearly seventy miles of freeway travel required.

When I tell my husband and daughter my plans, they both give me that eye roll I'm getting used to. I ignore them, pull on my riding leathers, and start Izzy. As I crest over that anticipated overpass where the 134 freeway arches wide and sweeping to meet up with the 5, I back off the throttle. Behind me, impatient drivers honk and swerve around. But I take the high, curving bridge at a pace I can handle and I'm ecstatic when I arrive at the shop. The mechanics there check my tire pressure and assure me I'm set for the ride.

Next, I head up the freeway toward Castaic Lake. I hold tight when cars whip past, the wind thumps my chest, gravel stings my shins, when my breath grows loud inside my helmet as fear spikes and then eases, spikes and eases. My hands freeze in the death clench. I concentrate with laser focus, trying to anticipate drivers that might make sudden lane changes, scanning the road surface for potholes or seams. I keep glancing down at the speedometer to make sure I am going fast enough but not too fast. My foot poised over the clutch, ready to shift into getaway mode. My right hand covers the brake, ready to apply pressure the entire ride. When I pull off the freeway at the exit for the lake, I stop to catch my breath. My ears are ringing. The ride took less than an hour, but the thirty-six miles have exhausted me.

The ride home is less fraught; I begin to settle in. I continue to squeeze the handlebar grips, but my breathing is more regular and my shoulders relax. I pull into a gas station by my house to fuel Izzy before tomorrow's big ride. The tank full, I turn toward home, and that's when it happens. I was warned about this. No biker escapes it. In slow motion, barely moving, the bike's weight gets away from me. I don't know if I'm angled too far to the left, or if I've hit an oil slick on the pavement. Whatever the reason, I panic as Izzy and I lean precariously, ungainly to the left. I try to grab her, to force my will onto her, to make my muscles stronger than her heft. But I fail. Right near the gas station, we're going down and there's nothing I can do to stop it. We slam together into the concrete.

My heart thumps as I jump off the bike, trying to figure out what to do. I try to lift her, but the helmet obstructs my vision. I rip it off and then the gloves. Behind me, a woman chides her husband. "For goodness sakes, help her." A man comes over from where he was pumping gas and helps me right the bike. I'm about to get on and ride away before my damaged ego can get further mangled.

"Maybe you should rest a minute," he suggests. "Have some water."

I sit on the curb in front of the gas station's convenience store. My hands shake. My mouth is dry. It feels as if all my blood has been exchanged for electricity. I am awash in shame. I don't look like the badass biker chick I'm trying to become, but some kind of poseur who can't control this machine, a pathetic girl trying to do something beyond her ability.

This happens to everyone, I remind myself. It's to be expected. It has nothing to do with being female. When my breathing slows, I examine Izzy. Her side-view mirror is bent. The handlebar scratched. Otherwise, she's in better shape than me. Eventually, I wash my face in the bathroom, slurp water from the faucet, and put my helmet back on to ride Izzy home.

• • •

The alarm rings at 3:30 AM. I dress in the dark and ease Izzy out the driveway so as not to wake my husband or daughter. I ride down the freeway, over that daunting overpass. At this hour, no one is around to honk at me. A light rain starts falling, another first. I'm surprised by how little light my headlamp provides. I'm reminded of E. L. Doctorow's quote about writing a novel. "It's like driving a car at night. You never see further than your headlights, but you can make the whole trip that way."

When I pull up to the Love Ride staging area, I show my parking pass and am waved into the secured perimeter. An older biker dude with a long gray beard helps me back my bike into the tight parking space. He can tell I'm a newbie. I join the other volunteers as we set up registration tables, drink strong coffee, and prepare the VIP area for Jay Leno and the other celebs. The fancy riders will be corralled in a separate parking lot, away from the rank-and-file bikers who will fill the entire four lanes of San Fernando Road for blocks. The VIPs will lead the ride, leaving in advance of the ordinary riders by five or ten minutes to make sure they're not caught up with all the rowdies. Rebecca and I, along with the shop employees, will ride up after everyone else has gone. As the cool damp morning breaks, the day becomes a bucking bronco ride, registering riders, herding VIPs, directing news reporters, working credit card machines that malfunction, trying to keep a smile on my face as the crowds swell and people want T-shirts in different sizes. Jay Leno walks through, escorted by Rebecca's father and an entourage. Cast members from *Sons of*

Anarchy and *Breaking Bad* wander, drawing admirers wherever they go. I feel the bass beat from the bandstand through the soles of my motorcycle boots and watch news reporters interviewing attendees.

Eventually, the roar of engines drowns out even the rock-and-roll din—all those bikes fired up at once. The registration area has emptied out. It must be time.

The VIPs have left without my noticing, but the huge crowd along San Fernando Road can probably be heard a mile away as it revs its collective motor. I go to the street to watch. Thousands of motorcycles rumble and start moving slowly, a fat writhing snake of iron and exhaust and noise and leather, a thunderous peloton gaining momentum. The moment feels epic. Goosebumps run up my arms as I watch this choreographed movement of energy and chrome.

Most of the riders are men. Most are on Harleys. A few busty women in heels perch on the "bitch seat." But a handful of women riders pass. I cheer them on. The ranks of motorcycles, like legions of an opposing army, keep coming and coming.

And then they're gone. A hush fills the early-morning street, the sudden absence of music and engine growl palpable. My ears are deafened by the quiet. Discarded raffle tickets and liability-release forms litter the asphalt, along with breakfast burrito wrappers, abandoned doughnuts, and used coffee cups. I return to my post to close down registration.

Rebecca approaches as I eat the peanut butter sandwich packed. I want to be sure I'm not shaky from low blood sugar when it's time to ride.

"I can't do it," she shakes her head. "I'm sorry, but riding is going to take more energy than I have." She arrived onsite at 1:30 last night and will have to see the entire event through, well into this evening. She's worried she'll be too tired to safely make the ride home.

My heart sinks. I'm not going to do the ride, even after yesterday's harrowing trial run. But on the heels of that disappointment is a flicker of relief. I'm not sure which feels worse: that Rebecca's not going to ride or that I'm glad to be off the hook.

"I'll go up in the shop truck," she continues. "You can ride with me if you like. Or you can ride with the employees. They'll keep an eye on you."

I think about going in the shop truck and know I'll be dissatisfied with myself if I take the easy out. I think about riding the motorcycle without Rebecca and I'm scared. I could just take Izzy and head home now. I never needed to go to the lake in the first place. I've already done it once.

I talk with Quentin, the salesman who sold me Izzy. He's been kind and encouraging throughout. But not today.

"Too much testosterone," he says, shaking his head. "You don't need to be messing with that. Just go on home."

His words remind me of being a kid, shooed away by the older boys at the empty swimming pools where we'd ride skateboards. I was usually the only girl. And with his comment, a light switch is thrown and I want to go more than I've ever wanted to do anything. I want to prove that I can ride like everyone else.

I line Izzy up with the employees' bikes, trying to keep my breath steady. Just as we're about to leave, someone gets a message that there's already been an accident. A rider went down on the 5 freeway and now the whole tangle of bikes is slowed up. We decide to take an alternative route to the lake, avoiding the main ride entirely.

The seven of us take off in staggered formation. I'm one from the end. When they bank into the turns, they don't back off the throttle. I try doing the same. (Braking in the arc of a turn on a motorcycle is highly dangerous. You need to gauge your speed and slow, if required, before you enter the turn.) I'm totally getting it. I'm able to keep up.

We fly up the 210 freeway, a living organism made up of seven parts all moving and working together. Watching the back of the rider in front of me, I sense what he's going to do next by the angle of his head and the way he holds his back. Before the leader even puts on his indicator to move over a lane, the rest of us are following suit, smooth and easy, a communication not of words but of telepathy, action, and grace. As we ride, my fear from the morning evaporates. For the first time I feel a deep sense of belonging. I am part of something bigger than me. I experience magic and elegance and cooperation and joy. I have been a loner most my life. This kind of collective, wordless ballet is mystical. Transcendent. For the forty minutes we ride, I am both in sync with the others yet piercingly focused on my own experience, alive to the moment, and acutely present every inch of the way.

We park the bikes at the lake, and the mysticism vanishes the moment we turn off our ignitions. Everyone scatters. In comparison to the ride, the event itself is a letdown. The precision motorcycle drill team is interesting enough and the band rocks the lakeside. Someone is thrown into the lake naked, and others get drunk. Tattoos are inked onto flesh and guys line up to take pictures with the Budweiser girls. Lines for the bathrooms, for the food trucks, for beer, wind through the dry grass. I help out in the T-shirt booth and let Rebecca know I'm leaving an hour before the event ends. I want to get on the road before these thousands of bikes start roaring home.

I join the southbound 5 and settle into a rhythm. I am focused, alert, and remarkably calm. I feel as if I've done something monumental.

At home, Hope, Jarrod, and J ask me about the ride.

"Amazing," I say, stripping off my sweaty safety gear and climbing into a shower. Later, checking the news online to see how many bikers actually participated, my stomach drops. The site reports that two Love Ride participants died on the 5 freeway on the way up. All that time, people were partying and having fun, buying T-shirts, drinking beer, and two people were dead. I've been high-fiving myself over my accomplishment all afternoon, ignorant of this fact.

There's a bad taste in my mouth and I don't know how to integrate this information.

I text Rebecca. She's just learned of the deaths, too. J and Hope are both horrified. I should get rid of the bike immediately. I am appalled that people died today doing something I also did. And yet I can't deny it. I still feel proud of myself for having done so.

In the days and weeks that will come, I will learn more about the deaths, the first fatalities in the nearly three decades of the Love Ride.

The victims were a couple. He split lanes next to a tanker truck, a maneuver that's highly discouraged. His handlebar hooked onto the rear ladder of the truck, pulling them under. I tell myself that such things can be avoided. I'd never lane-split next to a tanker. I don't even know how to lane-split.

But the truth is pounded home again. I am doing something lethally dangerous.

• • •

Two weeks later, I'm still working on my skills. After putting the bike down at the gas station, I've watched videos online to learn how to pick up a motorcycle. To do so, the person backs up to the bike and wedges her butt just beneath the seat and against the frame. Using the strength of her legs, and holding on to the frame with her hands, she rocks the bike again and again until she gains leverage with the rubber wheels pushing against the ground. Eventually, the momentum catches and she's able to stand it up. At least that's how it works in theory. God willing, I'll never need this information, but it's best to be prepared.

I've been told that Little T is a great ride. Its celebrated twisties and sparse traffic make it an excellent place to practice. I zip over there on a mellow Monday.

Soon, I am climbing a mountainous path that's more intense than expected. When I come to an overlook, I hit a wall of air. The Santa Ana winds have been channeling air and gusting throughout Los Angeles. They smash into me just where a vista point opens between mountain passes. I decide to postpone learning on Little T. I pull off and gently turn the bike. I'm barely moving, about to start down the hill, when it happens again. That damn slow-motion thing when gravity takes a hold of the bike and won't give it back. I feel her going. I am going with her. I try to leverage my 115 pounds to right the 550-pound machine. But down we both go. My hands scrape on the gravel. My leg is stuck underneath, bruised. Her mirror is again dinged.

I pull myself out and try to call my son Jarrod on the cell. I know he's nearby and might be able to help. But my phone can't get a signal in this mountainous terrain. I'm only a few miles from civilization and yet completely cut off. I see how I've overestimated my margin of safety.

One car passes. The driver and passengers crane their necks to look and keep going. I try calling again. No luck.

"Okay, girl," I say. "It's just you and me." I back my butt up to Izzy's seat and reach behind to grab her frame.

I squat for traction and start lifting with my rear, rocking her gently. My arms scream and my shoulders ache. I get nowhere. I walk away for a moment, breathe, try calling home again.

"We gotta do this," I tell her. "No one's coming to rescue us." I put my back into it, this time getting into a deeper crouch. I rock and I rock and slowly I start feeling momentum. My grip comes loose from her frame and I grab tighter than ever. "Come on, girl. Come on." I'm yelling now, trying to make this work. And then, it happens. She starts to feel lighter. I can feel her rising. Hallelujah. A little more. Just a little more.

I stand her up and set the kickstand, my arms shaking, my heart thundering. I did it. I picked up a fucking motorcycle. Five hundred and fifty pounds of iron.

The next day, my body will be screaming. My back. My butt. My hamstrings. My quads. Every cell has strained to lift this thing. The aches will eventually pass, but the triumph will be mine.

• • •

My son Jarrod takes the Rider's Edge class and gets his license. Now both my boys and I ride. He graduated college last spring and is living at home again, working at a gourmet café while he searches for a grown-up job. Some days I let him take Izzy to work. Occasionally, he calls as the workday is winding down. "Can I take her to Angeles Crest?"

Angeles Crest Highway is a test piece where fearless young riders in leather racing suits lean sport bikes almost horizontal into curves and record their exploits with Go-Pro cameras clamped onto handlebars or helmets. Similar to Little T, it's a mountain road with twisties and gravel, sometimes the road just a gap between boulders. The Crest is out of my league. Besides, he's younger and braver. I say yes because he asks only to go on weekdays when it's less traveled and not as crazy as on a weekend.

I'm at home on a Thursday afternoon when there's a commotion at the front door. It's Jarrod, wearing motorcycle gear, covered in dirt. He's crying. "I'm sorry," he says, taking off his helmet. "I'm so sorry."

I'm confused. "What?"

"I had an accident. I didn't mean to hurt her."

My heart starts pounding. "Hurt who? Are you okay?"

I get him to sit. Give him water. Strip off his safety gear. The full-face helmet has a horrific scrape from the face shield all the way to the back. His leather jacket is shredded clear through to the armored exoskeleton. He's shaking.

"I was on the Crest. A car. It cut in front of me. The road . . ." he gestures. "Two lanes down to one. I tried to stop. I tried. To brake. There was gravel."

My stomach knots.

He kicks off his shoes; his ankles are bloody. There's dirt in his hair, in his shirt, in his pants. Sand and gravel fall all over the hardwood floor as I assess his injuries. He had shoulder surgery a few months earlier but thankfully he went down on the other side. He's mostly okay. I clean him up.

"It's just cosmetic," he keeps trying to tell me about the damage to Izzy. "I didn't mean to hurt her."

"I don't even care about the bike!" I snap. "I'm just so grateful you're okay."

Eventually, we go to the driveway to assess the damage. *Cosmetic* doesn't accurately describe what I see.

One side is scoured down to the metal. The mirrors are broken, the taillight smashed, the "heavy breather" exhaust torn off the frame. I call Rebecca and she says she'll send a truck tomorrow to collect the bike. I draw an Epsom salts bath for Jarrod. Why did I let him take the bike? Why did I say he could go to the Crest?

In the coming days I'll talk with the insurance adjuster, with Tom, the head of service at the shop, and do some serious soul-searching. My son could have been killed. Or it could have been me on the bike. And though I'm relieved Jarrod is okay, another fact hits home.

My Izzy is destroyed.

Tom was amazed Jarrod was even able to ride her home. Her frame is bent. The brace that holds the fork in place was torn loose in the accident, thereby tweaking the fork. I choke up on the phone when the insurance adjuster gives me the news.

Realizing I'm a friend of the owners, the insurance adjuster scrambles to fix the problem. Eventually, he offers to have Izzy repaired if I'll make up the difference between what the insurance policy will pay and the cost to fix her. That's an extra $2,800 even when Rebecca and Tom agree to charge me only wholesale.

"I know you loved her," Rebecca says, "but you'll always be worrying if something from this accident has made her unsafe. Motorcycling is dangerous even when your equipment is in top-notch repair. You don't want to be harboring doubt on the road."

Everybody is agreed: I should let my Izzy go to the recycling bin.

I know that if Jarrod had been hurt, I wouldn't be concerned in the least about the bike. But Jarrod *is* okay and I am an experiencing a loss that cuts to the core. I feel ridiculous. I'm this upset over a motorcycle?

I'm aware that I sound as if I'm oblivious to the hazards. Why would anyone do this? I've just recounted two deaths and a serious accident involving my son, all of which occurred within in quick succession, each in close proximity to me.

Cheryl Strayed, the Pacific Crest Trail hiker, speaks of risk taking in general. "You say, 'I'm going to do this thing,' and then everyone is telling you the horror stories: about the person who got hurt, who got murdered or whatever. It's far, far more dangerous to get in our cars to drive across town to pick up the kids from school. But people aren't going to tell you about every accident they've ever heard about every time you get in your car."

I try to put her words into perspective, but I know that when I've driven across town to pick up kids from school, I've done so out of necessity. There is no necessity to put my life on the line on a motorcycle. There is no reason I need to replace Izzy.

Except that I do.

I walk into the shop for the first time since the accident and Quentin enfolds me in a hug. The guys there, they get it. I mourn Izzy beyond reason and explanation. This is the grief that tips the balance. I have lost my father and am not done lamenting his passing. I have just begun to see the depths of unhappiness I have sunk to in my increasingly desolate marriage. Grief accretes. With the demise of Izzy, I feel the preciousness of all that I have lost, a sharp thrust of absence and sorrow.

I gather myself up and return home in my car, reduced to four-wheel status for the foreseeable future. Izzy, with her solo seat, with her badass matte-black self, had given me something I desperately needed: myself. But now she is gone.

CHAPTER FOUR

THE BITCH IS BACK

◎

> To love someone fiercely, to believe in something with your
> whole heart, to celebrate a fleeting moment in time, to fully
> engage in a life that doesn't come with guarantees—these
> are risks that involve vulnerability and often pain.
>
> —BRENÉ BROWN

I sit naked in the bathtub sniffling, makeup smudged around my eyes, when J opens the door. He looks at me quizzically. "What's up?"

"I need you to sign us up for couple's counseling," I rasp out, reaching for a soggy tissue to blow my nose. "I can't do this any more."

"Things aren't so bad," he says. "We'll get through this."

"I'm not so sure."

He thinks that whatever is wrong will pass, that this is a phase I'm going through. And clearly, I'm the only one going through it. But night after night, I wake up and stare at the ceiling, feeling alone and alienated and unsure of how to proceed. I feel so distanced from him it hurts. I sleep on the couch most every night. Sharing a bed with someone who feels so far away creates a deep, abiding ache. It's one thing to be alone. It's another to be coupled and awash in loneliness.

It's not the first time we've sought counseling. I signed us up a few years ago when our middle son was diagnosed with an anxiety disorder and needed psychiatric care. The counseling helped a bit with my feelings of abandonment in dealing with our son's illness, but I had not then felt as desperate as I do now. Throughout the marriage I've been the motor behind things: deciding where the kids will go to school, what dentist we'll use, where we'll live, how we'll spend our summers, what we'll eat, how we'll pay for college, when counseling is needed. This time, I need to not be alone making the decision. I ask him to make us an appointment, hoping he'll recognize he's got skin in this game.

Weeks pass after the bathtub conversation. A month, maybe two. I bring up my request again. Eventually, he makes the appointment.

My unhappiness in our marriage first came up more than a decade ago, but after discussing it with J a number of times, nothing changed. I wanted him to acknowledge that our marriage wasn't ideal, that he held as high a standard as I did when it came to our couplehood. Once we were together on that same page, I thought, we'd come up with a plan to improve things. But my concerns were met with blankness, as though my unhappiness did not pertain to him. Sure, our relationship was not great, but whose was?

So I simply stopped mentioning my despair. What's the point in harping if a solution is not to be found? Besides, we were busy raising three children and keeping a roof over our heads.

But this time feels different. I am coming to the end of my rope. I may already be there.

• • •

We talk about the things you talk about in couple's counseling: the need to make time for each other, to go on dates, to partake in activities the other likes. We have both grown so used to doing what we want to do individually, this is a radical shift. He arranges an outing into the city to see a play, and I take his arm as we stroll to the theater. We play Frisbee at the park. I set up a beach day and we pack a picnic for two and bring the dog. I can't see that he's enjoying himself any more than I am.

I feel dead inside. I suspect he does as well.

I believe he views me as a wife and mother, not the interesting, creative person I know myself to be. He acknowledges me for the domestic tasks I accomplish, not for the human being I am. Likewise, I believe J has kept himself locked away in a shell of his own making, that he either doesn't know himself well enough to share that authentic self with me, or he doesn't care to. It's hard to love someone who won't show you himself, and it's harder still to feel another's love when you do not believe you're visible.

We try, but we fail.

Long ago I stopped hoping that the obstacles we faced as a couple might pave a path to greater connection. Though marriage handbooks speak lyrically about how every challenge can be a door to deeper understanding, my experience has been the opposite.

Instead of drawing us closer, moments of deep, frank discussion only push us apart, like the repelling ends of a pair of magnets. We keep digging ourselves in deeper.

The truth is, we're basically mismatched. I'm a writer who cares beyond reason about the written word. J doesn't read—not the literature I'm dying to discuss with someone, nor even my own books and essays that are like children to me. I plan ahead and dream big. He prefers to let things unfold and settles for what life provides. I appreciate quiet and a house that's ordered and simple. He keeps the TV on and favors piles as an organizational strategy. I strive to live within my means. He spends freely with credit cards. All these things might be surmounted, if abiding concern and kindness for the other are at the heart. But kindness and concern seem to have trickled away in recent years.

Still, I try what I've been taught in therapy: using "I" statements, recognizing I'm responsible for my own happiness, trying to be the person I'd like to be paired with. The result is an ever-deepening sense of aloneness.

By the time we make it to counseling, I am unable to picture a different outcome. We remain cordial with each other—to a fault. We're like roommates careful to not piss the other one off. This timbre is in biting contrast to the rest of my life that, in recent years, has become increasingly rich and comfortable and nourishing. I am enjoying the first full-time job I've had in decades, teaching at a university, working with creative writing students. I love spending time with our teenage children and the activities we pursue together: backpacking, hiking, music, discussing books and philosophy, running. I savor the group of friends who surround me, people alert to and interested in the larger world, and who are interesting to me. I feel amazingly blessed to be accepted and loved by so many.

But when I come home and chat with J, I feel empty. We talk about the house, or the dog, or the kids. If there is no domestic issue to discuss, we tell each other about the little stories we read online that day. Our crayon box of conversation topics holds only a few basic colors. The rest of my life is kaleidoscopic.

And while I realize this is truly a "first-world problem," I'm not alone with it. Turns out, this experience of dissatisfaction at midlife has a long history for men and women alike and often shows up in marital discord. In some ways, I'm right on schedule. How many movies have we seen in which a balding middle-aged man suddenly buys a sports car or begins an affair with his younger, blonde secretary? I'm not sure what the tropes are for women: Either we become the nagging housewife or the power-driven corporate woman. Or maybe we have a torrid affair.

What does a real women struggling with these issues in midlife look like?

"Women tend to use their associations and relationships with others to gain identity and self-esteem," I learn from Christiane Northrup, MD, author of *The Wisdom of Menopause.* Home and hearth often matter the most to us, even those among us with high-powered jobs or who have chosen not to marry. Men, on the other hand, derive their identity and self-esteem from the outside world during their prime years: from their job, their income, their accomplishments and accolades. But nothing stays stagnant.

"For both genders, this pattern often changes at midlife," Northrup writes.

In an ironic role reversal, women at midlife begin to direct their energies toward the world outside the home and family, perhaps for the first time. Men, meanwhile, are often tired of fighting the daily grind and want to draw their energies in, looking forward to retiring, caving up, staying home. Men begin to look for more satisfaction from their domestic relationships at the very moment women are biologically primed to start exploring the larger world. When the relationship is healthy and flexible, this shifting pattern can be easily absorbed. The man may cut back on working hours or retire and take up cooking and other domestic chores while supporting his partner's new outside interests, like starting a business or returning to school.

"Some [couples] are so energized by their newfound freedom and passion that they fall in love all over again," Northrup writes.

Some, however, do not.

• • •

Waiting to see our counselor the next week, a copy of *The Wall Street Journal* in the waiting room catches my eye. "The Gray Divorcés," the headline reads. I try to show scant interest, but I'm dying to read it. *Divorce* is not a word J and I have ever used, not a possibility I've allowed in my thinking. I can't even say the word aloud. Marriage is for life. That's what those vows meant. But now the word is hovering in my consciousness in a disturbingly frequent way.

I Google the article when I get home and learn that mine is the first generation more interested in finding personal happiness than in fulfilling marital roles, according to sociologist Susan Brown of Bowling Green State University, the lead author on a study about divorce among middle-aged and older adults. Among people fifty and older, the divorce rate has doubled over the past two decades, her study found. In 1990, only one in ten people who got divorced were aged fifty or older; by 2009 the number was roughly one in four.

And get this: "cheating doesn't appear to be the driving force in gray divorce." Infidelity was cited among the top three reasons only 27 percent of the time in Brown's study of older divorcés. So much for any ideas of a bodice-ripper affair.

"Marriages that in previous generations would have ended in death now end in divorce," the article quotes Betsey Stevenson, assistant professor of business and public policy at the Wharton School of the University of Pennsylvania, who studies marriage and divorce.

"In the past, people didn't live long enough to reach the forty-year itch. 'You can't divorce if you're dead,'" says Ms. Stevenson. The fact that many more women work outside the home and might be able to support themselves financially is also part of the equation, giving women options that previous generations might not have had.

The drive to find happiness before it's too late, though, seems to be a primary reason. Many of these divorcés may have twenty-five to thirty-five years of productive life ahead of them when they begin questioning if they want to spend that time with their current mate. And it is women, interestingly, who are the ones mostly initiating these breakups. Among divorces by people ages forty to sixty-nine, women reported seeking the split 66 percent of the time, according to an AARP study.

I am shocked to read there are so many women like me going through upheavals like this. I live in a bedroom community where most of the couples are intact, where my friends and I volunteer on the school council, run book fairs, oversee Halloween carnivals. The few divorces I'm aware of happened long ago and most of the partners have since remarried and now show up, four parents to a child, for school functions.

Do I even want to consider divorce?

An unprecedented 48.5 million women are now in midlife in the United States, reports Northrup. "This group is no longer invisible and silent, but a force to be reckoned with—educated, vocal, sophisticated in our knowledge of medical science, and determined to take control of our own health." The doctor/author herself went through a divorce at midlife after a twenty-four-year marriage. Her sentiments echo those from *The Wall Street Journal* article. "With most couples for most of human history, 'till death do us part' was twenty-five years," she says. But life expectancy in 1900 was forty-seven. "You saw your first grandchild being born and then you died. So we have really created this whole other stage [in life]. And quite frankly, if we do not step out of our comfort zone now," then when will we?

I ponder these things. I am forty-nine, married nearly twenty-five years. How many years do I have left? How do I wish to spend them?

Some of this dissatisfaction women experience at midlife has to do with biology. It's no secret that relationship crises are usually attributed to the crazy-making effect of hormonal shifts that occur at this time in life. These hormone-driven changes affect the brain, giving women sharper eyes for inequity and injustice, and voices that insist on speaking up about what they see.

"As the vision-obscuring veil created by the hormones of reproduction begins to lift, a woman's youthful fire and spirit are often rekindled, together with long-sublimated desires and creative drives. Midlife fuels those drives with a volcanic energy that demands an outlet," writes Northrup.

The brain chemicals that turned women into wonderful nurturers and doting caregivers during the childbearing years drop off in midlife, leaving us with the same basic hormonal makeup we had at about age eleven.

In other words, when those hormones start to wane, watch out, because "the bitch is back." That's according to writer and humorist Sandra Tsing Loh, who tells of her own struggle with hormonal changes in *The Atlantic*. "If, in an eighty-year life span, a female is fertile for about twenty-five years (let's call it ages fifteen to forty), it is not menopause that triggers the mind-altering and hormone-altering variation; the hormonal 'disturbance' is actually *fertility*. Fertility is The Change," she writes.

"It is during fertility that a female loses herself, and enters that cloud overly rich in estrogen. And of course, simply chronologically speaking, over the whole span of her life, the self-abnegation that fertility induces is not the norm."

I spent my young adult life striving for what's been called the American dream. A nice house, a responsible spouse, the 2.3 children who do well in school and have possibilities of eclipsing their parents' lives. Those nurturing hormones helped in that pursuit, but they also excised the flinty dopamine, thrill-seeking drive right out of me, replacing it with a thick, soft blanket of estrogen. By my late thirties, I had morphed into the head room parent for my kids' grade school, a woman who cooked homemade play-dough and wore Winnie-the-Pooh jumpers paired with sensible shoes. I was Estrogen Woman with a large *E* emblazoned on my chest. Any kind of risk-taking impulses went underground. I fed that sensation-seeking part of me by attending graduate school, writing books, learning to play the cello, discovering subtle ways to experience risk. Which makes complete sense: To be a good mother, those other drives needed to take a backseat.

The awakening I'm now experiencing is abrupt and disconcerting. No wonder it looks to others like a midlife crisis. But I'm not *acting out*. In a very real way, I'm *coming out* as who I really am.

In Loh's 2014 book, *The Madwoman in the Volvo: My Year of Raging Hormones*, she becomes embroiled in an unexpected affair with her longtime manager. Together they leave their respective marriages, both of which included young children. They start a new life together and live, thus far, happily ever after. I love the romance of that plot. Wouldn't it be wonderful if some handsome stranger would show up right about now? I know it's not that simple. I helped build this dying marriage. Who's to say I wouldn't do the same thing yet again?

But I know one other thing for sure: I'd love for a man to look at me in *that* way. As if I matter. As if what I have to say is important. As if I'm attractive.

In my early twenties, when I married, I saw myself as unattractive and, frankly, damaged goods. The late teens and early twenties is a time when female self-esteem is at its nadir. I had been neither cute nor popular in high school. The young women in glossy magazines not only didn't look like me, but also hadn't experienced what I had. Thus, I was sure, I was not attractive. Which was fine as long as I was paired with someone who made me feel secure and safe.

I had faced difficulties in childhood that had bewildered and challenged me: I tended my siblings in the absence of a healthy mother, particularly caring for my youngest brother, who had mental health issues and ended up in juvenile hall, foster care, and then California Youth Authority before joining the ranks of the homeless. I had been the one to call for help when our mother became psychotic, suicidal, or otherwise dangerous and our father was away on business. In high school, when I first thought I had found someone who would stay by my side through these kinds of difficulties, I became pregnant and was quickly abandoned by that young man. I carried the child to term and relinquished him for adoption. Returning to high school after a stint in the Teen Mother program, I'd faced ostracism on campus. I had navigated these challenges alone and feared the rest of my life would be equally hard and lonely.

When I met J, I believed I'd found the Golden Ticket, someone who would stay by my side when the next round of challenges appeared. I would never again have to be as afraid and alone as I'd felt in childhood. Someone would always stand by my side.

Not the best reasons to wed, I agree, but that's what drove me.

But I'm not that person anymore. I know my worth, or at least, I have a better sense of it. That I am intelligent I learned when I attended graduate school some years back. That I am ambitious and hardworking I learned when I became a freelance writer to stay at home with my kids. I managed to write and sell three books while juggling enough freelance gigs to pay the kids' school tuition bills. That I'm a good mother and role model for my children I learned as they developed and began to look up to me.

The one thing I never learned, though, is that I might be desirable, someone to be wanted for more than her skills in the kitchen.

Built more like a teen boy than Marilyn Monroe, I do not have a va-va-va-voom figure. Living in Los Angeles, where breast enhancement surgery is close to the norm, I have often felt inadequate with my lean, athletic build. No cleavage to parade in a low-cut blouse, no filling out tight sweaters in a specifically female way. Recently, I brought this up with J. Though I don't remember what we were discussing, I *do* remember his response: "Yeah, for years I had hoped you'd get a boob job, but then I just got used to things as they are."

Since I married young and experienced scant dating, I had (and still have) no idea what my value might be on the dating market.

So now I'm left wondering about such things. Am I attractive, even as I approach fifty? And if I am, what does that mean in the divorce consideration? I know women who would divorce only if they knew there's someone better waiting for them. That's not for me. If I strike out on my own, it's going to have to be for reasons other than another man's bed. I need to do this for me.

• • •

A few days later, an insurance adjuster issues a check for the lost Izzy and I think about buying another motorcycle. Rebecca has been suggesting a larger bike that would be more comfortable, but I'm not sure. I scan the bike inventory at her shop and pick a day to test-ride a few. Quentin meets me. I trust him; he sold me Izzy. That had been the first time I'd ever ridden a bike larger than the bantam Buell Blasts from my introductory weekend.

That day months ago, Quentin had trusted me to ride safely on the large, loud motorcycle I'd soon adopt. He'd let me take her on my own. I felt heartened by his faith. However, he came searching for me when I didn't immediately return to the dealership. By the time I pulled up, Quentin was circling back on his own bike. He set his kickstand next to me.

"I was worried maybe something happened," he said. He hadn't even taken the time to put on a helmet.

That night, a tiny spark of a crush started to develop for this man who was completely unlike me. A Delta blues singer and guitarist with long, sand-colored slicked-back hair and tattoos covering most exposed flesh, he is the polar opposite of J. Perhaps that explains it. J believes me so capable and self-sufficient that the thought I might need help never enters the equation. I was touched by Quentin's concern. Over the months that have passed since then, we've engaged in a mild flirtation. He seems to perk up whenever I stop by the shop. He makes me blush.

Unable to decide on a new bike, I take a loaner so Rebecca and I can continue riding. I'm always on the lookout for my next motorcycle. Whenever I see one that draws my eye, I think, *Wow, I like the profile, I like that look.* But when we get closer, I see it's just another version of Izzy. Eventually, I decide that I'll simply make myself a new Izzy. I buy a brand-new Iron model from Quentin and have the dealership change out the stock pipes like Izzy. They also change the handlebars. Again, to be like the old Izzy.

Not having her to ride has been painful. Without the passing glances of other motorists, I feel like I'm starting to disappear. Most of my life, I've wanted to fade into the background, to be quiet and unobtrusive, to take up as little space as possible. Suddenly I want to be seen and heard.

The new bike I christen Izzy Bella.

• • •

Meanwhile, my crush gains steam. I ask my therapist a few weeks later, "Can I have an affair and live with myself?" I tell her about Quentin, though I'm still determined that the word *divorce* has no place in my vocabulary. "Maybe a little affair would take away my discomfort with the marriage, might make all of this go away?"

I tell her about the dreams that have been plaguing my sleep and the sparking desire I feel. I'm not so much convinced it is Quentin

I'm running toward as much as the sadness at home I'm trying to escape. Whatever the reason, something has to change.

Sure, the grass is always greener somewhere else, she tells me, but an affair is not an accurate appraisal of another option. "What about just leaving your marriage?"

"That seems too harsh, like that would hurt J too much. With an affair, I might be able to get some of what I need without hurting him, too."

"But if you're miserable, don't you deserve a chance to be happy?"

"I guess. But not at someone else's expense."

I have worked hard for emotional balance, for a sense of integrity and peace, for a kind of clearheadedness that requires my ability to face myself in the mirror each morning. Could I have an affair without giving that up? My therapist suggests I take the coming week to think about it.

· · ·

At couple's counseling that week, I want to scream in frustration when J monopolizes the time, repeating the same stories about what a poor wife I've been, how I don't appreciate him. I'm confused why he wants to stay married when he thinks so poorly of me. Our therapist tries to cut him off to give me a chance to speak.

"I'm not done talking," he says.

· · ·

Thoughts of Quentin keep distracting me when I should be focusing on my marriage. He invites Rebecca and me, along with a bunch of the guys from the shop, to see his band perform one night. He's on a stage only a few feet away from me, rocking his guitar with his pelvis. This is killing me. He smiles and winks in my direction. Later, without my knowledge, Rebecca tells him I have a crush and reports his response back to me.

He may be edgy and a bad boy, but when it comes to marital fidelity, he's a stickler. "She's cute and interesting and I like her a lot. But I cannot get tangled up in anything like that."

And, as it turns out, I discover I'm not the kind of person to start an affair. I don't have it in me. It's clear in no time: Nothing's going to happen.

• • •

Nearly a year earlier, J had booked a family cruise. Ten days in Alaska to celebrate our twenty-fifth wedding anniversary and his birthday. In the past twenty-four years, we've taken only one family vacation that didn't involve tents, a Coleman stove, and sleeping bags. The kids are leaving home soon. If we're ever going to do a proper family vacation, now's the time.

But I can't bear the thought. I ask him to cancel the cruise.

It's not that I don't want to go to Alaska, or that spending time with the kids wouldn't be ideal. I just feel sick at the idea of publicly celebrating our twenty-fifth wedding anniversary. I don't want to keep going with the terse conversations between us in therapy, straining the frayed threads of affection that are supposed to tie us together as we maintain a facade that everything is fine. The duplicity eats me alive.

Perhaps we find ourselves stuck in these roles because we don't know any others. My parents did not have a good marriage. My mother's severe bipolar disorder made such a thing impossible. Still, they stayed married until my mother's death, because that's what Catholic couples are supposed to do. J's parents had a downright ugly marriage. His mother regularly spoke ill of his father. She'd been railing for a divorce for a decade before I entered the picture. Every year, the date of their anniversary was pointedly ignored. And yet they, too, remained married until his mother passed. Her animosity reached even beyond the grave with a stipulation in her will that excluded her husband entirely from her estate.

Given our models, how were J and I to know what a good marriage felt like or looked like or how to construct one? We knew only that marriage is supposed to be for life. When I gently introduced the fact that we were both miserable and maybe our marriage had run its course, the ire and rage directed at me was epic.

J never followed up on canceling the cruise. He was determined we were all going to go. The night he selected for our anniversary celebration was to be the formal night on the cruise. My daughter and I dressed in floor-length gowns. J and our sons wore suits. We looked stunning as a family. But I felt awful. I was supposed to be a woman celebrating twenty-five years of married love and yet I felt so estranged from this man and so hushed about my own unhappiness I was close to violence. The pretend-it's-all-okay vibe was no longer working. I plastered a smile on my face to make the night unfold as easily as possible, but when I got into an argument with one of the kids after dinner, the feeling of disconnect only grew.

J and I retreated to our stateroom. Anniversary balloons adorned the door. The room steward had folded bathroom towels into kissing swans and placed them on our bed as a special reminder of our anniversary. The falseness of the entire night cleaved my chest. J went out to get a drink. I stripped off my lovely gown—worn less than two hours—and looked at my naked self in the mirror. I was an attractive, fit woman, but the stress of the last few years had inscribed a deep worry line between my brows.

I wanted to break the mirror. I wanted to cut the dress I'd just worn to shreds. I wanted to jump overboard.

And then the scariest thought of all came. I had stopped using alcohol and all mind-altering chemicals when Jarrod was an infant twenty-four years earlier in the hopes of maintaining my sanity. I was determined not to follow my mother down the rabbit hole. Sobriety had been a wonderful gift that allowed me to be the best mother I knew how. But sitting in that stateroom, my gown a puddle on the floor, makeup smeared, every fiber in my body started to scream: I want a drink. I need a drink. I need to *not* feel this.

Had there been alcohol or drugs in the stateroom, I would have used them.

Just wait for it to pass. This will pass.

Fortunately, it did.

But I came to a moment of critical self-discovery, seeing clearly for the first time a truth that had nipped at my heels for more than ten years and that I had, until this moment, refused to see. I could *not* have an affair and stay emotionally balanced and sober.

I couldn't stay married, either.

• • •

"The Gray Divorcés" article I'd read offered a statistic that stayed with me: The vast majority of divorcés ages forty to seventy-nine (80 percent) consider themselves, on a scale from 1 to 10, to be on the top half of life's ladder. Furthermore, 56 percent even consider themselves on the uppermost rungs, at levels 8 to 10.

That's what I want, to be as close to that top rung in as many parts of my life as possible. Sure, we can't have joy and good things at every moment of every day. But I was not willing to settle for a life partially lived. I want to be awake and alive and tuned in to every part of my life. I want to be happy. I deserve to be happy.

So now I just have to find out what it takes to get there.

• CHAPTER FIVE •
IF YOU'RE HAPPY AND YOU KNOW IT

Our risk is our cure.

—LEE UPTON

"Female Motorcycle Riders Feel Happier, More Confident and Sexier Than Women Who Don't Ride," reads the press release from a motorcycle manufacturer detailing a study said to demonstrate this finding. Though it's a blatant effort to sell motorcycles to a mostly untapped market, the study nonetheless offers interesting insight.

Describing the responses of some two thousand women—half motorcycle riders, half not—the 2013 study finds that riding a motorcycle greatly improves a woman's feelings of overall self-worth. More than twice as many women riders report always feeling happy, nearly four times as many say they always feel sexy, and nearly twice as many always feel confident. Most important to me, more than half of women riders cite their motorcycle as a key source of happiness, and nearly three in four believe their lives have improved since they started riding.

Obviously, motorcyclists don't have a monopoly on happiness. Many factors contribute to feelings of wholeness, completeness, and joy—the stuff I'm after. According to psychologist Mihaly Csikszent-mihalyi, one of the most crucial components of happiness is what he calls "flow state."

As he describes it, flow is the mental state in which a person performing an activity is fully immersed in a feeling of energized focus, completely caught up in and enjoying the process of the activity, not thinking about its potential outcome or payoff.

When in a flow, "nothing else seems to matter; the experience itself is so enjoyable that people will do it even at great cost, for the sheer sake of doing it." You're so wholeheartedly immersed in what you're doing that you cease to be aware of yourself as a separate entity. You lose yourself in the experience.

And if you're like me, you might also forget to eat and sleep.

This is how I feel when riding Izzy Bella. I don't wish I was somewhere else or doing something else. I'm fully present and focused to a single point of consciousness. I also try to tap into this pointed focus when I run with Rebecca or have deep conversations with close friends. Backpacking and hiking, writing, reading, knitting, and dancing around my kitchen chopping vegetables for soup can bring on the same state.

But when I go home after a flow-state adventure, I feel the disparity between that engrossed, tuned-in aliveness and the leaden numbness that surrounds me in my marriage.

Some might argue that since I spend the majority of my time doing things that provide deep and abiding happiness, I shouldn't complain about the times I don't. But that's a sticking point. The more joy I feel, the more capacity for joy I possess, and the more aware I am of the parts of my life that chafe. Looking for joy now that I see the bareness of my marriage feels riskier than ever—and more important.

Risk taking is one key way to access this flow state, and there are many outlets to attain it. The commonly held idea is that risk takers are motivated by a pathological need to exorcise deep-seated fears or are compensating for underlying flaws. But Csikszentmihalyi sees just the opposite. The risk taker's enjoyment derives not from the danger itself, he maintains, but from her ability to minimize it. Rather than experiencing a morbid thrill from courting disaster, the risk taker enjoys the perfectly healthy, positive emotion of being able to influence potentially dangerous forces.

"What people enjoy is not the sense of being in control, but the sense of exercising control in difficult situations," he writes.

But here's the catch: It's not possible, Csikszentmihalyi says, to experience a feeling of control unless you're willing to give up the safety of protective routines. Only when a doubtful outcome is at stake, and you're able to influence that conclusion, can you know whether you're in control.

· · ·

I completely understand that my immersion in the motorcycle culture and my father's death are eternally entwined. A year after buying my first motorcycle, I still grieve my father's passing even as I discover a new freedom. There is no longer a parent watching over my shoulder to see if I am being the good Catholic girl, fulfilling the saintly aspiration my parents sought for me. I was named for Saint Bernadette, who had visions of the Virgin Mary and dug a spring in Lourdes, France, whose waters are said to have miraculous healing powers. My parents had been told they couldn't have children. Twelve years after they married, and four years after they adopted my brother Frank, my conception was, for them, a divine act. I was to be their holy child, the one who redeemed others. Though they never said so in as many words, I believed I was the one who was sent to heal my ailing mother—an expectation I repeatedly failed to meet.

Being the incarnation of all things holy has become a burden. I am ready to give up my saint's stained halo and the desire to be flawless. To do so, though, requires I also give up just about everything I think I know about myself.

I have taken the first step. J and I got into an argument recently over Hope's cell phone bill. Just another of the daily challenges that married people with children face, but for me, it was the breaking point. Our arguments had always gone around in circles, lasting for hours and getting us nowhere. The futility was too much.

"I'm done," I told him. "I can't do this anymore."

He sputtered and got angry and didn't want to believe me. "After all I've done for you," he scolded.

But I repeated myself a few days later when we met with the couple's counselor. "I no longer want to be married."

"We might as well quit therapy, then," he said, and turned on the deep freeze.

It had taken months to summon the words, to rally the courage to spit them out. I didn't know what would come next and I wasn't quite ready to move on. Hope was a senior in high school. J and I had decided we'd stay in the same house, living together as a family, until she graduated. But he'd told the kids and both his and my family about the pending separation without discussing it with me. I was furious.

• • •

Though I've given up my saint's halo, I still find solace in spiritual practice. I'm leaving this weekend to spend Rosh Hashanah with a group of women in a rented house in Ventura, a beach town midway between Los Angeles and Santa Barbara. I need some time to center myself. The plan is to have a simple Rosh Hashanah dinner on Sunday night and then take a high-speed catamaran to Santa Cruz Island—one of the amazing Channel Islands off the coast. We plan a day of hiking and open-water kayaking, a way of communing with God through nature and starting the Jewish New Year.

I am obviously not Jewish, but I join in the evening's ritual meal with delight, asking questions about the food, the holiday of the New Year, the coming of Yom Kippur (the Day of Atonement), and its rituals. Why do Jewish holidays always start at sundown when, as Catholics, we always started our holy days with the new day? When the sundown tradition is explained to me, I welcome the idea of walking through the darkness, waiting for the light of the holiday to bring illumination into my life.

One of the women explains tashlich, a ritual performed on Rosh Hashanah in which participants gather up leftover challah from the meal and carry it to running water—a stream, a lake, or the ocean. People then cast the bread upon the waters, letting go of sins from the past year. Our group isn't planning to undertake this ritual tonight. But for me, it strikes a nerve.

I feel a need for forgiveness and ask the ladies if they'll join me in the rite of tashlich. We take flashlights to the beach a block from the house, feel the sand that had been hot enough to burn our feet only a few hours earlier now cool and damp between our toes. The moon is almost nonexistent. The ocean's waves make a lacy scrim barely discernable in the flashlights' dim glow.

As a kid, my siblings and I made communion wafers out of Wonder Bread, its texture perfect—soft, white, pliable—to form little discs. This challah, though, feels coarse with sharp crusts like the pieces of glass that feel lodged in my lungs whenever I think about divorce. I tear the bread into little pieces, lots and lots of pieces for all the things I need to let go.

First off, being a devoted wife. I toss a piece into the ocean. I spent twenty-five years faithful, giving my heart and soul to my family only to find myself profoundly alone at the end of each day. This is especially true over the past decade when I have been unable to ignore the constant, low-grade ache of loneliness. To stay in the marriage and fake devotion is to do us both a grave disservice. But I mourn the wife I set out to be.

I heave another piece of bread into the ocean—my ambition to be a perfect mother. J and I raised three wonderful young people. The work we did as parents is a testament to our love of them and our desire to be the best parents we could, an aspiration that trumped our need to be good spouses. I will have to give up the mantle of the virtuous mother. A good mother doesn't leave her children's father.

She keeps the family together at any cost, is the glue that binds it all together. But I lost my glue long ago.

I pitch bread for the marriage I thought I was building all those years, for the household we created. Another piece of challah for the many hardships we weathered: J's almost fatal pulmonary embolism, Neil's near-drowning at age three and, in high school, his diagnosis with a severe anxiety disorder. Then there was the death of J's mother and the passing of my father. We'd been able to endure those hardships as a couple, difficulties that might have ended our marriage long before. But rather than strengthening the bond, the troubles piled on top of each other, burdening our relationship with a weight we couldn't escape. My sin, I suppose, was in letting it happen, not speaking up sooner, not knowing how to redirect the trajectory.

I lob bread for the young woman I was when I paired up with J at twenty-two, impressionable, looking for security at any cost. I chuck another piece for the older, wiser, and flintier woman I've since become, staring down the barrel of fifty. Bread tossed away, like the hours of my life, the dreams and hopes I must relinquish in order for other, new ones to arrive. I empty my hands of the challah.

• • •

Getting comfortable on the motorcycle is helping me become more at ease in this flow state. So much of my past has been spent striving—for an education, the right career, a good marriage, the best opportunities for my children, material goods, a sense of security. But I now see I placed too heavy a value on achieving those goals. Getting the things I want in life does not always fulfill me. Nor does it always work out.

As a young family, J and I struggled; we saved and sacrificed to buy a modest starter home when Jarrod was just one and we were still in our twenties. Two more children arrived and we lost that house to foreclosure eight years later when the real estate market plummeted. Still, unanticipated blessings followed that difficult experience. But only after I gave into the devastation and finally let go.

On the day I drove away from that home we'd painted and land-scaped and built a patio for, we started over with nothing in savings, ruined credit, and three small children to raise. I felt failure, awash in shame.

We were sure we'd been cheated by the system. We'd played by the rules, saved diligently, been frugal, and still lost. However, I found the courage to make a decision I would never have made otherwise. I applied for a graduate program in creative writing, taking out student loans for the whole experience. Assuming debt seemed a risky course. But believing that I had nothing left to lose, a vitally enriching career became mine.

I take solace from one of Csikszentmihalyi's discoveries about flow state. When a person's life makes sense, he explains, the "fact that one is not slim, rich, or powerful no longer matters. The tide of rising expectations is stilled; unfulfilled needs no longer trouble the mind. Even the most humdrum experiences become enjoyable."

I'm praying that this new perspective will pay off. Because, as Csikszentmihalyi reminds me, flow experiences are not necessarily pleasant at the time they occur. "The swimmer's muscles might have ached during his most memorable race, his lungs might have felt like exploding, and he might have been dizzy with fatigue—yet these could have been the best moments of his life." Gaining control of one's life is never easy, and many times, quite painful. But in the long run, optimal experiences add up to a sense of determining the content of one's life. And that, he argues, "comes as close to what is usually meant by happiness as anything we can conceivably imagine."

• • •

Yom Kippur approaches and I decide that since Rosh Hashanah was so helpful, I'll observe the atonement holy day as well. I find it odd that Rosh Hashanah, the New Year, precedes the Day of Atonement, that the sweetness of the New Year comes first, apples dipped in honey, when the fasting had yet to begin. But maybe that's human nature. We need a taste of the sweetness to lure us into doing the hard work.

I go to Catholic Mass in the morning on Yom Kippur and pray not in words but in silent groans that express unfocused desires. The Day of Atonement, I learn, is a time to ask to be released from any contracts we've been unable to keep in the past year. I entered into my marriage contract willingly and spoke those vows. But I see now I was not sufficiently formed at the time to understand their full meaning. I was a woman with considerable emotional wounds. The daughter of a mentally ill mother who used alcohol to medicate her symptoms, I was desperately seeking a man who would keep me from going crazy and perhaps get me to tone down my own drinking. Too frantic for someone to save me from myself, I was unable to make those vows in a substantive way. Kneeling at Holy Redeemer Catholic Church on Yom Kippur, inviting divine absolution and love, I come up with the words to ask that I be released from that contract.

Then I ask for the courage to release old loyalties, to let go of the conflicting values that have kept me locked in place, to find a new belief system that might see me into the next part of my life. I can't see what that new life looks like just yet, but I can feel it taking shape somewhere beyond my field of vision and I want to open my arms to greet it.

I don't hear angels singing God's acceptance of my request, nor do the heavens part and doves descend. After I've destroyed a boxful of tissues, I leave the church, my heart half a gram lighter.

Yom Kippur is a day of fasting. But as a Catholic, I've always been terrible at abstinence, claiming hypoglycemia or any excuse rather than admit that hunger makes me irritable, anxious, and scared. But this day feels important. I need to atone for my part in the end of this marriage. So I fast. Oddly, it is not nearly the ordeal I feared and that tells me something crucial. Yes, there is a mild headache as the day wears on. My stomach groans and I feel a bit weakened. But the hours pass. I feel good, as if I'm doing my part in the process of absolution.

I ride Izzy Bella to the "break fast" meal with the same group of women from Rosh Hashanah. The power of my motorcycle seems to balance the sense of weakness and hunger. Without the bike, I sometimes fear I might cease to exist. The taste of food is heavenly after a day of abstinence, the flavors made richer by hunger.

A few weeks later, during a four-hour car ride in which I'm held captive, J hammers me with demands. We have kept separate finances for most of our marriage since we couldn't agree on how much debt each was willing to live with. He took on the household expenses, while I paid for the kids' activities—private school and later college, dorm fees, music lessons, tutoring, summer camp, clothes. Since I don't want to be married to him, he tells me, I am to pay my own utilities, health insurance, food, and gasoline. I will learn later that he took me off his work-sponsored health insurance without telling me.

The next morning, I pack a small suitcase. In previously discussing what we'd do with the house, J had made it clear that he was not going to leave it without a court order. I'm too worn out to fight him anymore. I tell Hope what is happening. She and I hold each other, gripping on. I don't want to leave her and Jarrod, our dog, our home. The idea that we could abide amicably until Hope finishes high school in seven months is untenable.

I move out of the family house into a one-room guesthouse with a fold-down bed, a tiny kitchenette, and gorgeous west-facing windows that paint the wooden floors golden in the afternoon light. The new life I cannot yet see is gaining an outline.

• • •

Flow, according to Csikszentmihalyi, "is what the painter feels when the colors on the canvas begin to set up a magnetic tension with each other, and a new *thing*, a living form, takes shape in front of the astonished creator."

I feel nothing as glorious living now on my own. I am depressed and tired of waiting for the tide to change and my outlook to improve.

Contrary to what we often believe and sometimes mindlessly seek, flow moments do not occur when we're passive, simply enjoying ourselves in a receptive mode, like lying on a South Seas beach and breathing in beauty. It's not something that happens *to* us; it's something we *make* happen. Optimal moments typically occur when our body or mind is taken to its limit in a voluntary effort to accomplish something difficult and worthwhile. "For a child, it could be placing with trembling fingers the last block on a tower she has built, higher than any she has built so far; for a swimmer, it could be trying to beat his own record; for a violinist, mastering an intricate musical passage. For each person there are thousands of opportunities, challenges to expand ourselves," Csikszentmihalyi says.

This, I suspect, has something to do with what the addiction specialist Lejuez told me about the "learned industriousness theory." Our personalities, our brain chemicals, our bodies: They all fire up and feel good when we challenge ourselves and lose ourselves in what we're doing.

Riding my motorcycle can still trigger terror at what I am doing. But when I get into a flow state, my fears, my grief, my worries about how I'll survive now that I've left my marriage—all these are out of sight, out of mind. But that flow is cut off when I stop riding and find myself again in a state of anxiety. The more comfortable I get in the saddle, the more I renew hope that things will improve. I may have to use calm breathing exercises and talk myself down to get to that place. Once I'm in that flow, it turns out to be eminently worth the effort. The same is true for all risky endeavors. The focus required is so intense that in that act of focusing, our fears and worries slip out the back door, leaving only concentration and a sense of wholeness.

And that—wholeness—is precisely what I'm after, even as I'm not sure what I'm doing. In order to leave my marriage, I have to embrace the fact that such a choice will hurt me financially, socially, and emotionally. It's likely I will lose the house we bought, triumphantly, after the hideous foreclosure. Likewise, the cost of living separately will require financial sacrifice. Can I trust that I'll be okay, that my decision will not ultimately cost my children? Financial advisors tell us all to be more conservative with our investments as we age. But there's no way around this risk, this gamble of losing out, if I wish to be fully alive.

Next there's the emotional estrangement. My sister called a few days ago when she'd heard about the split. Hoping for a few words of consolation and compassion, I was stunned to hear her admonish me. "You can't expect to do something like this and not have people be mad at you," she said. The same thing from my oldest friend. "Let me get this straight: You're leaving your marriage because your husband is boring?" My stepmother, at first seeming supportive, went on to tell me how much she misses my father. "Not a day goes by that I don't talk to him, don't think of him. Still," she said, "I'm so glad he's dead and not here to see what you did to poor J."

I feel shunned, adrift, and begin learning that authenticity comes at a price. Will I have the inner resources to pay? Over the coming few months, family and friends break into two camps: those who want to remain friends with me, and those who need to keep their distance, as if divorce fever is a virus that is contagious.

And yet, the science of flow teaches that all these risks may be worthwhile. I need to keep in mind that optimal experiences are an end to themselves. I am standing up for myself, claiming myself. That is my reward.

My heart on many days feels as if it is made of Jell-O, warm and creepy Jell-O that leaks all over me, staining my hands that artificial red as I try to force it back into the shape of a heart. The stickiness is everywhere.

Yet, in my new place, I enact fresh rituals. I light candles and meditate and allow myself to feel as deeply as I can. I walk to the grocery store and buy only what I can carry home, a reminder that I'm on my own now and need to care for myself. *Give us this day our daily bread.* I cook in much smaller quantities—dinner for one—and am learning to find joy in doing so. I live a block from my daughter's high school and invite her to join me for homework, dinner, or a sleep-over regularly. I help her with college applications. I'm learning how to be an active mother even when not sharing quarters with my children. And I ache in a new way—not the old familiar ache of loneliness within a coupled facade, but the ache of reconstruction.

I remember reading about caterpillars turning into butterflies. It's not like the caterpillar gives up one leg—*I can manage without one leg this week*—in exchange for, say, a wing, allowing transformation to happen little by little, piece by piece. No. The caterpillar basically becomes mush, ceasing to exist as a caterpillar during the time of transformation, becoming a blob of plasma for as long as it takes to re-form as a butterfly. I'm in that amorphous state. Neither wife nor single. Neither full-time mom nor absent mom. Neither the scared young girl who said "I do" in a church all those years ago, nor the woman who is learning to live fully on her own.

It's a tender-to-the-bone kind of transformation filled with ragged edges and messiness. But it's real and feels genuine. I'm grateful for tashlich, for flow, for Rosh Hashanah, for Catholic Mass, for Yom Kippur, for my rituals that are being redesigned to fit this new reality. I am grateful for my children's willingness to try to understand my choice even though it hurts them. These are the ceremonies and graces that will one day deliver me into my nascent, new life.

Csikszentmihalyi writes that a person who has achieved control over her psychic energy, and has invested it in consciously chosen goals, cannot help but grow into a more complex being. "By stretching skills, by reaching toward higher challenges, such a person becomes an increasingly extraordinary individual."

Further, Csikszentmihalyi gives me a great gift in the form of a story about an indigenous tribe, the Shuswap, in British Columbia. The elders of the tribe noticed that at times, the world became too predictable and all the challenge and excitement began to ebb out of life. Without challenge, the elders knew, life for the tribe would lose its meaning.

To upset this complacency, every twenty to thirty years the elders decided the entire village should move. The entire population relocated to a different part of the Shuswap land, forcing the tribe to confront new landscape, new problems in procuring food and water. As a result of that upset and change, life regained meaning and value. The tribe members felt rejuvenated and healthy.

· CHAPTER SIX ·
MALE APPROVAL AND SEXUAL POWER

Opportunity dances with those on the dance floor.
—ANONYMOUS

As a teenager, the names *Fonzie, the Fonz, Arthur Fonzarelli,* and *Henry Winkler* could all rocket me to a fourth dimension. I was a tomboy, a girl who competed and was ranked nationally in skateboarding slalom, a young lady more comfortable in a pair of Vans slip-ons and corduroy OP shorts than kitten heels and skirts. I liked to hang with the guys at empty, abandoned swimming pools getting "vert" rather than go to the mall with girlfriends to shop. But when it came to having a celebrity crush, I was about as girly as you can get.

I bought fan magazines, went to every movie Henry Winkler made, read his biographies, toyed with acting because that would put me in the same mental territory as this man/character/dream figure. Though the Fonzie character was my favorite, Winkler didn't have to be Arthur Fonzarelli to make me swoon. He played a Vietnam vet in the 1977 film *Heroes* that I practically memorized. I bought a sweater and shirt just like he wore in the movie. I had a sense that I knew him, and that he understood me. If we were to sit down and talk, I believed, we'd pick up a conversation that had already been in progress.

Perhaps I was searching for male approval. My father was a wonderful, loving man. But he was preoccupied caring for my mother, traveling for business, watching out for my youngest brother who was fast becoming a juvenile delinquent, trying to tend the five basically motherless kids in our family. All this while he strived to keep food in the kitchen cabinets and making sure we went to Mass on Sundays. I'm sure, in some way, my father would have given me that approval if I'd known how to ask, but I didn't. I was afraid and uncertain, convinced that the disappointment of not receiving his approval would be worse than never asking.

When I couldn't get the approval I was looking for at home, I sought it with my skateboard and the grudging respect I earned from the boys. Male approval was male approval, after all. But soon, even that power faded and I looked where young girls turn next for that anointing: my own sexual power. Only, in adolescence, I didn't really know that's what I was reaching for.

• • •

The desk of Alex, the chrome and pipe specialist at Harley-Davidson of Glendale, features a picture of Fonzie sitting on a Triumph motorcycle with a girl wearing a skirt sitting on the back, holding on to him fetchingly. The photo surfaced from the auction catalog when the actual motorcycle was found in someone's garage after years of storage and neglect. I was hanging out with Alex while my bike was being serviced. I hadn't thought about my Fonzie obsession in decades.

"I always wanted to be Fonzie," Alex said of the TV character whose last official appearance dates back nearly thirty years. Alex is almost ten years younger than me and must have gotten in on the tail end of the *Happy Days* era. "He was just so cool."

I nodded. "I always wanted to date Fonzie," I replied, plunking myself into the proper gender-specific role. As a girl who'd grown up in the '70s, I couldn't rightly wish for more than that. Yet I couldn't explain to Alex that my yearning was deeper, more visceral. I wanted to consume Fonzie—just like the Holy Communion I took each week at Mass—and by ingesting him, to engender in myself the qualities I so admired.

The conversation went on to other motorcycle-related subjects, but something was amiss. I'd just lied to Alex and, more important, to myself.

"Actually, I take that back," I clarified, knowing the truth didn't matter to Alex but it did to me. "I wanted to *be* Fonzie, too."

After that conversation, I decided to look deeper into my Fonzie obsession. Certainly, the Fonz has been an important role model, demonstrating what it meant to be immune from peer pressure and true to one's self. That made perfect sense at an age when my identity was forming. But now I was in midlife with established demographic markers—professor, author, homeowner, mother of three—when coolness seemed radically beside the point. Yet the more I thought about my long-forgotten Fonzie fascination, the more I found the qualities he'd embodied as important as ever. I was grappling once again with issues of identity.

Alone for the first time in my life, I now make my home in a one-room apartment settled above a garage, just like Fonzie. Riding my motorcycle, I wear boots and a black leather jacket, just like Fonzie—though to be fair, I wear spring dresses and lace blouses when not on the bike. I am learning to make my way through life as a solo person, no longer tied by traditional family bonds, but a loner like Fonzie. I feel myself channeling some of the energy, the chutzpah, the generosity of spirit I found in the character. In short, I find myself *needing* to emulate Fonzie in order to survive.

My phone rings one evening while cooking dinner.

"Hello," a gentle male voice speaks. "This is Henry Winkler."

I almost drop the phone. "You just made my night," I say.

Weeks ago, I'd told a writing colleague, who coauthors his Hank Zipzer series of children's books, that I'd love to chat. I never thought he'd actually call. He graciously agreed to schedule a phone interview. I try not to gush.

• • •

By the end of my sixteenth year, I gave up my skateboard and Levi's 501s for high-heeled Candie's sandals, makeup, and giggles. I wore Calvin Klein must-lie-prone-on-the-bed-to-zip-them jeans. I learned to toss my hair and came to understand that boys didn't want to hang with girls at empty swimming pools if they could make out with them in cars.

If that's what it took to have male energy in my life, I was game.

That first boyfriend, who seemed like the only person in the world who knew the details of my home life and who was concerned about me, pressured me into having sex when I'd been just as happy to cuddle. And just like that, my life changed permanently. Ugly notes were left on my high school locker, cruelties whispered by former friends within earshot. That was the surface damage. More injurious was the cloud of shame surrounding my sexuality that would shadow me for the next thirty years.

I finished my education and was married upon graduation to the most Richie Cunningham–type man I could find. No more bad boys for me! I never lived away from home, didn't date widely, and chose as soon as possible what seemed the only safe role available. In short order I became a mother and settled in. Long gone were both extremes: the tomboy in torn Levi's, as well as the girl surprised by her budding sexuality, unsure what the sensual realm entailed other than trouble.

My life choices after high school were exactly what my father would have wanted. Traditional Irish Catholic to the core, he prized the virtue of motherhood above all else and was most pleased with me when I fulfilled that role. I wanted his approval more than anything. On the other hand, he disapproved of my writing. When my first book was published, I'd included just a few sentences about my mother's mental illness and the quality of silence that had filled our home in the narrative about knitting. He was so angered by those words that he didn't speak to me for two years. I tried through my writing to get him to see the "real" me, asking him to acknowledge who I was. But he preferred the construct he'd already created: the good wife and mother to his grandchildren, the docile and obedient woman he'd hoped I'd become.

• • •

But the motorcycle changed everything. The minute I got the machine to skim smoothly over the blacktop, I was hooked. The genie was out of the bottle and not about to go back in. As I began to master the bike, a more complete version of myself fused. Weaving through orange cones on the training range, I sensed the two parts of me work in tandem for perhaps the first time in my life. I felt as weightless and graceful as a dancer, executing moves of precision and elegance, as feminine as possible, while also aware of the brawn and boldness required to get that machine to do what I wanted.

When I interview Henry Winkler, I ask him about his experience with the motorcycle. I'd heard he was terrified of it.

"Not terrified," he explains. "But I almost never rode the motorcycle. I think I rode it for, like, twelve feet. But I *was* intimidated. I did not think that I could ride it with the internal confidence of not spilling it. I did not think I could figure out the hand, and the hand, and foot, and the hand, and the gear, and the speed, and the brake."

I am ashamed of the hint of smugness I feel, hearing this. No wonder getting my motorcycle endorsement at the DMV felt so great. I had mastered a skill even he had shied away from.

So what was the draw of the motorcycle for the Fonzie character— the outlaw persona, the macho element, the beauty of the mechanics?

He laughs. "All of it! He rode a motorcycle, loved it, loved just sitting on it."

I know the feeling. Not overnight, but fast enough to draw strange looks in my suburban world, leather boots and a jacket appeared, followed by a matte-black machine. The approval I'd craved from my father, my husband, and men in general was now rising up from within me. For the first time in my life, I didn't simply want to be the Fonz. I had, on some psychic level, become him.

• • •

For me, perhaps the motorcycle is a metaphor. To be clear, it isn't an act and the clothes aren't a costume, but simply protective gear, not unlike the padded shorts I wore as a skateboarder. And because I have never again since high school actively sought to appear overtly sexual in my manner of dress, I can wear my black leather gear with no self-consciousness.

At least, that's what I thought.

I was dressed in my leathers one day at Rebecca's shop, looking at helmets and chatting with the guys. Quentin introduced me to one of his biker friends.

"You ride?" the friend asked, probably wondering if I just sat on the back of some guy's bike.

I nodded.

"She also runs marathons," Quentin added, as if that explained the motorcycle thing.

The friend did what no one had done to me in decades—the slow up and down with the approving nod. Every inch of my thighs felt lit in neon.

"I can tell," he said. "With legs like that, you could cut diamonds."

I was so embarrassed I fumbled my words and dropped my helmet. (Dropping a helmet can compromise its integrity and is a huge no-no.) I scrambled to leave as quickly as possible.

That moment of male attention, after years of actively avoiding it with mom-type jumpers and loose-fitting clothing, felt unfamiliar and unpleasant, tinged with something akin to disgrace.

I was able to identify the source of my shame, and within a day or two to let it go. The sexual vibe given by the leathers, I decided, was a vibe others were adding, an identity I did not have to be categorized by. The safety equipment I wear is not meant to be someone's sexual fantasy. If there were a female Fonzie, I reflected, she would totally blow off this guy's sexualized read of my manner of dress.

And so I did, reclaiming a sense of my own sexuality and attractiveness. A few weeks later I allowed my daughter to pick out jeans for me a full size smaller than I usually wore. Thanks to the years of running, I could comfortably downsize. At first, I felt silly, like I was trying to be younger than my years, a "cougar" in the making. But compliments followed, and others encouraged me to play up the figure and features I'd worked hard to preserve. Soon, I was able to recapture a bit of the teen girl I'd left behind, the hybrid tomboy and sex kitten, but who could still own both parts of herself.

• • •

When Neil, away at college, called to ask about the separation between his father and me, he asked a question. "Mom, did the motorcycle have anything to do with it?"

"Of course not," I replied, which was the truth. But not the whole truth. The motorcycle had allowed me to reconnect with the part of me that had lain dormant all those years. I had found myself again—a self my father did not want to meet, a self that hadn't fit with my husband for at least a decade.

I am alone on most days, now. After two decades raising three kids, the sound of backpacks hitting the kitchen table after school and the sight of dirty socks on the living room floor are no longer part of my life. A motorcycle doesn't keep me warm in bed and isn't a lot of fun to confide in. But like Fonzie, I feel okay being on my own now and whole again for the first time in a very long time. Beloved. Anointed, finally, if only by myself.

Alas, it's a fleeting sensation. Six months later, a setback will come out of the blue and challenge all the advances I have gained.

CHAPTER SEVEN

TOTALLY HOSED

Anything that is successful is a series of mistakes.
—BILLIE JOE ARMSTRONG

I hit a ninety-one-year-old man Saturday night. There's no other way to say it but to spit it out. I hit a ninety-one-year-old man with my car and the guilt and shame of feeling wrong and flawed to my very core do not want to leave. The words, the images, keep repeating in my head.

I was driving down a dark street just a block away from a bustling urban area when, out of nowhere, no crosswalk in sight, he was in front of me, tottering across the street with a cane. I don't think he even glanced in the direction of my headlights. I slammed my brakes and yet, the nightmare still unfolded. His body slammed against my windshield, starbursting the glass. The smell of brakes filled the air. He tumbled to the asphalt where he lie unmoving, almost in a fetal position, before me.

I flew from my car with a howl of a banshee. *Help! Someone: Please. Help!* In that instant, I believed I had killed him. And that my life, as I'd known it, had just ended. One moment, everything's fine. The next moment, nothing will ever be the same again.

Bystanders gathered. A young Armenian man came to help and put a jacket under the older man's head. A woman called 911. I couldn't do a thing but stand there and twitch. I had completed a Red Cross course only days earlier and knew what I was supposed to do: identify myself as someone with first aid training and ask the man if I might help. But I could not even approach. I walked back and forth between my car and where the man lay, unable to do anything but shake and cry. The young man caring for him stopped his ministrations long enough to tell me that I needed to calm down and breathe slower. Sirens wailed, red and blue lights filled the pitch-dark night. One of the bystanders brought me a bottle of water. "It's going to be okay," this nameless, faceless person told me.

A female police officer approached. *What happened?* I told her. *Was he crossing left to right or right to left?* I had no idea. I was just driving and suddenly he was there. *Using your phone at the time of the accident?* I had the earbuds in and was listening to Pandora, and if the truth be known, I had glanced at a text message only a few minutes earlier. But at the time of the accident, the phone was pumping out music by the Gaslight Anthem. She brought me a second bottle of water and asked for my license, registration, and proof of insurance.

A male police office took photos of my windshield. He measured my skid marks. *How fast were you going?* I didn't know. I'm not a speed demon, was not in a rush to get anywhere, but odds are I may have been going over the speed limit. The male officer put his hand on my shoulder. *You must have good reflexes. Your skid showed you tried to stop.* Both officers told me the same thing. *This is why they're called accidents.* And while I appreciated their desire to help me feel better, I needed something else entirely. I wanted to be told unequivocally that it wasn't my fault.

The paramedics, meanwhile, moved the old man onto a back-board, attaching a cervical collar, asking him if he knew where he lived. He was alive. One of the officers told me that he didn't seem hurt. No blood. No broken bones. He wanted to go home, not to the hospital.

How can a ninety-one-year-old man suffer a trauma like the impact of a 2,500-pound car and not be dead?

Come to think of it, what was a ninety-one-year-old man doing alone at night in the middle of a dark street? A sizable crowd had gathered, but no family members appeared. No one seemed to know him. I answered more questions, called my friend Kitty to ask her to come and be with me. I still could not stop shaking and repeated to anyone who would listen. *I thought I killed him.*

The paramedics put him in the ambulance and took him to L.A. County hospital. How could I find out his condition? The female officer gave me her card with a case number handwritten on the back. Since tomorrow was Sunday, and Monday would be a holiday, the police department's communication's staff wouldn't be in until Tuesday. I could call then and learn his status.

We see this all the time, she tried to reassure me. *We had one of these just earlier tonight, a few miles from here.*

She said I could leave. How could that be? Surely, they needed to arrest me. But I got into my car and tentatively pulled away. I had driven less than a quarter block when she pulled me over. *Please get out of the car and follow me.*

I didn't smell alcohol on your breath, but for protocol's sake, I need to give you a field sobriety test, she told me. *Please, test everything you can,* I wanted to say. I was shaking violently, but I was sober. She instructed me to put my ankles together and follow her pen back and forth with my eyes.

I was guilty. Of what, exactly, I didn't know. But I waited for her to pull out the handcuffs and take me away. Certainly, you can't plow down a ninety-one-year-old man and not be guilty of something. But she finished the sobriety test and told me for the second time I could go.

I went to Kitty's house a few blocks away and called my insurance company and felt the guilt building. Maybe I hadn't been on the phone at the time of the accident, but how many other times had I used my phone in traffic? Surely, that was evidence against me.

Only days earlier I'd bragged to a friend that I had a perfect driving record—no accidents and one moving violation in twenty years. Maybe this was divine retribution for that hubris. Plus, I'd been stupefied by grief in the days and hours leading up to this accident.

Four days earlier, I'd passed my fiftieth birthday. A pathetic mantra had taken root in my head. *Fifty and divorced. Fifty and alone. This is not how I thought my life would unfold.* Other recent events put that self-pity in perspective. Last week, I'd learned that friends had lost their twenty-year-old son to suicide. Erik had struggled with depression and mental illness for years and the pain had finally become too much. I'd spent the previous Friday, the day I'd learned of his death, in quiet mourning, canceling all appointments to hold him and his parents in my heart. And then, the next morning, I'd gotten the text I'd been dreading from my friend Emily. Her precious son Ronan, whom I'd held and carried and fed and loved, had just died from the Tay-Sachs disease that had started to consume his neurological system before he was even born. He was a month shy of his third birthday. A mutual friend was en route from Phoenix to be with Emily in Santa Fe, but I was stuck in L.A. So I'd spent another Friday, the day before the accident, at home, stopping life long enough to feel deeply this second loss, to be with Emily in my heart.

These losses all started to become too much, the pain of the divorce, the loss of my children in my living space, even the loss of my little dog, Sami, since my rental didn't allow dogs. My heart was shattering into bits too small to ever piece back together.

Not an hour before the accident, I had attended the memorial for Erik. He was the same age as my own children. His buddies spoke so eloquently of him, and I held my friends, his parents, as they shook with their own grief. Had I been too addled with heartache to be driving?

Worse, still, was the simmering old guilt. I was oblivious to its presence until Kitty pulled me up short. As I blathered on about how I must somehow be to blame, she cut me off. *You are no more responsible for this accident than you were for your mother's illness.* She wouldn't let me look away. Kitty, like me, shares a history of maternal mental illness with traumatic institutionalizations, violence, and suicide attempts. She knew exactly what the voices in my head were telling me.

Later that night, another friend did me a similar favor when she, too, spoke firmly. *You cannot afford to give these voices room in your head. You simply cannot let them take over.*

I lay in bed that night, seeing the nightmare images over and over again. And then the words of one of my favorite authors, David Foster Wallace—who also suffered from mental illness and committed suicide at the age of forty-six—came to comfort me. In a commencement speech at Kenyon College, he told graduates about the power of thought. "Learning how to think really means learning how to exercise some control over how and what you think. It means being conscious and aware enough to choose what you pay attention to and to choose how you construct meaning from experience. Because if you cannot exercise this kind of choice in adult life, you will be totally hosed."

So I began to construct meaning, separate from the feelings that were flooding me. The accident had taken place in a heavily Armenian neighborhood where people are joined tightly by culture and stand up for each other. I was clearly not Armenian and had hurt one of their own. Yet, not a single person from the gathered crowd accosted me, yelled at me, or in any way challenged me. Rather, they brought me bottles of water and told me it would be okay.

Every time the words and images provoking guilt intruded—*I hit a ninety-one-year-old man*—I countered with a piece of evidence.

It's Monday now and I still don't know the condition of the man. I pray he was released that night and that, if he suffers cognitive impairment that would have put him in the middle of a dark street, this accident helps his family seek the help he needs. I pray that he's still alive because a part of me is convinced I killed him. And I pray that I may be free of the guilt I cannot seem to shake.

But I'm not there yet. The sound of sirens in my neighborhood sets off flashbacks. The red-and-blue police lights spin in my head. I know there's no one who can tell me what I desperately long to hear—that I'm not to blame—so I guess I'll have to settle for knowing I am powerless to stop bad things from happening.

I did not have the power to stop my mother's mental illness. I did not have the power to stop this accident from occurring. But I was given the power to arrest my own nascent alcoholism. And thanks to friends, I'm learning to stop the destructive, guilt-focused thinking that tries to pull me down.

But the whispers are still there. I still don't fully believe I couldn't stop my mother's illness. I cannot completely embrace that degree of powerlessness. How am I to make peace with a world filled with such random horror? I'm trying but cannot fully let go of the what-ifs— what if I'd taken a different way home, what if I'd not stopped to visit Kitty instead of going straight home that night? Because if I admit I'm *that* powerless, then I also have to make room for the tragedies that happen to others—babies who die of neurological disorders, and young men who kill themselves because the pain of living is simply too great. And I have to acknowledge that such things may visit me, too. So the choice of how to think about this accident, how to construct meaning from it, is mine alone. If I'm not in control of accidents and mental illness, then bad shit can happen to me and the ones I love at any moment. And if I am in control of such things, I'm hosed by guilt. Which will it be?

In the days following the accident, I learn more. The man was hospitalized for five days with a contusion to his skull and two broken ribs. My insurance company interviewed me and came to the conclusion that I had not been at fault. But then the police department issued its own report: I had been driving too fast for conditions and was at fault. Their decision stunned me. Hadn't the man been dressed in black, crossing the street in the dark, no crosswalk or intersection in sight? There was no way I could have seen him until the last moment. The report did not claim that I was speeding.

Meanwhile, calls and letters from an attorney hired by the man's family started to arrive. I was being sued for damages that exceeded my policy limits.

I ended up talking with the officer who'd investigated the accident. In a clearer state of mind, I clarified what I knew and what I suspected about the man's state of cognition. She did a deeper investigation, and though she shared none of what she learned from that investigation, she eventually amended her report to say that no fault could be assigned. There's relief in that, but I still want to be told flat out that it's not my fault. I want the officer's vindication, as if it will also hold me not at fault for the demise of my marriage, my mother's illness, and all the other horrible, sad things in life.

This is the meaning I construct from these events.

Sometimes life goes incredibly well and we're filled with light and joy. And sometimes, the loving of each other becomes painful and fraught. We struggle on. We try to love each other as a response to depression and illness. We try not to hit each other with cars. We try not to create additional damage. We fail to live up to our own ideals. Yet we succeed, every so often, in being fully human and alive, even when the pain of living feels as if it might destroy us. And with so much stacked up against us, sometimes all we can do is hit the open road. For me, it's time to pack up and see what's out there in the big, bad world.

CHAPTER EIGHT

LEAVING HOME

Once we believe in ourselves, we can risk curiosity,
wonder, spontaneous delight, or any experience that
reveals the human spirit.

—E. E. CUMMINGS

Day One: *Friday, August 23*
Hollywood, California, to Cedar City, Utah: 472 miles

I wake at 3:00 AM, certain I've slept less than an hour since I turned
out the light. The adrenaline has been too much. It's been rousing
me every few minutes. I keep thinking about what I may have forgotten or worrying yet again about some far-flung-but-certainly-
pending tragedy I cannot possibly control but which, if I worry about
it hard enough, I hope to avert.

Without turning on the light, I dress in my armored textile riding
pants and jacket and gather my things that have been packed, waiting
by the door, for days.

Creeping down the steps of my studio apartment and past the Cal-
ifornia-perfect pool shaded by citrus trees and bougainvillea, I lug
everything I hope to need for this journey. The night is black and
utterly silent—amazing considering the place is only a few blocks

off Hollywood Boulevard. I move past the main house, the home of friends who gave me shelter when I separated from J nine months ago. Their dogs bark from inside. I was hoping not to wake anyone, to make as little fuss as possible.

I've been striving to make as little fuss as possible my entire life. But there's something about this trip – about being seen and heard on a motorcycle—that I hope will make me more comfortable with spreading out and genuinely owning my life.

I pull up to Rebecca's house at three thirty. I've been parking my motorcycle at her place since the separation, as I don't have safe parking in Hollywood. Working by the beams of our headlamps, I strap down my T-bag, a smallish soft-sided piece of luggage that slides over my sissy bar. My tank bag attaches with magnets and allows me to read driving directions through the clear plastic sleeve. I check my tire pressure and figure out how to use the Bluetooth device that will let me communicate with Rebecca on the road. I put on extra clothes, worried I'm not dressed warmly enough. It's chilly now and at speeds of seventy will be even colder, yet the day will be in the hundreds by the time we hit Vegas.

We sip coffee, exchanging few words. This five-thousand-mile journey has been a year in the making.

During these final preparations, I'm heartened to realize I know a thing or two about what I'm doing. This aptitude surprises me. I can't help acknowledging that this entire journey has been basically a fluke. Even my friendship with Rebecca is a coincidence. I was the head room parent at the K–8 parochial school both our kids attended and talked her into being the room parent for one of the grades. I knew her to say hello on the schoolyard, but not much else. One day, I emailed a few friends to see if anyone wanted to trot around the high school track with me. One of them was also named Rebecca. "I don't think you meant this for me," the motorcycle Rebecca wrote back. "But I'd love to join you for a run." Soon, we were meeting three and four times a week to run together, but as novices, we couldn't jog and talk at the same time for lack of breath. We wore headphones for at least a year while we pumped our arms and legs around a track. Eventually we turned off the music and started talking.

I initially thought we had little in common. But there's something about sweating next to someone who is struggling just as hard as you, breathing heavily, working intensely, one of us feeling strong one day, the other feeling strong the next, that opens up a kind of willing vulnerability. If you don't have to at look someone, you say things you might keep hidden in a face-to-face setting. We gradually talked of ever-deeper things, exploring ourselves and our lives. We told each other just about every secret we might otherwise hold closely.

• • •

Our motorcycles are finally balanced and packed. We nod at each other and fire up the bikes. Rebecca takes the lead. The first stop is a gas station near the 210 freeway in Pasadena where we meet Edna and George, who will accompany us on part of our journey.

Originally, Rebecca and I had planned to do this trek alone. But George and Edna asked if they could ride to Milwaukee with us. We agreed, knowing that we might be grateful for their help on the road. We have a lot to learn. But by the time we turn our bikes back west and head home some nine days from now, we had better know what we're doing. We're going to be all alone by then.

"Do we know where gas is at each stop?" I quiz George under the jaundiced fluorescent light of the gas station. Since I am on the bike with the smallest tank, I need to ensure we stop every 120 miles or so. The others are on much bigger bikes with ranges of 200-plus miles and may forget that I will run out long before them. I carry a siphon tube in my tank bag in case. If I were to siphon a little gas from Rebecca, we might both make it to the next station. I'm praying we won't need to use it.

George has done much more cross-country motorcycling than the rest of us and is a small, sinewy man, with a long salt-and-pepper ponytail and weathered-brown skin, a stunning blend of Native American and Japanese heritage. He smiles at Rebecca and me with wrinkled, kind eyes, nodding at my question.

"We'll stop in Barstow," he tells me. I am comforted to have this one bit of information.

The plan for today will take us through Las Vegas and then up to Cedar City, Utah, where we're expected by friends of Edna and George who will give us hospitality for the night.

"But first we'll stop for lunch at Whiskey Pete's in Primm," Edna says, referring to the little Vegas-wannabe town populated with low-rent casinos just over the California-Nevada border. We're going to meet up with an Australian couple there, also part of Edna and George's extended two-wheel coterie.

I knew Edna for a number of months before I realized she was George's wife. She's model tall to his compact stature, platinum blonde to his weathered brownness. They've been together for more than four decades, since Edna was fifteen. George is riding a big, older Harley Ultra Classic. Edna's ride is just a bit more petite, a custom-built Barbie Harley. A Barbie doll is embedded on each side of the sparkling Pepto-pink gas tank. Edna's glitter-pink helmet and bubble gum–colored leather gloves are perfectly matched. She loves when little girls in cars see her, point at her, and wave. She always waves back. Over the course of this trip, countless men will ask to take a picture with her and her bike. She will accommodate them, but it's waving to the little girls who don't know until they see her that they can grow up to ride Barbie Harleys that will give her the most pleasure.

I am a woman who plans things down to the most microscopic detail. I have long believed that if I worry enough about something, I can keep it from happening. As a kid, my mother's chaotic behavior startled and often frightened me. My response was to try to manage my surroundings, to be as certain as possible as to what was to come.

This trip, I begin to see, is going to be an uncomfortable exercise in letting go, in welcoming the unknown.

Still, what surprises me most is the fact that I'm here in the first place. As I have explored my new obsession with motorcycles, I've tried to sculpt this passion into some kind of coherent narrative, to find a way that it might add up and finally make sense. So far, I have failed. One thing I *have* learned, though, is that I am a novelty seeker, and in life, that's a good thing.

I imagine a twelve-step meeting in which those who share this trait tell our stories to each other, trying to understand how we got here and how to make sure this trait serves us rather than destroys us.

Hi. My name is Bernadette and I am a neophiliac.

Defined as a personality type characterized by a strong affinity for novelty, neophilia is at one end of a continuum experts call novelty or sensation seeking. It's a subset of what psychologists have named "The Big Five" inventory of personality traits. These five include (1) openness to experience, whether one is inventive and curious, or more consistent and cautious; (2) conscientiousness: one's inclination for efficiency and organization, as opposed to being easygoing and careless; (3) extraversion: whether one is outgoing and energetic or solitary and reserved; (4) agreeableness: how friendly and compassionate versus analytical and detached one is; and (5) neuroticism: one's degree of sensitivity and nervousness compared with feelings of security and confidence. You can take the Big Five personality test here: www.outofservice.com/bigfive/.

Risk taking and sensation seeking are part of openness to experience. This trait is characterized by an appreciation for emotion, adventure, unusual ideas, and art; unquenchable curiosity; and a draw toward a variety of experience.

When it comes to the terms *risk taking, sensation seeking,* and *novelty seeking,* a number of psychologists and psychiatrists all seem to be studying the same attribute, calling it by slightly different names and considering the trait in different ways in relation to overall personality studies. No matter what we call it, neophiliacs have a tendency to seek varied, novel, complex, and intense sensations and experiences and often take physical risks for the sake of having them. These experiences may take the form of extreme adventure activities such as skydiving, snowboarding, and mountain-climbing. But the trait also expresses itself in unsafe drug, alcohol, or tobacco use, gambling and stock market speculation, and reckless sexual exploits. Men generally score higher than women for the trait, with sensation seeking typically increasing during childhood, peaking in the late teens or early twenties, and thereafter decreasing steadily with age.

Interestingly, researchers have found that those who demonstrate this openness to experience trait often align with liberal ethics and politics and enjoy thinking in abstractions and symbols. Those on the other end of the spectrum hew to conventional and traditional interests. Generally, they prefer that which is plain, straightforward, and obvious over the complex, ambiguous, and subtle. Closed people prefer familiarity rather than novelty and are resistant to change.

"Novelty seeking is the fundamental trait, and risk taking is one of its manifestations," says Winifred Gallagher, whose book *New: Understanding Our Need for Novelty and Change* focuses on this trait. As a species, we're highly neophilic—lovers of novelty—but as individuals, we differ by degree. Novelty seeking refers to the intensity of your attraction to things that are new and different. Someone at the low extreme of the spectrum avoids novelty and prefers the familiar, while someone at the other end actively pursues novelty and is bored with the routine. Most of us, of course, fall somewhere between those two poles.

Sensation seeking isn't simply craving new experiences and going after them, but the emotional intensity, energy, and concentration we bring to the experience and the passion that invigorates the pursuit, whether in work or sports, relationships or the arts, driving style or food preferences.

It doesn't matter if one is drawn to explore the great outdoors or the great books, "by becoming more curious and interested in life, you'll also have a more curious and interesting life," says Paul Silvia, psychology professor at the University of North Carolina at Greensboro. "The tendency to either approach or avoid novelty is the most important stable behavioral difference among individuals in the same species, period."

When it comes to risk, we have to weigh our choices. Deciding to try something new might reward you in many ways: prestige, money, career success, or maybe a fabulous lover. Or, you could end up unhappy, frightened, broke, or humiliated.

Learning that novelty and anxiety are a package deal makes me feel better. Though I'm not as terrified each time I get on Izzy Bella these days, the fear still lurks. So why would anyone—why would I —try scary new things when fear is blocking the way? As it turns out, emotions like surprise, curiosity, and interest are more satisfying for some of us than fear is daunting, and that attraction pulls us over the fear threshold. These buoyant feelings are what inspire us to lean into something new. "Like a sip of champagne, bubbly curiosity lifts us out of quotidian reality and a business-as-usual mind-set and slips us into the *approach* reaction with the unfamiliar," Gallagher says.

So what's the difference between novelty seeking and risk taking? Gallagher believes risk taking is a specific form of novelty seeking in which the novelty you seek is an intensely exciting, arousing experience. One's reaction to a roller coaster is a good gauge of that person's degree of risk taking. Do you say: *Get me out of here?* or *I'll try it once?* or *Let's do it again?*

Initially I'm stumped because I'm not a big fan of roller coasters or anything that combines the pull of gravity with perilous drops. So how and why do I find myself in this category?

• • •

We take off from Pasadena into the darkest, coolest part of the night. We've downed a fair amount of coffee but I'm already exhausted for lack of sleep. I've been packing for days, agonizing over what to bring, discarding what wouldn't fit in the compact bag, making last-minute purchases like heavy gloves for when we hit the Rockies and Yellowstone, panicking about what I have forgotten. Cold-weather clothes fill most of my bag: leather jacket, down vest, long underwear, ear and neck warmers, a rain suit. I may need these items only one day of this trip, but I'll be grateful to have them if the weather turns harsh.

The first hour on the ride is uneventful. The sun is not even tickling the horizon yet and the morning is cool, but I'm warm. And relaxed. And soon very, very sleepy. Motion is supposedly a reliable hypnotic for a restless toddler but I never sleep on planes or in a car. Still, I cannot keep my eyes open. The thrum of the road with the drone of my pipes creates a kind of white noise that lulls me toward Mr. Sandman. I shake my head and try to perk up. I don't think I'm in any danger, but I keep waiting for the fog in my head to clear. I drift into the fast lane. I sit up straighter and force myself to pay attention. But then, I'm ahead of Edna and fast approaching George's rear fender. How did that happen? I ease into my place in the formation, but George drops back to gesture if I'm okay. I nod that I'm fine. Falling asleep easily is not part of my nature.

Thankfully, he's been around tired bikers enough to know the signs. He signals for us all to pull to the shoulder.

"You need to walk around, have something to eat," he tells me.

I'm embarrassed. I hate to be the one responsible for everyone having to stop. I am most secure when I serve as a knowledgeable, astute member of the team. I hate feeling like the weak link. After some food and a brisk walk, though, I am alert again and grudgingly grateful he made the call. I would have risked my safety not to draw attention to myself. What a ridiculous, humbling thing to admit.

After the fifteen-minute break, we're back on the bikes. The sun is starting to warm in the east, the darkness seems less inky. I'm finally out of danger. But I also acknowledge that my need for perfectionism and self-sufficiency is going to kill me if I'm not more careful.

• • •

I learn that people who share similar sensation-seeking drives tend to be more romantically compatible with each other, and that divorced males score higher than single and married males. Divorced and single females score higher than married females.

The term *neophobe* applies to individuals on the opposite end of the spectrum—those who exhibit a strong desire for safety and predictability. Neophiliacs and neophobes together account for 15 to 30 percent of all people overall, approximately 10 to 15 percent on each end of the continuum. "The remaining 70 to 80 percent are moderate neophiles of different degrees," explains Gallagher. This refers to people who "want to be neither scared stiff by too much novelty and change nor bored stiff by too little."

Though there are different lenses through which to examine a person's drive for novelty, a lot of the experts tend to agree on the basics: While risky behavior can be detrimental to the individual (and, it must be noted, behavior that is too cautious may likewise be detrimental), both traits can be beneficial to society at large. "Whatever the costs for a particular person, particularly at the continuum's high and low ends, the roughly 1-5-1 proportion of those who generally approach, weigh, or avoid new things is good for the commonweal," according to Gallagher. Bold adventure seekers may live too fast and die too young. But they also explore, experiment, and otherwise push the envelope for the rest of us in productive ways, she says. "Like individuals, societies struggle to balance the need to survive, while prioritizing safety and stability, with the desire to thrive, which requires stimulation and exploration."

• • •

"Well, hello there!" the Australian motorcycle couple enfolds Rebecca and me in hugs as if we're long-lost family rather than friends of friends they've just met. They've been coming to California for decades, renting motorcycles and often touring with George and Edna. We're standing in the casino parking lot in Primm, amazed at how hot the day is already at 10:00 am.

"Let's get some food!" they say in unison.

We settle for an IHOP located inside the stale-smoke casino. There isn't a bathroom inside the restaurant—the casino wants you to wander past as many slot machines as possible to find it. I locate the bathroom, wash my face, apply sunblock to the little patches of skin that are exposed. In my snug motorcycle gear, I walk back through the casino. Some of the men eye me: with awe, appreciation, intimidation? They take more notice than I'm used to. The women, on the other hand, seem to make an effort *not* to notice me.

If I were dressed as my everyday self, I wouldn't get these looks. Or maybe that's not true. During the course of my marriage, I learned to turn off the sexual-awareness meter that we all developed in puberty. From age twenty-three on, I stopped noticing men. They were off-limits. And since I was in the "off" position, they stopped noticing me, too.

Or so I thought.

Earlier, Rebecca said she caught glimpses of the faces of truckers who passed us on the highway. "They really perk up when they see Edna's bike. Then they almost do a double take at the two female bikers following her."

I hadn't noticed. In fact, I thought of myself as rather androgynous when I was on the bike.

• • •

Gender, as it turns out, has a lot to do with the concept of novelty seeking. For both sexes, novelty seeking peaks in adolescence and declines with age—"even Keith Richards has slowed down," Gallagher notes. That said, lots of research shows that deliberately engaging with new challenges, even things as simple as trying a different restaurant or gym routine or taking a community college course, is a great way to improve your well-being and protect your mental and physical health. "So, ladies of a certain age," Gallagher proposes, "why not learn to fly-fish or ride a motorcycle? If not now, when?"

The major difference between the genders in this realm is that women are more sociable, and men have higher levels of testosterone and lower levels of monoamine oxidase A, two brain chemicals associated with risk taking. This could help explain why more men than women are interested in extreme sports and the Special Forces. That doesn't mean women wouldn't be interested in such exploits, however. Just note the number of female astronauts, West Pointers, and mountain-climbers. "I suspect women motorcycle riders would be in there somewhere too," Gallagher notes.

The more intellectual, emotional form of novelty seeking, openness to experience, refers to one's degree of curiosity, imagination, creativity, insight, and preference for variety. "Some studies show that many women who score high in novelty seeking manifest the tendency in unconventional lifestyles or hobbies, globe-trotting," she says.

Biological as well as cultural influences can incline some populations to be more enthusiastic about new experiences than others. While the frequency of a gene linked to novelty seeking varies greatly around the globe, among Westerners of European decent, its prevalence comes in at a substantial 25 percent. By contrast, it's rarely found in culturally conservative China.

It seems our ancestors' novelty seeking was boosted by the modern nervous system's sophisticated circuitry for the regulation of dopamine, one of the brain's major chemical messengers that referees our emotional responses to the world. Dopamine is critical in the seeking and processing of novelty and rewards. But how we process that neurotransmitter can vary from person to person. An individual's dopaminergic makeup can help explain why one person is eager to explore new things while someone else might see only the risky downside involved.

· · ·

We enter Las Vegas just past noon when the city's mien is at its most brutal and unflattering. This gambling and sex spectacle in the middle of the parched wasteland has never appealed to me. I prefer to feel centered and grounded, but Vegas is obviously designed to distract and dazzle. Gratefully, the plan is to roll on through.

But then a construction zone chokes four lanes down to two, and George pulls to the side and comes to a stop. There's barely a sliver of shoulder. Rebecca and I pull up behind with traffic passing only an arm's distance away. Edna has to get off at the next exit to make her way back to us. George's engine has quit. We edge up snug to the K-rail erected to provide a safety barrier for the construction workers.

As George starts pulling out tools, my heart sinks, worried this experience is going to be like everything else. As a kid, it seemed there was always something that interfered with my plans. Birthday parties canceled when my mother was sent off to Camarillo State Mental Hospital again, outings aborted when my younger brother ran away or was arrested. When I was accepted into graduate school, I waited until the very last second to prepare. I was certain something would come along to destroy my chance to have that experience. I seem to have spent my life waiting for the one thing that was going to torpedo whatever hopes I'd tentatively begun to imagine into existence. When one's dreams are forever being thwarted, you learn to deny them, or at the minimum, not take them seriously.

I am trying hard not to throw in the towel when we've hardly even crossed the state line. But the words keep running through my head: *Who do you think you are, that you should deserve this?*

With the highway traffic flying by and gusting us with wind and road debris, George tinkers. I try not to panic. Within fifteen minutes, the problem is fixed.

• • •

There's another aspect, too, to this kind of risky behavior that feeds our need for sensation. Though we are biologically programmed to seek out what's novel, modern life seldom gives us reasons to truly put our lives on the line. As a result, humans take what are, in most modern cases, unnecessary risks because the craving for adventure still runs strong in our genetic makeup. As a society, we laud our risk takers, showering praise and adulation on them. Race car drivers, astronauts, mountaineers, and explorers are seen as heroes (and heroines) to many in our culture. This positive social reinforcement is a powerful force, basically guaranteeing that that genetic disposition will be passed along.

Some social scientists speculate that novelty seeking may be the result of having more leisure time than our ancestors. Free time, together with brains wired for risk and a social milieu that feeds off novelty, makes a powerful concoction.

In fact, it's one of the reasons people love horror films so much. People who would never engage in high-risk activities themselves often take vicarious excitement from movies. Nothing is going to jump off the screen and get us, so we can fill that need for a little burst of fear, a moment of panic, a release of dopamine and adrenaline, all safely contained within a benign environment, thereby allowing us to get the "fix" our biology craves.

Michael Apter, research psychologist and author of *The Dangerous Edge: The Psychology of Excitement*, describes the appeal of risk taking as the "the tiger in the cage" phenomenon. Risk seekers desire the danger and thrill of the tiger, but they also want the safety of knowing the beast can be contained.

In fact, many people who love to take risks are characterized by a consuming desire to control their own destiny. Though others imagine they have a latent death wish, the truth is that they are actually passionate devotees of living life to its fullest. By taking part in activities in which they could be injured or killed, and then drawing back from the brink through their application of skill and discipline, they tap into a level of awareness and alert presence that can make life seem that much sweeter. Risk takers are not interested in dangerous activities, per se, but in experiencing danger that they can control and master to the utmost degree.

Is it ironic that scientists find risk seekers to have a strong need for control in most or all areas of their lives? In fact, some experts suggest that taking risks may bring periods of welcome abandon to individuals who have trouble letting life simply unfold.

People, perhaps, somewhat like me.

• • •

We cross the short pie wedge of Nevada and enter Utah. My arms ache, my back is sore from holding my shoulders upright. My legs knot from being held in a static position. This is the longest day riding I've ever experienced. We approach Cedar City when George pulls off the highway.

"We just passed a sign for Zion National Park," he says. He's going to call Roger, who will be hosting us tonight and who ostensibly knows this area better than we do, to see if we have time to explore it.

Zion is one of my favorite places on the planet. A magical space composed of towering sandstone cliffs in red, beige, and peach, it's a slot canyon with a distinctive Narrows, a gorge with walls more than a thousand feet tall cut through by the slender Virgin River. One must wade or swim to fully hike the terrain. But right now, I just want to stop and rest. It's only midafternoon and I'm shot. I could kill for a bed. Or even a floor, any horizontal surface. I'm relieved when George finds out that we can't actually ride our motorcycles into Zion. Everyone, cars and motorcycles alike, must park outside and take a shuttle. He's still ready to go to Zion, but Rebecca and I—the tired ones—talk him out of it.

The automatic door of the largest garage I've ever seen opens as if of its own accord when we pull up to Roger and Crystal's place. In their airplane hangar of a garage, there's room for all four of our bikes. We park, unload, find the rooms they've set up for us. I'm out cold in minutes.

Dinner is served at six thirty. Hamburger Helper and an iceberg lettuce salad. I'm immensely grateful for their hospitality. Over dinner, Rebecca and I listen to stories Roger and George share about being stuck on the road with fellow bikers, the lengths to which both have gone to help stranded fellow riders. The many nights sitting on the side of the road with a friend's broken-down bike, keeping each other company. They crack themselves up with tales of a guy named George Sanchez and his unreliable Sportster.

"Why did you keep riding with him if he was always breaking down?" I ask Roger.

"He would have stayed with me, too."

I ponder this simple algebra of connection.

• • •

Apter tells a story about what he calls "edgeworkers"—those who voluntarily adopt experiences that take them to the "edge" of life. He says that edgeworkers recognize one another, despite great differences in lifestyle and social location. He cites gonzo journalist Hunter S. Thompson, progenitor of the term *edgework*, to explain how Thompson won the confidence of the Hells Angels when researching his first book:

> I just went out there and said, "Look, you guys don't know me, I don't know you, I heard some bad things about you, are they true?" I was wearing a fucking madras coat and wing tips, that kind of thing, but I think they sensed I was a little strange . . . Crazies always recognize each other. I think Melville said it, in a slightly different context: "Genius all over the world stands hand in hand, and one shock of recognition runs the whole circle round." Of course, we're not talking about genius here, we're talking about crazies—but it's essentially the same thing. They *knew* me, they saw right through all my clothes and there was that instant karmic flash. They seemed to *sense* what they had on their hands.

Those who are interested in pushing boundaries, even when they are scared to do so, may be in some kind of psychic communion with others of their tribe. It provides a form of community that may be lacking in much of modern life.

• • •

"So," Roger turns to me. "What kind of work do you do?" In this group, I'm the odd one out, definitely not part of the tribe. Everyone, other than Rebecca, who owns Glendale Harley, earns a living with their hands. Rebecca is accepted despite her outsider status by the beloved nature of her business.

"I write books and I'm a college professor," I say. Roger asks more questions, and when my background as a former book critic comes up, he pauses.

"That would mean you've read something like a hundred books in your life!" he exclaims, unable to believe that such a thing is possible. "I've never read a book all the way through," he confides.

Roger and Crystal have embraced different risks from the ones I have chosen. The same goes for George, Edna, and Rebecca. But as motorcyclists, we're all the same. We find ways to feed this need, not only because we're biologically compelled to, but also because it's actually good for us.

Cutting-edge neuroscience demonstrates that novel experience can improve our mental and physical health well into old age, Gallagher reports. Which makes total sense. When we do something new, learn something we didn't know before, we create new neural pathways, develop new skills. We come alive in a new way and develop neuroplasticity. "Research now shows that adults of all ages who want to maintain sound minds as well as sound bodies should rise from their ruts and exercise both," she writes.

Each time we cultivate our neophilia by trying something different, we make it easier to take the next step away from dull routine. We all seek novelty in our own ways. The one thing that seems clear, though, is that it's healthy and life expanding to embrace novelty.

Researchers who investigate quality of life find that the skillful exploitation of the novelty effect can help us wrest more enjoyment and productivity from daily experience. Economist Tibor Scitovsky studied the relationship between happiness and consumerism. He argued that buying lots of inexpensive "pleasures"—fresh flowers, a piece of dark chocolate, a special meal—evoke deep appreciation and are intensely satisfying. These things are a far better investment in one's quality of life than spending on "comforts"—serious, expensive things like a deluxe car or an expensive couch. He also supported the idea that we enjoy a pleasurable event even more when we take a short break in its midst. A few moments of pillow talk during sex or a pause during a massage enhances the experience. This is because that time-out interrupts the adaptation process, so we can re-enter and re-appreciate the initial arousal of the activity's delights.

And it's arousal rather than adaptation that is often what pulls us into pleasurable activities. Someone who's terrified to hike alone or to speak in public will not adapt to that fear and will make a conscious effort to avoid it.

On the other hand—Gallagher uses the example of a hoarder—another person may stay aroused by utterly boring objects: old mail, newspapers, bottle caps, pencil stubs, and respond to them as if they were novel, not dismissing them as others would. "Then, too, some of us adapt to stimulating things that, being dangerous, should have remained highly arousing."

It's this precarious balance between what's new and exciting and what feels okay to do that equals a healthy degree of sensation seeking.

Gallagher's words about her own quest for novelty come to mind as I fall asleep. "Novelty-seeking is the spice of my life. I live in different places, both of which are extreme—NYC and remote Wyoming—because I get bored easily. For me, novelty seeking is more a matter of openness to experience than extreme risk taking. I love the research and reporting involved in producing a book, because I get to learn new things and think new thoughts every day. Then, I get to create something new out of it all!"

CHAPTER NINE
MATCHY-MATCHY

I've been absolutely terrified every moment of my life
and I've never let it keep me from doing a single
thing that I wanted to do.
—GEORGIA O'KEEFFE

Day Two: Saturday, August 24
Cedar City, Utah, to Jackson, Wyoming: 521 miles

The phone alarm chimes in the blackness of early, early morning. I have slept deliciously hard. I inch my way off the limp air mattress partially deflated during the night and try to stand. My back hurts, my hamstrings yowl, and my ears still ring from the roar of my pipes. I make a note to bring earplugs on my next road trip. The idea that Rebecca and I could chat via Bluetooth or that I could listen to music while riding is a joke. I may have to ditch those doggone pipes after all.

In the rooms nearby, I hear the others gathering themselves. I struggle with my T-bag. To get anything out of it, I pretty much have to dump the contents and then shove it all back in. So much for my pretrip obsessive organizational system. I select clothes for the day: Armored pants. A fresh T-shirt and socks. I wedge my feet back into the motorcycle boots. I can't believe we're going to do this again. I put two ibuprofen in my tank bag for later.

As I dress, I notice the guest room decorated in a pale blue country theme. A rocking chair perches in the corner, a cross-stitch sampler hangs on the wall. Depictions of fairies are everywhere—paintings, figurines, and a particularly large sculpted wood sprite holding a translucent bubble the size of a cantaloupe. The room is harmonized and color-coordinated and sweet. Safe.

There was a time I aspired to a life like this, predicable and innocent. When my kids were little, I insisted on matching towels in the bathroom and cute little soaps. I sewed window valances that matched bed comforters and carpet tones. As if such coordination could keep away the scary things.

My need to be so matchy-matchy came from the chaos of my home life as a child. Not only did nothing match in the physical world but also nothing *felt* as though it matched: not the emotions that swirled around, dangerous and caustic one moment, kind and warm the next, nor the devout religiosity in which everything about my childhood had been steeped, intending to keep us all safe.

My father had been raised in an institutional home in Ireland—picture a Dickensian poorhouse for kids—and had been considered an orphan, though he had living parents. Together, the government and church had been in the business of taking away children who were thought to be in moral danger from their families. Since my alcoholic grandfather had abandoned his family (single mother = moral hazard), my father and his siblings had been shipped to various institutions to be raised by Catholic sisters, brothers, and priests who were paid a stipend per child. When those children reached the age of sixteen, they were ejected from the protective system to fend for themselves. My father didn't meet his own brothers until he was ten. His sister Carmel died of tuberculosis in one of those homes.

Up until a decade before his death, my father couldn't speak with any candor about his upbringing. "It was like being sent to a reform home," he told me, something to hide from others because it reflected poorly on oneself. Amid that discomfort—family removed, disgrace added—religion became a deep and abiding comfort for him in a world that was bereft of softness. Perhaps one of the religious sisters or brothers had been particularly kind to him. Perhaps God himself reached out. He tried to bring that degree of security to our family life via recited rosaries, novenas, and family prayers declaimed on our knees before an altar and crucifix each evening.

My mother, meanwhile, had been the untreated victim of childhood sexual abuse, the youngest of ten children in an Irish culture that kept things about sex hidden, shamed, and hushed. At the age of ten, she had seen her father (the likely perpetrator of her abuse) struck by a bus and killed. If she harbored guilt and anger for the abuse, how might his death have complicated her recollection? Whatever she thought, one thing was indisputable: She developed severe emotional problems and medicated herself with alcohol and psychotropic drugs. The fact that my parents were able to meet, marry, move to the States, and raise five children was a miracle in itself, though their union left their children with more than a few scars. For me, there was confusion about what was real and what was the cleaned-up face we were supposed to show the world. Every Sunday, you could find us lined up, youngest to oldest, in a front pew at Holy Family Church. Shoes a little scuffed maybe, hair not always combed, hoping that looking good enough would mean that the difficulties and ugliness that took place during the week might fade into the background, a grape juice stain mostly removed, leaving only a ghost of itself.

As a young mother, I had been convinced that it was up to me to keep the whole family together and unified through my singular efforts. To let go, to see how events might unfold if left to their own devices, was to invite chaos at best and mental illness at worst. "Raising you kids did this to me," my mother often said of her bipolar condition. And I believed her. If I had been able to relax and let go during my children's young years, to relinquish the control I held on to for dear life, what was to prevent the same specter from visiting me?

Ironically, this is what I find myself struggling with now. Can I finally let loose all the constraints I've placed on myself and see what's really here? Am I able to risk knowing who I really am?

Upstairs, Roger and Crystal have been awake for some time, brewing coffee and preparing breakfast. Though last night we'd urged them to sleep in and let us leave quietly, they'd insisted. "We don't get visitors that often. We want to see you off."

Last night, Roger had given me his card. "You get stuck anywhere in the country—anywhere at all. You call me. I have a truck. Tools. I can be there before you know it. And I know people everywhere."

I tuck his card into my tank bag. I am grateful for his kindness but unused to strangers pledging extreme offers of help.

We all converge at the breakfast table. I pour a cup of coffee. After yesterday morning, I worry about being lulled to sleep again. And though I don't want to have to pee ten minutes into the trip, I pour a second cup to err on the side of wakefulness. Fox News—anathema to a dyed-in-the-wool liberal like me—plays on the television. I have to reconcile my political views with the straight-up kindness and hospitality this couple has extended. We're on the bikes by 4:30 AM, waving good-bye. Next stop: Beaver, Utah.

• • •

As I ride, the color-coordinated room comes back to me and I contrast it with my motorcycle riding. It's more than just facing my fears. I'm jonesing for a kind of vulnerability, a willingness to allow others to see me in a compromised, don't-take-a-picture-of-me-now state. A willingness to finally let the world know I'm not perfect and I don't have the answers. Part of it has to do with my readiness to ask for and receive help and encouragement from others. Usually, I want to be seen as an expert before I've even learned the subject. And that ego-preserving state has kept me, over the years, from doing many things I would have liked to have done.

In my early twenties, I trained seriously to be a professional dancer. Then I got my chance: an audition at Disneyland. I was nervous but prepared. As the audition became more competitive, I lost my nerve. I didn't want to be one of those escorted from the stage, publicly acknowledged as not having the goods. Within seconds, I convinced myself that I didn't want the job. I was better off in my cocktail-waitress life. Before anyone had a chance to reject me, I picked up my bag and sauntered away.

And I never tried again.

I'm staring into a nasty bit of truth: I am naturally good at many things. But if you ask me to do something I don't innately excel at, my first instinct will be to shut down. My second instinct will be to come up with creative reasons why I can't possibly accept the challenge.

But now in my middle years, I realize I have a third option. If I can shut down the judgmental voices in my head long enough, another voice sometimes speaks in a timbre so gentle it's easy to miss.

It's okay to try it and not be good, this voice whispers. *You might like it.*

Rather than spending energy bemoaning what doesn't come easily or getting angry with others who seem to do what I want with ease and confidence, I realize I have a better option. If I am willing to spend the energy and resources necessary to master something that catches my attention, I now understand that I can do it.

As I was getting ready for the hospital to give birth to Hope, my youngest, my brother Brendan called to wish me well. "You going to ask for anesthesia?" he asked. I'd delivered my older children without drugs, and I hoped for the same experience this time. He thought that was a good thing, if possible. "It's important to feel all of life as it occurs." His words stuck with me. I have spent decades trying not to feel big portions of my life, trying to hide from what feels frightening or beyond me or challenging in uncomfortable ways.

But something has changed, and I don't know exactly what. How have I become this woman, crossing the country on a motorcycle, embracing risks I would have run from in my younger years?

I have some thoughts. I saw how my children struggled with learning, how they persisted and grew from the experience. They may not have known how to draw, but they noticed how much better their fifth attempt to draw an apple was than the previous four. My friend Nancy, who put herself through medical school as a single mother of four daughters, used to say that intelligence isn't knowing everything. It's the awareness that we're capable of learning what we don't know.

• • •

Though sleepy, I do a marginally better job staying alert as we ride out of Cedar City. The morning is cool and I've made a point not to overdress; that helps. We've barely left Cedar City when we stop in Beaver simply because everyone from back home has told us we need to stop there. This tiny town has gained fame from its "I (heart) Beaver" souvenirs. We pass through the little hamlet long before any of the souvenir-hawking businesses are open. But at a gas stop I scope out the limited selection of Beaver-related items in the service station. I pick up a rubber bracelet imprinted with I ♥ BEAVER and then a bumper sticker, wishing I could buy them for someone with a playful spirit at home. I'm a little embarrassed by the thought. I consider myself a feminist, someone who has a sex-positive outlook, and the beaver jokes feel a bit like teen-boy humor. Yet, I'm also kind of tickled by the silliness of it all. There is something about my life that has squelched the fun out of me and robbed this double entendre play of its inherent lightness. I want to discover what this kind of play is about. I feel giddy when I touch the words *I ♥ BEAVER* cut into this bracelet, followed immediately by a static cling of shame. I leave the gas station with no Beaver-related merchandise.

Eventually, the sun rises and the morning unfolds. We're riding along Interstate 15 with a posted speed limit of seventy, which means we're doing eighty or more. When we descend into the Utah Valley and Provo in late morning, the stark beauty smacks me awake. The sky's bright blueness hurts my eyes. The clouds are whiter than any I've ever seen, shamelessly unambiguous against their cerulean background. It's as if all the clouds I've known before had been hiding behind a kind of modesty scrim, and now, for the first time, I see them naked. I can't stop staring.

We pull off the interstate north of Provo at the Timpanogos Harley-Davidson dealership. When we turn into the parking lot, we find wall-to-wall Harleys about to depart for a charity ride, almost all ridden by men. The few women present are mostly passengers. As we park, guys wanting to take photos immediately approach Edna. A woman rider with such a girlish bike is clearly a novelty here. Still, I'm heartened to know that the number of women motorcyclists is now rising. According to the Motorcycle Industry Council, "In 2014, the estimated number of motorcycles owned by females is 14 percent, a 50 percent increase over the last 10 years."

• • •

Rebecca and I ramble through the shop, get coffee, rest. The dealership is amazing with lots of glass and weathered steel, a mash-up between rustic and ultramodern. There's even a restaurant that makes the best skinny little French fries I've ever tasted.

Back on the road, we continue half an hour into Salt Lake then east on Interstate 80, climbing Parley's Summit to seven thousand feet. When we cross the border into Wyoming, almost immediately we see huge, ambling bison. They're not running free, ruling the Great Plains as I'd hoped. They're corralled, zoo-like, in a pseudo nature preserve next to the interstate where we pull off to get gas.

The bison are slow-moving things—or so they appear. But don't be fooled. Bison can outrun humans, sprinting as fast as forty miles per hour. More people are injured in Yellowstone National Park by bison than by bears.

I expect them to stink but they don't, or maybe we're not close enough to know for sure. They're sizable: A bull can weigh more than eighteen hundred pounds and stand six feet tall at the shoulder. Bison once roamed the American prairie by the tens of millions and provided a way of life for the Plains Indians. But European settlers hunted them to the brink of extinction. According to the International Union for Conservation of Nature, only fifteen thousand of these animals considered "wild" remain free ranging and not confined by fencing. Tribes of the American plains once relied on bison for food, shelter, and clothing and as a powerful spiritual symbol. But now, corralled behind this fence, the bison seem disempowered, domesticated in a way that makes me uncomfortable.

I think of what I've learned about the dearth of female road trips and why taking this trip is so important to me. As women in this culture, have we been corralled and kept penned in like these bison?

But then another thought enters: Is it possible we have corralled ourselves? In what ways have I constructed my own enclosure?

• • •

After we top off, George approaches a man in a pickup truck. "Is there a good little diner to get something to eat around here?"

He gives us directions to Lucille's.

We park the bikes, strip off layers—the day has gotten hot again—and settle into stiff chairs with plastic cushions around a wobbly Formica table. Looking at the menu, Rebecca and I realize we're not in California anymore. Both Edna and George are accustomed to road food. Rebecca and I—runners, yogis, hipster spinners—are a bit prissy in our food choices. We're mostly vegetarian, farmers' market shoppers who prefer organic, non-GMO produce, especially kale. Here our choices seem to be French fries versus potato salad as a side with a traditional hamburger. Then I notice a green salad with chicken on the menu. That might do the trick.

"Does the salad come with iceberg lettuce?" I ask the waitress, trying to sound as if I'm simply inquiring and not making a damning statement on the nature of iceberg lettuce.

"Yup."

"Is there some way to get a different kind of lettuce?" I ask.

"Let me check with the cook. I think we have some Rogaine in back," she answers.

Rebecca and I look at each other, suppressing the reflex to laugh.

"Uh, I mean romaine," she checks herself.

I remind myself that just because we do things in California a certain way doesn't mean the rest of the country has to follow suit. I hate myself for it, but I still want my dark leafy greens. Turns out they're all out of romaine. I order the salad anyhow and make a note to pick up apples on our next provisions stop.

George pulls out his maps. "How 'bout we take Highway 89 instead of the interstate?" he asks. "The view and empty roads will be gorgeous."

Rebecca raises her eyebrows at me. We both glance at Edna. Why not?

• • •

The sparsely traveled two-lane highway weaves into Utah, through Richfield (population 160) and Randolph (population 470), then returns to Wyoming. We travel north up the flat trench between mountain ranges. The day is unmercifully hot and I'm sweating inside my safety gear. We occasionally pass bikers attired in short sleeves, half helmets, and light shoes. I wish I could be that cavalier, but thinking of my family, I'm glad I opted for safety over comfort.

The miles tick off the odometer and I realize I'm riding on automatic pilot. It's a dangerous lapse. Balanced on two wheels at seventy miles an hour, it's necessary to be constantly on alert. But we've been at this so long now that it's hard to pay attention the same way I did at the beginning. In many ways, that's like life. With something new, we perk up and focus. Once we get used to it, we acclimate, we adjust to the newness, whether it's something wonderful or tragic.

Interestingly, though, I learn it's often easier to adjust to new but unwanted parts of life than to the new, positive things.

"We all have an inner thermostat setting that determines how much love, success, and creativity we allow ourselves to enjoy," writes psychologist Gay Hendricks in *The Big Leap*. When we exceed our inner thermostat setting, we'll often do something to sabotage ourselves, causing us to drop back into the old, familiar zone where we feel secure. Hendricks uses his own experience as an example, citing a time when he was feeling good and yet found himself manufacturing a stream of painful thoughts and images precisely because he *was* feeling good.

This phenomenon is borne out in the world around us with studies of lottery winners. One of these studies found that more than 60 percent of the winners had blown through the money within two years and returned to the same net worth as before their big win. Many ended up worse off than before they won. The idea that we are worthy of having our dreams come true, that we deserve good things, often runs counter to what we have been taught or what we think we know about ourselves. This is because our inner thermostat usually gets programmed in early childhood before we can think for ourselves. And once set, if not questioned, this mind-set will hold us back from enjoying all the love, financial abundance, and creativity we might otherwise claim.

As an example, Hendricks cites the early days of the steam-powered train, when scientists wanted the speed capped at thirty miles an hour because they believed the human body would explode at speeds greater than that. "We're approximately at that same stage of development with regard to our ability to feel good and have our lives go well," he writes. "In the face of so much evidence that life hurts and is fraught with adversity on all fronts, having a willingness to feel good and have life go well all the time is a genuinely radical act."

• • •

I'm floating off on these thoughts when I see George pull over to the shoulder. Edna and I follow suit. He gestures back down the highway where Rebecca has pulled over, five hundred feet behind, and is getting off her bike. We turn around and return to find Rebecca loosening her helmet.

"It just stopped running," she says. I boomerang from pride in resetting my inner success thermometer to the thought that this trip is the worst idea of my life. Rebecca's bike is nearly new, with fewer than five thousand miles on the clock. All along, Rebecca and I have reassured ourselves we'll be okay because we're on new bikes. What could possibly go wrong?

She pulls out her phone and calls her brother-in-law, Paul, a certified mechanic working at her shop. "We're somewhere in Wyoming," she tells him. The day is exquisite. I see a photo op and park Izzy Bella in the middle of the deserted highway and take pictures of her, all tricked out with her luggage and accessories, looking like a real road warrior. I'm working to distract myself from the dread that is building. Paul asks George to check the connection at the battery terminals. George locates a wrench in his kit, unlatches and raises Rebecca's seat. A couple of twists of the wrench snugs the cable connections.

The bike fires right up. We're good to go.

• • •

Before starting this trip, I contacted C. Robert Cloninger, professor of psychiatry, psychology, and genetics at Washington University in St. Louis. Cloninger is known for his research on genetics, neurobiology, and development of personality. He developed a well-respected measure of personality traits that includes risk-taking variables.

Like the Big Five personality traits I considered earlier, the psychobiological model Cloninger created is yet another way to look at the same terrain. By contrast, his model includes four dimensions of temperament: novelty seeking, harm avoidance, risk dependence, and persistence. He also developed character models to measure self-directedness, cooperativeness, and self-transcendence, and these elements shape the first four dimensions. (You can test yourself at https://tci.anthropedia.org/en/.)

Three of these traits are crucial to create a risk-taking personality, he explains.

1. Low harm avoidance: someone who is outgoing, risk-taking, and optimistic. If I were on the other end of this spectrum, he tells me, I would be shy, fearful, and apprehensive.

2. Novelty seeking, which can involve being impulsive and disorderly versus being orderly and rigid. A person who ranks high in novelty seeking and low in harm avoidance would be characterized as a thrill seeker, both impulsive and risk taking.

3. These emotional drives are then regulated by character traits—one's conscious goals and values, and one's capacity for self-regulation. Being self-directed, for example, means a person is responsible, purposeful, and resourceful. On the other hand, those who score low in this attribute would present personality disorders characterized by traits such as blaming others and aimlessness.

Once Cloninger has gone through this matrix with me, he takes what little he knows of my life from our conversation to try to assess what category I best fit. "So, if you are high in self-directedness, as most people with your academic achievements are likely to be, then you would have the ability to judiciously regulate and express your emotional drives."

If, on the other hand, I had ranked high in novelty seeking and low in both harm avoidance and self-direction, I would present an impulsive personality disorder, he predicts. The quality of self-direction increases with age from twenty to forty-five, then levels off at the high level of maturation, he explains.

By contrast, novelty seeking and harm avoidance do not follow a consistent direction with age, and there is little difference between the genders in this respect, except women are a little more harm avoidant and a lot more reward dependent and cooperative than men.

He explains the frequent relationship between passionate temperament profiles (low harm avoidance, high novelty seeking, high risk dependence) and creative characteristics (self-directedness, cooperativeness, and self-transcendence).

"So risk taking is related to creativity," he boils it down for me. "You might even think creative writers tend to become bikers!"

• • •

But now, out here in the wilderness, all that knowledge doesn't feel very relevant. We've moved further into Wyoming and Edna's trip-stopping flat tire has just occurred, leaving us stranded and alone. A storm is moving toward us, we can't raise a cell phone signal, and gunfire cracks somewhere in the tree line. At this moment, being a risk taker doesn't seem like such a great personality trait.

George eventually gets a hold of an Auto Club operator. By figuring out where and when we last got gas, he's able to get a bead on our location. A tow truck is on its way, though it might take an hour or more to arrive.

"Go on, you two," George tells me and Rebecca as the rain clouds loom even closer. "There's no point in all of us getting wet."

Edna concurs. "Really. We've done this before. We'll have the bike towed to Jackson and meet you at the motel. We'll be there before you know it."

Rebecca and I recall learning about the biker ethic of not leaving companions stranded the evening before with Roger and Crystal. I want to be a responsible rider who sticks with disabled comrades. But the sound of gunfire is raising the hair on the back of my neck and that storm looks far too ominous. A pickup truck, the only vehicle we've seen in the hour or so we've been stranded, passes, then circles back. Two middle-aged men greet us. They confirm the obvious: We're basically in the middle of nowhere. "A hundred miles, actually, from the middle of nowhere." There's a Harley sticker on the back window of their truck. They offer to stay with Edna and George, to give shelter in their truck if needed. Nightfall is approaching fast and they urge Rebecca and me to keep moving toward Jackson. We take their advice.

I've been picturing the ride into Jackson Hole, one of the most anticipated scenic moments of this trip. Now, I no longer care. The rain starts to pelt as we ride the curvy road. It stings my exposed wrists, smears my face shield, drips down the back of my neck. Goosebumps cover my skin; my teeth chatter. We could stop and put on our rain suits, but that will make us even wetter, so we power on. Stopping for gas in Jackson takes my last ration of strength. My legs are shaky and my hands tremble from low blood sugar. By the time we pull into the motel parking lot, we've clocked more than five hundred miles for the day and are absolutely numb with exhaustion. I hope Edna and George are okay.

We check into our rooms, twist off our boots, and shed our drenched riding clothes. Changed into dry jeans and shirts, we return to the front desk for recommendations on a good place for cheap eats. As we get a list of local food joints, the tow truck pulls into the lot, Edna's pink bike tethered to the bed, still as sparkling as a Rose Parade princess.

Once Edna's bike is unloaded, the four of us amble to get something to eat. Here we are, in one of the most scenic destinations in the west, and we're too damn tired to appreciate any of it. We pick the closest restaurant we can find.

"What in God's name was going on with the gunfire?" I ask as we settle into a nondescript Mexican restaurant booth.

George raises an eyebrow and Edna shrugs. "No idea." It's a mystery that will remain unsolved.

CHAPTER TEN

RIGHT ON TIME

The adventurer gambles with life to heighten sensation—
to make it glow for a moment.
—JACK LONDON

Day Three: Sunday, August 25
Jackson to Cody, Wyoming, via Grand Teton and
Yellowstone National Parks: 229 miles

Staying in a Motel 6 is never a lovely experience, and this is probably the ugliest, most uncomfortable Motel 6 I've ever been in: all modern edges with shiny surfaces, no sense of gentleness or comfort. No box spring for the bed; the mattress simply rests on a hard-looking platform. Harsh fluorescent lights. The bathroom is spitefully bare-bones without that most treasured of amenities, a tub. But for about ten hours, we get to be off our bikes, out of the rain, out of the alternating hot and cold wind, with bellies full and a horizontal padded surface on which to lie down. Sheer exhaustion is the most wonderful soporific. After a satisfying dinner, Rebecca and I are out cold.

Last night at dinner, George, Edna, Rebecca, and I brainstormed how we might move forward given Edna's hobbled bike. She learned from the tow truck driver that any repair shop who might be able to deal with her tire will be closed today, a Sunday, and likely the next day as well. She was able to get names and numbers of locals who might have a lift to change the tire or have access to a new tire. But if Edna and George are delayed longer than a day or two, they'll have to abandon the trip altogether and turn back. They are both expected in Santa Barbara within a week to run motorcycle security for the Avon Walk to End Breast Cancer. Plus, staying in Jackson would be an expensive proposition.

Jackson is a major gateway for millions of tourists visiting nearby Grand Teton and Yellowstone National Parks and the National Elk Refuge each year. This is the only location on our journey we had to book a hotel ahead of time and then paid double what we're paying in other places for a Motel 6, the cheapest digs we could find. Staying for more than a few days might quickly wipe out a cross-country motorcycle budget.

Though we've been calling it Jackson Hole, I learn that name is a misnomer. *Jackson Hole* refers to the entire valley in which the town of Jackson is located. The term *hole* derives from early trappers and mountain men who entered the valley from the north and east, descending relatively steep slopes, giving the sensation of entering a hole. These low-lying valleys are surrounded by mountains and contain rivers and streams, which make good habitat for beaver and other fur-bearing animals.

But given the cost of food and lodging here, I imagine the only fur-bearing animals we'll see are of the human variety adorned in pricey coats. High-end ski resorts like Aspen and Vail come to mind. According to the chamber of commerce, a strong local economy, primarily due to tourism, has allowed Jackson to develop a large shopping and eating district, centered on the town square. That, along with a sky-high cost of living, means most of the people working in Jackson cannot afford to live here. But the real abomination is the fact that this amazing natural beauty is at arm's reach and yet stores and galleries hawk cheesy mimicry, fake imitation Indian crap, and Mangelsen images.

Last night we came up with the plan for today. Rebecca and I will ride through Grand Teton and Yellowstone while George and Edna see what can be done to fix tire. We tried to talk George and Edna into doubling up on George's bike, joining us to see the national parks. They insisted that since they've been in this part of the world many times before, they'd rather spend the time getting the repair completed. Rebecca and I, who have never been here, should go on ahead. If all goes well, Edna and George will meet us in Cody, Wyoming, at the end of the day. If they strike out, Rebecca and I might then choose to turn back to Jackson after seeing the national parks to wait with them. Or we might decide to forge ahead on our own. George and Edna will be fine either way, they assure us.

By the time we're ready to set out, I am bundled beyond recognition. Though the day might be reasonably warm in parts of Yellowstone, there is a 60 percent chance of rain coupled with morning and evening temperatures that are frigid on a bike. I'm wearing long underwear under my armored textile pants, with a rain and wind-resistant liner zipped in as a midlayer. On top, I wear a thermal layer, a woolen shirt, and a down vest beneath my leather jacket. My hands are sheathed in heavy leather gloves with liners. Two pair of woolen socks smother my feet, which are crammed into motorcycle boots. When we wave good-bye to Edna and George, I am the Pillsbury Doughboy trying to mount Izzy Bella.

Leaving town, we pass the Million Dollar Cowboy Bar, one of the few landmarks that had topped Rebecca's must-do list when we'd planned out our route, renowned for its line dancing, barstools shaped like saddles, the famous country music acts that have performed there, and the general wildness said to occur. I'd been the one asking for Yellowstone and the Rockies—the big-ticket items. But we were all exhausted last night and never made it to the bar. It's early now and the Million Dollar Cowboy Bar is shuttered. I regret we didn't motivate ourselves sufficiently to fulfill Rebecca's meager wish list.

Heading toward the Tetons, I'm intensely aware of the gratitude I feel for Rebecca. She's walked me through some of the most difficult experiences of my life, the person who got me on a motorcycle in the first place. It was this time of the year—late summer—two years ago that I first learned to ride while I watched my father die. Rebecca was steadfast in her support, as I had been for her a few years earlier when she left her marriage of eighteen years. She was with me when, even as I grieved my father's passing, I also discovered a new freedom.

Rebecca and I enter Grand Teton National Park within an hour. These rugged peaks jut up abruptly to the west, some of the summits snowcapped even in August, as the rising sun throws its pinkish glow on the base of the mountains. The colors slowly climb the magnificent hillsides, tossing out hues of honey, mauve, and gold. We stop at a vista point to take in the view. The Teton Range spans forty miles and is characterized by three distinct spires. The name is attributed to early-nineteenth-century French-speaking trappers—*les trois tétons* (the three teats)—later Anglicized and shortened to *Tetons*. The morning has not warmed up much yet, but stopping to take in this sight heats our enthusiasm. The peaks are breathtaking.

After photos, we roll north toward Yellowstone. I have wanted to visit here since I was a kid watching Yogi Bear and Boo Boo in Jellystone Park. I grew up camping, hiking, and exploring Sequoia National Park in central California. I knew that the picnic basket–stealing cartoon bears were nothing like life in a real national park, but the grandeur of Yellowstone, even through that cartoon medium, always beckoned. It was a place I longed to see. And today is the day.

Riding into Yellowstone, the road changes from being relatively straight with gentle, sloping curves to a barely perceptible climb; then, almost without knowing it, we've entered Yellowstone.

The leaves are just beginning to change colors and we ride through vast openness, punctuated now and again by shadowy areas; at an elevation of nearly eight thousand feet, the terrain is broad and plainslike. In California, at this altitude, we'd see many more peaks.

We make it to the site of Old Faithful just as the geyser, known to go off every ninety-one minutes, is getting ready to blow. We rush over, ungainly in our bulk, to see the show. I seem to have developed a knack for ending up at the right place at the right time. For years I worried about being late, trying to wrest control from the hands of a clock. But now when I let go, all the pieces simply fall into place. This amazes me. Even though I was certain that leaving my marriage while my daughter was still in high school was the worst case of abandonment, I see now that it needed to happen when it did. Showing up at Old Faithful at this exact moment reminds me to trust this path and to keep moving forward.

My cell phone rings just as Old Faithful exhausts itself. Through some miracle of networking among the locals of Jackson, Edna and George have been able to source a tire and someone who can put it on. They'll meet us in Cody later today. Our plans are back on track. "Trust" seems to be the lesson of the day.

Rebecca and I loop to the Old Faithful Inn, possibly the largest log building in the world. The inn is gape-worthy with its multistory lobby, flanked by long frame wings containing the guest rooms. It is one of the few log hotels still standing in the United States and one of the first of the great park lodges of the American west. When the Old Faithful Inn first opened in the spring of 1904, the fact it had electric lights and steam heat was a big deal. Now, though the look is down-home rustic and hints at a hardscrabble life, the amenities are all twenty-first century.

I scurry to the bathroom to strip off some of the many layers I'm wearing. Rebecca and I order food. Though riding a motorcycle can't possibly burn all that many calories, it's a tiring way to travel. Every time we stop to eat, I'm famished.

Riding the rest of the way through Yellowstone takes the entire day. What looks like a short jaunt on the map is actually quite different. The roads are twisty, and with all the tourists, it's slowgoing. Which is a bonus for us, offering more chances to turn off at waterfalls and to appreciate the bison and elk in a more natural habitat.

Three-quarters around the Yellowstone loop, all the cars in front of us come to a stop. Red-and-blue lights of an emergency vehicle flash up ahead. I worry someone's been hit by a car, but as we get closer, I see a park ranger stopping traffic so bison can safely cross the road.

I think of Yogi Bear's "Mr. Ranger, sir," and smile. We idle our bikes, inching forward, observing the impressive creatures, their placid eyes juxtaposed against their intimidating bulk. We curve toward the southern exit of the park and skim along the edge of Yellowstone Lake, mentally recording vistas of twisted, regal trees, wind-polished stone, and spacious alpine meadows before descending toward the barren plains of Cody.

I start to worry that we're taking too long and that our trek is holding up George and Edna. Making it through Yellowstone took so much longer than I'd anticipated. The sun is lowering in the west as we pull up in Cody. I take out my phone, certain there will be irate calls from them wondering where in the world we are. Turns out, they called only two minutes earlier. When I reach them, I learn they, too, just this minute made it to town. Again, my concerns are unwarranted: Whatever it is we think we are doing, wherever we are expected, as grace would have it, we are right on time.

We find a gingerbread-looking family-run motel on the edge of town. The young couple that owns the place offers us a hose and rags to wash down our bikes. Clearly, they're used to hosting motorcyclists. They also tell us about the rodeo tonight. As much as I'd like to experience a rodeo, we're all too knackered. Though we didn't ride that many miles today, with all the creeping traffic and distractions— glorious and mundane both—the attention required was intense and meant we were in the saddle for the majority of the day.

After a shower for the humans and the bikes alike, then a brief rest, we wander down the street to the famed Irma Hotel for dinner. George and Edna ride on George's bike, but Rebecca and I prefer to walk, stopping to take touristy pictures with statues of bears. The Irma Hotel is a landmark built by William F. "Buffalo Bill" Cody, the city's cofounder who named the inn after his daughter. The bar, made of polished cherry wood and mirrors, is the focal point of the restaurant and was a gift to Buffalo Bill by Queen Victoria. It's odd to imagine such a pairing. And yet, who's to say how life will gift us, or from whom? I think of the place I've been living, of the great friendships

I've been graced with. When I keep my heart open, who knows what other gifts might arrive?

Day Four: Monday, August 26
Cody, Wyoming, to Wall, South Dakota: 428 miles

This is the first morning I've woken feeling ready for what might come. My muscles have finally settled into the pattern of riding hundreds of miles a day. Miraculously, my legs, back, and forearms don't ache. I am becoming seasoned.

We down some coffee, munch Lärabars, pack our bikes with Edna and George, then hit the road. Our first stop, Sheridan, Wyoming, is 120 miles or so away, so we'll need to plan a gas stop. As we leave Cody, I figure the morning's ride will be uneventful. We just need to get to the next location.

How wrong I am.

East of Cody, the road rises and bends. As the twists become tighter, we lean gracefully into each curve, moving like ice dancers across the asphalt, four of us swaying in choreographed, effortless unison. The pattern of our movements is mesmerizing. We travel in perfect harmony, synchronized grace made visible. The canyon walls rise up right around us and the vistas become spectacular. We've entered Bighorn National Forest, one of the oldest government-protected forestlands in the United States. The light of the morning, combined with the shadow of the canyons and the magnificent views, and coupled with our feeling of nimble flight, creates a magical aura. The air smells of pine and soil and sunlight.

This forest lies well east of the Continental Divide and extends along the spine of the Bighorn Mountains, a mountain range separated from the rest of the Rockies by Bighorn Basin. Elevations range from five thousand feet along the sagebrush and grassy lowlands where we entered to thirteen-thousand-plus feet on top. Fifteen thousand miles of trails weave through this stunning preserve.

We take U.S. Route 14, known as the Bighorn Scenic Byway, through the middle of the thirty-mile-wide woodland, a road that's closed in the snowier months of the year. By the time we reach the top, the temperature has plummeted to the thirties and we're all grateful to have motorcycles without sensitive carburetors that might cough and choke at elevation. What scant traffic there is comes to a stop so that cattle may cross the highway, herded by cowboys on horseback and dogs. We try to stay warm, balanced on our bikes, and I'm grateful for the heat rising off my pipes.

This day, for me, becomes emblematic of the whole adventure. There are days when you know something amazing is expected, like seeing Yellowstone yesterday. But days like today, when you're not expecting anything out of the ordinary and yet are graced with wonders beyond your imagination—just the feeling of serendipity that comes with the experience cannot wipe the smile off my face.

After the glories of Bighorn National Forest, as we descend into Sheridan, the temperatures quickly rise. It has taken us all morning to go only 120 miles, and by the time we stop for lunch, the day is in the hundreds. We eat at a little diner and run into two men also en route to the Harley gathering in Milwaukee. One rides a '70s vintage Harley that lost its brakes as he was coming down from the Bighorn Mountains. The thought of descending that mountain with no brakes terrifies me. Over sandwiches and fries, he tells us how he's been looking for a mechanic in town to help him out. His younger companion is on a Buell sport bike, a family member of the Harley clan though it looks and rides nothing like a Harley. We will see these men almost daily until we hit Milwaukee. With each stop, we're running into others who are part of the summer migration to Harley Mecca.

• • •

The wonders of western Wyoming are breathtaking. Eastern Wyoming, however, is an unlovely creature. After the joys of the morning, we settle into the numbing grind and cross the South Dakota state line, which promises "Great Faces, Great Places" and more hot, flat tedium.

We pass through the Black Hills and then enter the Badlands and their rugged beauty. The geologic deposits here are said to contain the world's richest fossil beds. Ancient mammals once roamed the area. I can almost picture them: rhino, wooly mammoth, giant tapirs, a saber-toothed cat. The park's 244,000 acres protects an expanse of mixed-grass prairie where bison, bighorn sheep, prairie dogs, and black-footed ferrets are supposed to live, but today we see little moving. The most memorable part is the deep silence that surrounds us. Amid the tall grasses, emptiness from horizon to horizon.

Next up is the ritual pilgrimage to Sturgis, South Dakota, home of the annual motorcycle rally held in early August since 1938. Originally created to showcase stunts and races, Sturgis has evolved into one of the largest motorcycle rallies in the world. My friend Emily, whom we'll stop to see in New Mexico on the ride home, was taken to Sturgis as a nine-year-old by her Lutheran-minister father. Emily lost her leg as a young child to a congenital defect and then developed a mad yearning for motorcycles. Though she and her father, I imagine, could not have been more out of place at Sturgis, with its beer-swilling, sunburnt, bare-bellied biker crowd, I have always loved the story of her father's unstoppable desire to please her, a desire so strong it carried them here.

By the time we reach Sturgis, the cleanup from the event a few weeks earlier is complete. I've seen photos, though, with the streets so lined with motorcycles it's amazing anyone can get a bike in or out. Hotels and motels within a hundred-mile radius are booked months in advance. I imagine the thundering pipes and the craziness of the parties. I adore picturing little Emily and her dad among that bacchanalia, but not me.

Today, thankfully, it's quiet.

We take an obligatory photo by the Sturgis bar, purchase cut-rate T-shirts at the souvenir shop, and stop at the Sturgis Harley-Davidson so George can top off his oil. As we have come to expect, more than a few male bikers request a picture with Edna and her Barbie bike.

Then it's back on the bikes and the continuation of one of those days that stretch on forever. We pass the turnoff for Mount Rushmore and decide that we'll save it for the return trip.

As I ride, the words of Lejuez, the addiction specialist, come back to me. Many people who embrace risk are either running toward or away from something, he'd said. Into which category do I fit? Yes, I am running away from the saintliness aura I had bought into as younger woman. But I'm not running toward its opposite, a kind of reckless decadence associated with both midlife crises and motorcycles. I am running away from a marriage that had begun to suffocate me, but I'm not looking for the arms of a new man to throw myself into.

So, what then, *am* I looking for?

Lejuez called on his expertise in addiction to help me understand risk taking. He explained that, from a learning perspective, there are two reasons why someone might use drugs. The first is positive reinforcement. It's what we think of with drugs: the high, what feels good about it. But even more influential is negative reinforcement, the idea that we might be removing something bad or unwanted in the process.

To illustrate, he conjured up heroin users. If they're experiencing withdrawal and they use again, another dose of heroin will take the pain of withdrawal away—that's negative reinforcement, taking something bad away. But this process occurs on more than a physiological level; there's also a very strong emotional component. Cocaine addicts, for example, might find the drug eases their depression and makes them feel saner and more normal than without it. Likewise, people who suffer from anxiety attacks but don't know what's happening. They're walking around and all of a sudden their chest feels tense, they may experience heart pain, and they think they're having a heart attack or going crazy. A drug like heroin can medicate that. Heroin or cocaine might be medicating emotional symptoms, blunting an emotional response, as much if not more so than meeting a physiological need.

The same thing happens with risky behavior like motorcycling. "You could argue that the 'high' someone gets from that kind of activity may be needed because they're not feeling a lot of reinforcement in other parts of their life. It brings an excitement, a new group of friends," he told me. I consider the thrill of the ride plus all the new people I've met, people quite different from those I knew previously in the world of writers and academics. All act as positive reinforcements. My world *does* feels larger.

"But it also removes something, a negative," he continued. "For example, imagine someone in such a rut they don't know how to say no to that rut. They're the person who does this or does that and everyone has this expectation of them. That becomes a negative." If that person finds a new love, like motorcycling, they're suddenly so motivated by it that they get busy and are finally able to say no to the things they wanted to say no to all along. Through their new passion, they can make those things go away.

I consider how unhappy I'd been in my marriage. I'd aimed for perfection, character impeccability, and exactness, all the while feeding a subterranean desire to be the saint for whom my parents named me.

How many saints do you see on Harleys?

Though most people might label this scenario as a form of avoidance, Lejuez reassures me that our escapism reflex is probably one of the body's most powerful and important responses. "In many cases, we think of avoidance as a bad thing because you're not doing the things you need to do." But avoidance really just means being able to make a choice that allows you to avoid something you don't want before it happens. Sometimes this is a good thing. You're avoiding all numbness and disconnectedness that's built up over time and engaging in something to turn the tables. This is also accompanied by a release of endorphins and an increase of serotonin.

"Never underestimate the value of making negative things go away," he said.

Lejuez talked about learning theory and what's officially called *punishing a behavior*. When an alcoholic gets sober, for example, that person is punishing the addiction behavior. "*Punish* sounds so pejorative, but it just means what we do to make something stop." If you punish one kind of behavior, though, you have to reinforce and reward alternatives. If you don't reward the alternative—for example, taking care of and praising yourself for avoiding an addiction while addressing underlying issues—you may end up simply suppressing the drive until even more damaging behaviors arise. Think of people on a diet. They do what they're supposed to, they strive to be "good," and then one day, they just say, "Forget it! I'm going to do what I want." There's "this explosion of selfishness because they didn't take the time to look out for themselves from the start."

Though I hadn't considered it before our conversation, I asked Lejuez if there's a connection between my own two-decade abstinence from alcohol and drugs and my desire to ride a motorcycle in my late forties. "In your case, you can make the connection from an unhealthy escape/avoidance behavior to a healthy escape/avoidance behavior." This, he said, is an important lesson. "Every one of us has had things that have crept into our lives and have taken over. We wish we could find a more healthy way." It's crucial, he said, to know that healthy alternatives are possible, that we can find new, enriching ways to meet these needs.

Throughout South Dakota, I keep seeing signs for a place called Wall Drug with the promises of free coffee to newlyweds and military personnel, free ice water to anyone who asks, the best pies in the country, the largest drugstore ever. We follow these signs, like Burma-Shave ads, for more than a hundred miles. By the end of the day we hit the little town of Wall. We're weary and wiped out, susceptible to the lure of all that advertising.

Wall Drug is a cowboy-themed open-air shopping mall, unabashedly tacky, consisting of a drugstore, gift shop, restaurants, western art museum, chapel, and an eighty-foot brontosaurus. In *The Lost Continent*, humorist Bill Bryson writes that "it's an actual place, one of the world's worst tourist traps, but I loved it and I won't have a word said against it." *The New York Times* reports that it takes more than $10 million a year and draws some two million annual visitors. Wall Drug earns much of its fame from those billboards we passed. They pepper a 650-mile-long stretch of highway extending from Minnesota to Montana.

We snag motel rooms, shower, and go in search of the best dining option along the single street of restaurants and extended drugstore offerings, including, what I'm told, is an impressive art collection. By the time we leave the restaurant, though, it's no later than 8:00 PM on a summer's night and yet all of Wall has closed down. We haven't yet seen its storied attractions beyond the tasteless diner. Just like we bypassed Mount Rushmore and skirted the Black Hills, we've missed our chance to see the Largest Drugstore in the World. But we got the magic of Bighorn National Forest this morning, and that's more than enough.

• CHAPTER ELEVEN •

ON TO THE PROMISED LAND

> But if you never did anything you couldn't undo
> you'd end up doing nothing at all.
>
> —ANNE TYLER, *Ladder of Years*

Day Five: Tuesday, August 27
Wall, South Dakota, to Albert Lea, Minnesota: 461 miles

The hotel clerk in Wall, South Dakota, amazes me. When we arrived late yesterday, hair plastered to our heads, a necklace of salt around our necks, holes burned into my textile armored pants from where my leg drifted too close to my exhaust, we looked as if we'd been through a battle. She, on the other hand, was the picture of cool leisure. Her hair coiffed to perfection, a blouse so crisp it appeared constructed of a fine-grade cardboard, her lipstick applied just so. Sure, she'd been sitting in the small air-conditioned hotel office while we'd been pounding out hard miles. Seeing her was like encountering a gorgeous hothouse flower in the midst of a refugee camp. I was aware for the first time of how bedraggled we'd become.

Her freshness inspired me. After dinner, I took out the Tide Pods I'd packed a week earlier after Rebecca had put me in charge of sundry supplies. She'd suggested the little self-contained detergent balls, rather than liquid detergent that might spill, or dry detergent that could dissolve if our luggage got soaked. I put my few things— underwear, socks, T-shirts—in the bathroom sink, filled it with water, and added one pod. I happily washed my things, anticipating that clean smell next to my skin.

The pod, though, was apparently made to wash an entire load of laundry. I washed and rinsed and washed and rinsed and still couldn't purge the detergent's slimy slickness. I showered, washed my hair, enjoyed the smell of a clean body, at least, as my clothes sat in yet another sink full of fresh water. And then I rinsed again. I finally had to put the clothes in the bathtub and add sufficient water until they were soap-free enough to hang dry. (Note to self: Next time, a little bar of soap rubbed on the clothes in the sink should suffice.)

We wake early in the morning, hoping to get a jump on the heat that promises to be brutal. We seem to have arrived in the plains states in the middle of one of the summer's most intense heat waves. I go to the front office to check out the complimentary breakfast buffet. That same clerk is there, her face open and welcoming, a toothy bright smile, looking ready in case a camera crew should arrive at any moment. I am wearing clothes that, while not exactly dirty, qualify as less than clean. The things I'd washed last night aren't yet dry. I examine the breakfast offerings: coffee that smells burnt and looks like sludge. Wilted Danish. Plain bagels, precut as if we needed instructions on what do with a bagel, are hardening in the morning heat.

"I'll make the coffee," I tell Rebecca when I return to our room empty-handed. "Have a Lärabar." I extend one of our few remaining lifesaving goodies. We can hear George and Edna readying them- selves next door. His incessant coughing, especially in the mornings, is worrisome. At every road stop, George reaches for a cigarette. My own lungs seem to clog in sympathy, listening to him hack.

My mother, who'd once been a professional singer, died of lung cancer. I saw lung disease rob from her what little remained in the wake of the bipolar disorder—the rosiness in her cheeks, the strength to climb stairs, the breath with which to sing. The cancer stole everything, that is, except the desire for another cigarette. The afternoon after she'd had surgery to remove one and a half lungs, she was begging the doctors for a cigarette, extracting the oxygen tube from her nose to insist. She smoked until the day she died in her midfifties.

Before we roll, we look at a map.

"Can we stop for lunch in Mitchell?" I request. "Mitchell, South Dakota, is about half a day's ride from here."

"What in the world's in Mitchell?" George asks.

I stammer as I try to explain. One of my favorite singer-songwriters, Josh Ritter, wrote a song, "Other Side," in Mitchell. In an early, unpolished recording of the song, he talks about a cross-country trek bringing his brother to college on the East Coast. Stopping for the night in a budget motel in Mitchell, he marveled at the massive Flintstone characters he could see from the motel's parking lot. "People from Canada must think we're nuts!" Ritter had said. I don't care about seeing Flintstone characters, but the idea of being in the same backwater town he'd been in, breathing the same air, feeling the same sun, appeals. The crew agrees: lunch in Mitchell.

We mount the bikes and take off. I stream the entire Josh Ritter songbook through my Bluetooth device, catching only the occasional lyric over the thunder of my pipes. One song, about Lawrence, Kansas, another meditation on a Midwest town, loops in my head.

> *Preacher says that when the Master calls us,*
> *He's gonna bring us wings to fly*
> *But my wings are made of hay and cornhusks*
> *And I can't leave this world behind.*

I savor the song as we pass unrelenting fields of cornstalks, flanked by massive spools of hay stacked like jelly rolls, forgotten by the side of the road. I remember the crisp woman in the motel. I am not cut out to be like her. This is just a fact. Like the backcountry folk Ritter writes about, I, too, possess wings made only of humble hay and gritty cornhusks. Yet maybe it is this very cornhusk quality that allows me to feel the air thump my chest, to fully take in the smell of the grasses and alfalfa and the way the scents warm as the sun rises, to see the sheen of the macadam increase with the heat, to feel the deep thrum of my motorcycle hard along the road, and to notice my hands lose feeling from the nonstop vibration of holding on.

I move my body to get more comfortable. If I hold the grips by only my fingertips, I can raise my back almost upright from my normal pitched-forward posture. That position feels like heaven. For a while. When it gets tiresome, I try the opposite, extending my legs onto the highway pegs along the fork, and leaning back a tiny bit, the lip of my pelvis hard up against the back of the seat.

Everything is bathed in gold this morning, a life so real and precious I, too, cannot leave this world behind. Even for the promise of— what? A picture-perfect afterlife? Or this mortal one in which I might stay crisp and clean all the time? I'll take the life I have, this one right here with seared pant legs and less than clean T-shirts, with stinky socks and grime under my fingernails. Though I still fantasize of one day becoming the embodiment of pristine womanhood (if not saint-hood), the truth rides shotgun with me this morning. For perhaps just this one moment, the woman I am is exactly the woman I wish to be.

Miles and miles of prairie lurch by.

We hit Mitchell just in time for lunch. I'd posted on Facebook earlier this morning that we're in South Dakota and friends have replied that we *must* see the Corn Palace there. But first I want to find the Flintstone characters and look for the budget motel where Josh Ritter stayed. I do a Google search on my phone for "Flintstones, Mitchell, South Dakota" but come up with a blank. Hungry and tired, Edna, George, and Rebecca find a patch of shade for a little relief from the pounding heat. George smokes a cigarette while Edna and Rebecca down water. I try different keywords but still come up empty.

"Let's just go to the Corn Palace and while we're there, I'll figure out what happened to the Flintstones."

The Corn Palace in Mitchell takes pride of place in this city of fifteen thousand. It's open to the public and the kind volunteers who serve as docents will be happy to tell you, if you ask, "Just what *is* a corn palace?" that this is the world's *only* corn palace. That, however, doesn't answer the question. With its turrets and onion domes, the Moorish revival architecture of the exterior is completely sheathed with cobs, husks, leaves, and corn silk. If it's made of corn or other grains, it's used here. (As a native of Southern California, I'm reminded of the Tournament of Roses Parade where all the floats are decorated exclusively in flowers and plant material.) The smell of popcorn is immediate and overwhelming. With more than five hundred thousand visitors annually, the Corn Palace—part coliseum, part basketball arena, part multipurpose auditorium—serves as a venue for concerts, sports, and exhibits, as well as the focal point for the annual Corn Palace Stampede Rodeo and Polka Festival. (I'm having trouble picturing a rodeo inside what looks to be a high school gymnasium gussied up in corn husks, but I couldn't have imagined a corn palace in the first place, so I chalk it up to a lack of imagination on my part.) But whatever it is, from my perspective, this kitschy monstrosity looks like the world's grandest bird feeder.

Sandwiches and air conditioning at a little café across the street revive our spirits as I continue Googling for my Flintstones. Finally, the mystery is solved. Josh Ritter must have been just as brain-fried as we are when he passed through this part of the world. Turns out that Fred, Wilma, Barney, and Betty are to be found in the Flintstones Bedrock City Theme Park and Camping Resort, located not in Mitchell but in Custer, South Dakota, some 316 miles in our rearview mirrors.

After lunch we step outside and the heat hits us like a sledgehammer. Rebecca and I break out our "hydration vests" made of black fabric and quilted with little pouches of water-retaining gel. We fumble in the bathroom, splashing water, trying to get the vests to soak up as much H20 as possible. Dehydration and heat stroke will be as serious a threat today as the speeding eighteen-wheelers and the monotonous asphalt. Leaving the café, my vest in place, trying not to drip all over the floor, I almost run into a man entering the establishment.

"Oh, little lady, you're going to be mighty hot out here wearing that." He points at my vest. At first sight, it must look like leather.

I squeeze its side and let water drip onto the hot concrete pavement where it begins to evaporate on the spot. "I hope not."

"Ahh!" he says. "Perfect. Wish I had one of my own today. Safe riding, now, you hear?"

Back on the road, the hydration vest helps for maybe the first hour but soon dries out, and the heat starts to bake my brain. Over the vest, I wear an armored jacket. The liner has been removed so air can flow through to the vest, though it still feels as if I'm wearing my own personal sauna. But safety is my priority. The list of experience I wish to have in this one cherished lifetime continues to grow. In the motorcycle safety class, I learned about the ways a motorcyclist can protect herself and I take them all seriously. Though my bike is matte black and I favor black clothing and helmet, I make sure to wear some kind of reflective gear when it's dark. A full-face helmet, while hot and uncomfortable, is the best safety choice. I bought the kind worn by professional racers to provide as much comfort and protection as possible.

Yes, it can be argued that no amount of safety gear can make what I'm doing completely risk free. That's valid. Yet I would argue that life *is not* safe and can *never* be insulated from every hazard.

There are no assurances, and given that hard-edged truth, I have only one option: to appreciate the moments of grace as they come along. I have been blessed to be as fully present as possible with my own children and then to send them on their way with the knowledge that we shared every moment we could and that's the best we get. And though I'd like to live to an advanced age, to see my children find their places in the world and launch their careers, to maybe one day bounce a grandchild on my knee, there are no guarantees. Yes, I could die on this motorcycle trip, get struck by lightning, or come down with a fatal disease tomorrow. All the more reason to grasp this present moment, and particularly those moments that are not exceptionally memorable.

It's unbearably hot right now, the sweat stings my eyes, and my riding clothes have become the Crock-Pot in which I'm slowly cooking. But my senses are tuned in 100 percent. I smell the prairie. I feel the heat rising off the asphalt. My eyes are focused on the road ahead, searching for potholes or cracks in the asphalt, watching for road debris or an errant vehicle. I am here, fully inhabiting my flesh and bones, an embodied spirit glorying in the sense details of being corporeal. This may not always be the case. But right now, I am present. I am alive.

• • •

By midafternoon, we're getting close to the Minnesota border. George pulls off at a rest station. I'm wobbly getting off the bike. One look at Rebecca and the others and I know they're also suffering with the heat. Walking into the visitors' center, we are greeted with the most delightful air conditioning. I never want to leave. The drinking fountain spews refrigerated water. Trying not to draw the attention of the ladies working behind the information desk, we douse our hydration vests. Eating dried fruit and nuts revives us a bit, as does the liter of water we each down.

As we leave, Edna notices a hose on the grass outside. She turns on the water and arcs the spray in our direction.

"Wanna *really* cool off?"

Rebecca steps into the spray. "Let me have it!" She raises her hands and pirouettes in the water's sweep. I'm next, squealing when the stream douses me. George takes the hose and sprays Edna down, and then it's George's turn. Eventually, we squish across the parched lawn to our bikes. Wet woolen socks slosh in hot leather boots. Sodden hair plasters drenched skulls. We look like the least badass bikers imaginable.

We mount the bikes just as a group of HOG (Harley Owners Group) riders pull up, decked out in their colors, undoubtedly en route to Milwaukee as well. We nod hello, ready to leave, knowing how ridiculous we look. We don't care.

George holds up a hand to ask us to wait. He fishes around in his saddlebag, pulls out a book, thumbs through it, then removes his helmet and puts it in his carrier. I notice a number of the other bikers who have pulled up are likewise sans helmets. George explained that he'd checked his HOG book to verify the helmet laws in the state we were entering. We find out later that evening that we'd ridden though South Dakota wearing helmets that weren't required by law.

I've been with hardcore bikers when we've passed into nonhelmet states. Within yards of crossing the state line, they stop and remove their helmets. I am always agog at the freedom and joy they feel doing so. Yes, I'd love to pull this bucket off. But I wouldn't consider it for a moment. My life—on or off the bike—is not assured. Still, I can take all precautions that increase my chances.

Only nineteen states and the District of Columbia require all motorcyclists to wear helmets. This, despite data showing that helmets drastically reduce the risk of injury. Helmets are 37 percent effective in preventing deaths and about 67 percent effective in preventing brain injuries. Who wouldn't want the extra benefit on their side? In states that require helmets, deaths and injuries typically drop when the law is enacted. The opposite, unfortunately, is also true in states where such laws are repealed.

We cross into Minnesota, the state where my soon-to-be ex-husband was raised. Both sadness and anger wash over me. There was a time when I loved this state. We visited it as a family and brought the kids a few times. But now I can't help thinking about the dark side of its midwestern values and the "don't ask for more than the world offers you" mindset. J was stuck twenty-plus years in a go-nowhere job, unhappy, yet unwilling to risk and change things. He thought that same mentality should govern our marriage. Right now, he's pissed as hell because I have shown the audacity to think I deserve better. To wish for a relationship with real intimacy, deep love, something more than "you agreed to this, so you're stuck with it." Being here again, under very different circumstances, makes me bristle.

We've been on the road for at least eight hours when we stop for gas and I search on my phone for nearby hotels. We've stayed at low-end lodgings the last few nights. I find a slightly more upscale chain and we agree to book it. As we pull up, I laugh. The hotel parking lot is filled to bursting with Harleys outfitted for cross-country travel. The hotel itself is basically an annex to the local Harley dealer that sits next door. We seem to have found the right place.

After dinner, Rebecca and I walk to the grocery store to refill our stash of dried fruit, nuts, Lārabars, and apples.

After a soak in the bathtub, I nestle into my nice hotel bed, appreciating the thread count of the sheets, the efficiency of the air conditioning, the firmness of the mattress, the wonder of pillows. I have laughed more today than I have in years.

Day Six: Wednesday, August 28
Albert Lea, Minnesota to Milwaukee, Wisconsin 367 miles

I don't move all night. There's something about physical and emotional exhaustion that brings a gift: the deepest sleep imaginable. I wake rested, ready to get going. Today we'll finally reach Milwaukee and get a few days of downtime. Though my body has at last adapted to the vibration and strain of controlling this nearly six-hundred-pound machine at high speeds, I still will be glad for the break.

At the serve-yourself-breakfast in the little dining room, we meet bikers from Vancouver, Mexico City, Idaho, and Alaska. All of us are on our way to Oz.

Unlike many of my fellow riders, I don't profess a particular loyalty to Harleys, even though making a cross-country trek to attend the company's 110th anniversary might suggest it. It's just a matter of circumstance. If Rebecca had owned a Triumph dealership, I'd probably be on a Triumph. Ditto Ducati or Moto Guzzi. I have a fondness for all beasts two-wheeled and motorized. I appreciate the fact that Harley-Davidson is one of a declining number of manufacturing ventures in this nation that's still doing well, and the all-American satisfaction in the bikes and their storied history.

The morning is cloudy and humid, still warm but not as scorching as yesterday. We ride. I keep experimenting with different ways of sitting on the bike to give my shoulders a rest. Before we left L.A., I did two modifications to the bike: the addition of highway pegs so I could stretch my legs on long runs, and a more comfortable Mustang touring seat, the cushiest I could find. It has a depressed center spot, nicely designed to cradle one's behind while offering in a little lip of a backrest. When I first bought Izzy B, I added a riser to her handlebars to bring them closer to me. But I still found I pitched slightly forward to reach the controls. Any time I ride, after an hour or two on the road, I feel intense pressure in my shoulders from holding my upper body upright. That riser modification to bring the handlebars closer, alas, was basically undone with the new seat that pushed me back by about an inch. My behind is now more comfortable, yes, but I have to reach even further forward to reach the grips. Which means that as I reach forward, different parts of my anatomy hit the seat and absorb the vibrations in a new way. Something I haven't thought much about until we start to cross the Mississippi River, the point of entry into Wisconsin.

It's about ten thirty. The morning is warming and the sun feels good on my face. Right here, with a row of semis to my right and traffic moving smoothly at eighty miles an hour, I feel a delightful sense of buildup. I'm sitting more forward than normal to reach the grips, but now, instead of feeling the strain on my shoulders, my consciousness is elsewhere. The sensation is downright pleasant. Okay, more than pleasant. I look at my fellow riders. Is it obvious what's happening? Slowly, hoping no one notices, I rock my pelvis subtly in time with the vibrations. Mild but very enjoyable waves of pleasure course through me. Then they build and I feel my eyes grow wide. Is this really happening? I'm having an orgasm on a bridge traversing the Mississippi in broad daylight surrounded by truckers. My back arches and my hands grip the controls. Waves of euphoria flood my blood with the neurohormones oxytocin and prolactin, as well as a healthy dose of endorphins. Tingles run along my arms and curl my toes in the heavy leather boots. A shiver makes me even taller. Truckers, cowboy-driven pickup trucks, and soccer moms stream past, unaware.

I've gotten away with something amazing. Right here, in public.

I've long suspected that it might be possible to orgasm on a motorcycle, with all the vibrations thrumming through one's body for long stretches of time. But it has not been my experience in the two years I've been riding, nor have any of the female riders I know ever mentioned anything about it.

Not that I asked.

Discussing sex and its shadowy backroom intricacies is not something I normally indulge in. I am of the belief that sex is an ineffable private experience and thus best left in the realm of the unspoken.

After the orgasm subsides, I need to process what just happened. Do I say anything? Is this normal? The last two years have all been about my journey toward authenticity. There's no authenticity in silence, in pretending things didn't happen, but how do I talk about this? Perhaps I've unknowingly morphed into some kind of lone cougar. Will I be picking up thirty-year-olds before this trip is over?

Male friends often joke about my motorcycle being a five-hundred-pound vibrator. I laugh, putting it in the category of just another urban myth. I didn't expect this.

Maybe it's the new seat? Or that I've been balanced on top of 565 pounds of vibrating iron for so long that this was simply inevitable? Or perhaps it might have to do with me beginning to rediscover my sexual self?

I have to admit that sex has been on my mind a lot since my marriage ended. Certainly a lot more than I expected. Just a few weeks ago I purchased condoms, something I've never done. There is no man, active or wished-for, in my life. Still, the condoms are a talisman, giving me some assurance that I won't be sexless the rest of my life. It seems I'm waking up from the deep narcolepsy to find myself in a new and unfamiliar land, utterly flummoxed to be here. I am celibate for the first time in my adult life.

I knew my marriage was over when I had sex with J for the last time, more than a year ago. I found myself completely incapable of giving in to the feelings of desire I'd always been able to jump-start in the past. I couldn't manufacture even the tiniest trace of yearning. Instead of appreciating the joys of touch, I became hyperaware of the gardener's leaf blower buzzing next door. I couldn't block out the stale taste in my mouth. I watched dust motes move under the ceiling fan, wishing it would hurry up and end.

For many years, sex had been the rubber band that held us together, the oxytocin producer that made us feel warm and loving toward one another. We used it to smooth the rough patches, and over two and a half decades and three kids, you can bet there were a lot of rough patches. Sex was the one area of our marriage that stayed good the longest.

Long after we'd stopped talking about the things that mattered, long after we'd gotten into the habit of putting the kids' needs ahead of our own, long after we'd prized our role as parents at the expense of our role as spouses, we could still communicate with this one physical act of expression. We might not have been able to say the words to support each other emotionally, to ask the questions that would bring about the disclosure of deep dreams and harbored hurts, but when given the chance to spend intimate time together, all those frayed parts didn't seem to matter.

That's not an altogether good thing. If our sex life hadn't been good, perhaps we might have sooner confronted the issues that bedeviled us. If this physical act of reconciliation had been less effective, maybe we would have demanded more from our marriage and worked to ensure that it met our needs. Or, possibly, the divide would have been apparent sooner.

And now I find myself orgasming on a motorcycle, buying condoms, embracing an awkward truth that keeps popping up in my dreams, as I ride, when I write and run and walk and eat.

I miss sex.

On a level that's deeper than physical, that's something other than loneliness, I am craving a man and the release within me of pure, fireworks-grade carnal desire. Which is fine, I guess, except that it's not what I expected at this point in my life and I am bewildered by the unrelenting nature of this drive I didn't anticipate.

Thankfully, it's good to know I'm not alone in this sudden craving. Though many women report a decrease in libido connected with hormonal changes during perimenopause, others, like me, report an increase in libido. Sexual drive, I learn, is shaped by myriad factors and complex interactions. If you're feeling engaged with your life and inhabiting yourself as fully as possible, your sex drive might surge like never before. Research shows increases in libido may be linked to the reduction of two kinds of stresses: (1) a decrease in anxiety about pregnancy and thus the ability to relax and simply enjoy sexual interaction, and (2) a decrease in child-rearing responsibilities that may have negatively impacted intimacy in a coupled partnership.

Though I'm no longer coupled, I can say without a doubt that unplanned pregnancy is no longer a concern and that the child-rearing details have largely left my life. Physically, I'm in the best shape I've ever been in, thanks to training for marathons, as well as backpacking. I'm waking up at fifty years old, suddenly ready to go, hoping to explore the world of sex I never fully examined when I was young and single. And yet, there's no one in my life to engage with in this way.

When I was in the process of separating, the thought of doing without sex wasn't even on my concern list. I just wanted out. Besides, society tells us that sex drive drops precipitously with age, especially for women. I honestly didn't think sexual yearning would be an issue. I'm like someone who's always been well fed and who then becomes surprised to feel hunger. I was also battling another, older myth that I had never fully wrestled to the ground.

My first sexual encounter occurred when I was sixteen and seeing a slightly older boy. After months of joined-at-the-hip dating, he pretty much demanded sex. I wasn't ready but was insecure and didn't want to lose him. I consented. From that very first experience, I bought into a dangerous stereotype: Sex was something women do *for* men to keep them happy, to keep them hanging around. Sex had very little to do with me and my own desires. Men, I came to believe, simply had this gender-specific, extraneous need and when women were feeling generous, we might consent to give them a hand, so to speak.

This misconception not only hurt women like me who might not fully embrace our own sexuality until midlife, but also harmed the men in our lives. All that time, I thought that by bestowing my sexual "favors" I was being a giving person, indulging his "special" biological wants. I placed men in a category that required they be grateful to me for my forbearance with their silly little desires.

How condescending is that?

"The first year is the hardest," a good friend who's been divorced for decades said of celibacy. "After that, it just becomes normal."

Her casual fatalism saddened me. It still does.

A fellow writer spent time in his twenties in Dharamsala, where he met another writer who'd become a student of Tibetan Buddhism. They talked of writing, and the student told my friend that he "didn't need the books anymore." Thanks to his spiritual advancement, he no longer had to create words and stories to feel fulfilled. My friend has been haunted by those words for the past thirty years. Every time he hits a dry patch in his creative life, he starts to worry. Because, though he may be a spiritual seeker himself, he still wants books in his life, he still needs them.

Like I still need sex. Partnered sex. The real flesh-on-flesh deal.

I crave touch. Being touched. And most especially, extending touch. I find myself looking at men in a new way, just looking at arms, or hands, or legs, and appreciating them like never before. What could feel better than a pair of strong arms holding me right now? What would be nicer to touch than a powerful chest? How much would I love to kiss that jawline with its five-o'clock shadow? (And let's be honest: How up in arms might I be if a man were writing this and describing in yummy details the body parts of a woman?)

Years ago I learned to avoid the allure of bars by picturing the alcohol stashed behind a wall topped with razor wire—there, but not available to me. I had similarly assigned the same restrictions to men while I was married, I just didn't realize it. I stopped noticing them or responding in any way. The sexually responsive part of me was completely shut down, turned off, totally unavailable except for one man in one clear-cut situation.

But now, everything feels cut loose, breaking apart. I'm noticing men (and women, too) as if they haven't been right in front of my face all these years. I'm newly aware of the raw sensuality that surrounds so many people. Over the past year and a half, Rebecca and I have been going to an upscale massage spa as a reward for our running efforts. My first visit there, just before my marriage ended, was amazing. Sitting in the Jacuzzi nude, watching the amazingly beautiful figures of other naked women in the sauna or steam bath, soaking up the joy of touch in the massage. It was my first experience of being fully *in* my body in years, maybe decades. I felt like I was finally coming home to myself.

At the same time, this newly revitalized in-my-body experience is a little disconcerting, like watching TV in black and white and then, suddenly, the Technicolor is turned on. Look, there's red! And orange! Have you ever seen such exquisite lime? Everyone around me has been seeing the colors all along. I try to figure out how to deal with the abrupt collapse of the wall that had unequivocally separated me sexually from every other being on this planet—Poof! Gone!— with no idea how to navigate this new terrain.

What I am finding is that celibacy is a bitch. Unbeknownst to me, it turns out I'm a very alive woman with—who would have guessed?—a strong sex drive. Someone who shares the human condition, complicated by all its messy and awkward wants and desires, with my fellow humans. That revelation is at once comforting and disturbing.

Plus, I have no idea how long I should prepare to wander in this unknown land of sexlessness. I wonder, from day to day, if I would be better off plotting a rendezvous or two of my own; I may do so yet. On other days, I embrace the yearn and try to appreciate its beauty. Still, I hold on to a package of condoms as a kind of promise. This celibacy phase can't last forever.

Besides: I always have my motorcycle.

• • •

We ride on toward Milwaukee. I'd asked to stop for lunch in Madison because I've heard it's such a great college town. As a professor, I'm always curious about the happenings at other college scenes. We leave the interstate at the exit we assume leads there but end up at some rural crossroads that's clearly not right. We're hungry and ask around for lunch suggestions, which put us at the Jet Room, a little restaurant inside the Madison Airport. As the four of us enter the Jet Room, I think about pulling Rebecca aside to tell her of my morning. But what would I say? *Would you believe I had an orgasm on the bike?* It seems like more than a lunch conversation, especially with George and Edna present. I'm not even sure I want to have the conversation at all. In spite of my awakening to new experiences, I still feel a residual film of shame.

We leave the airport, still hoping to see the college town, but follow yet another set of wrong directions that puts us ten miles further away than we intend. By the time we navigate our way back to the interstate, we've managed to make an entire loop around Madison without ever seeing it. That loop speaks to me of my own life. I may pick a destination, do everything in my power to get there, only to find myself circling my desire, never quite reaching it. When I'm smart, I eventually abandon the elusive desire when I realize it's not what I truly need. I have finally, at long last, learned to wear life like a loose garment. To let go when things are not falling into place. To stay alert for new things I wasn't expecting.

We finally arrive in Bookfield, the Milwaukee suburb where we'll base our operations for the next three days. Rebecca's college roommate and her family have offered to host us. Pulling off the interstate and trying to get our bearings, I see a Starbucks. Since leaving L.A. six days ago, it's the first Starbucks I've encountered. Realizing we've been that far off the radar gives me joy. I wish we could have made the entire journey without Starbucks.

The lawns here are uniformly trimmed and bordered, the streets overhung with mature trees. We pass Dairy Queens and kids riding home from school on bicycles, finally drawing up to Sue and Russ's home. We park, four Harleys abreast, under the basketball hoop in the wide driveway next to their large house. I take a picture of my odometer. Since leaving L.A., we've covered 2,463 miles.

Sue's two grade school–age sons greet us and show us our rooms. Mom arrives soon with arms full of groceries. We sit in her landscaped backyard, chatting, the others drinking wine. Sue's husband, Russ, will soon be home to start cooking. Sue's brought home real midwestern fare: steaks, corn on the cob, and potatoes.

I excuse myself and go up to the room I'll be sharing with Rebecca. Quiet, alone, I Google: "orgasm on motorcycle?" One woman's comment cracks me up: "Are you kidding? All the bashing around on my lady parts. No way!"

A guy answers the question in a different forum: "My last wife used to get off on the Harley vibration, but it was such a pain getting the 650-pound bike into the bed and then washing the oil and chain lube out of the sheets that we only did it that way a few times."

Another site says a motorcycle's vibrations can cause an orgasm but calls such occurrences "accidental."

Immediately I think: *I'm a freak.* And then I start finding comments from women who have experienced what I have, some as passengers, others as riders. One young woman confesses that it happens when her dad takes her out on his bike. She feels terribly conflicted. Another loves the back of her boyfriend's bike more than her boyfriend. I'm glad to know I'm not alone but suspect, by the few number of comments, my experience is fairly rare. I'm still not ready to say anything to Rebecca.

Eventually, we eat. I'm ready to fall asleep in my plate. After, I am asleep in two seconds, while visions of orgasms and motorcycles and men pepper my dreams.

• CHAPTER TWELVE •
THE UGLIES

Life is on the wire, the rest is just waiting.

—KARL WALLENDA

Day Seven: *Thursday, August 29*
Shelter in place, Milwaukee, Wisconsin

"All women are beautiful creatures, by virtue of their gender, their grace, their femininity. They were all created beautiful. Thus, none can be ugly."

So goes the sex-discrimination thinking at the heart of the Uglies, an all-male association made up of some of the most successful motorcycling men in the world. This exclusive posse includes rock-and-roll celebrities, producers, actors (including the late Larry Hagman), visual artists, and Fortune 500 businessmen. According to the group's website, the Uglies claim brothers in almost every state as well as France, Switzerland, Finland, Spain, and Germany, "along with a gaggle of Nomads that might turn up anywhere, usually when it's time for dinner."

The Ugly logo shirt—a skull and crossbones on a field of black—has been proudly worn at major Hollywood events, on stage at giant music venues, in the boardrooms of multinational corporations, on the floor of the U.S. Senate, not to mention barrooms and brothels from Hamburg to Honolulu. "Beneath that swag is a seething Ugliness that unites what otherwise appears to be a totally disparate amalgamation of riders," the website boasts. And though I've been warned that this is a rabidly all-male club, and that women are never welcome except as compliant arm candy, I am still dying to get my hands on a T-shirt.

I've met some Uglies back in Los Angeles, but I'm about to get to know more of them. We'll be spending much of this weekend with the club because Rebecca's father, Oliver, is an Ugly. If we're with Oliver, we're golden. Over the past two weeks, Oliver chartered a more casual route to Milwaukee, meeting up with Ugly brothers along the way. More Uglies are arriving in town by the minute.

Of course the question arises: How do I reconcile the fact that this is a gender-excluding society? Their motto—"Beauty is only skin deep, but Ugly is to the bone"—seems an odd contradiction to the exclusion of women. Yes, I know that the world of motorcycling is unapologetically sexist and certainly doesn't need me to help support it by yearning for its emblem of oppression. And yet, I find myself here, curious as to the macho mystique of this tribe, wanting to better understand the hormonal bonding.

We won't be meeting with the Uglies until later this afternoon, but thinking about such things spurs questions about how we're different, men and women, and how our experience of risk and life shape us, questions that have been with me since day one of this journey. While we've explored the reality that men tend to be bigger risk takers than women, I wonder about the benefits we sacrifice by remaining risk averse, just like I wonder what I'm foregoing by being excluded from the Uglies. My research and ongoing conversations with scientists provides key clues. "The Confidence Gap" in a 2014 issue of *The Atlantic* by journalists Katty Kay and Claire Shipman is particularly informative.

Androgen hormones are part of the answer. The male body pumps more than ten times the amount of testosterone than a woman's body, benefitting men with advantages in speed, strength, muscle mass, and a zeal for competition. This hormone also ties into risk taking. *The Atlantic* article cites recent studies at Cambridge University that linked high testosterone levels with an appetite for financial risk. Using saliva samples taken twice daily from high-income male traders at a London hedge fund, researchers found that on days when the men's testosterone levels started out high, they made riskier trades compared to days when the levels began low. This became a self-perpetuating cycle: When those risky trades paid off, the traders' testosterone level surged even more. One trader demonstrated a 74 percent rise in testosterone over a six-day period of gains. Thus, taking risks and seeing them pay off means a person is much more likely to continue taking risks.

Though I've read that women show an increase in financial risk-taking behavior (such as competitive bidding) during ovulation— they also perform better at sports, demonstrate improved visual acuity, score higher on tests, and display enhanced cognition. Still, they do not generally demonstrate the same levels and type of risk taking seen with testosterone-fueled men. If they have children, the desire to nurture and care for their offspring may be part of that equation, tamping down any risky inclinations. Still, that doesn't mean that risk of some sort is not good for them, only that they're not as biologically compelled to take the more hair-raising kinds of risks that men do.

But one thing seems certain: Avoiding risk altogether is actually an unhealthy state for all of us, male and female alike.

When we opt for security and risk-free choices, the likelihood diminishes that we'll take future life-enriching risks when they present themselves. If you're not used to stepping out of the controlled life you've built, the chances shrink that you'll do so today or even tomorrow. We accustom ourselves to staying small and contained. Just as the men whose levels of the neurohormone surges when their risk taking pays off thus creating a drive for still more risk, those who take fewer and smaller risks may see their lives contract, our desires shrink. Remember what you dreamed of when you were younger? Do you still have those dreams and desires that thrill and impel you? Or has life taught you to accept what you've been given and to ask for no more?

The cultural milieu in which we were raised, and the one in which we now operate as adults, shapes our reluctance. This tendency may play a bigger role in our hesitation to fully inhabit our lives and dreams than even biology. I'm personally fascinated by the findings of Kay and Shipman in *The Atlantic*. While their examination focuses on women in business, their conclusions shed light on women as a whole and our relationship with risk as seen through the lens of confidence.

Kay and Shipman report that, compared with men, women in the business world generally don't consider themselves as ready for promotions as their male counterparts. Women predict they'll do worse on tests than men predict of their own performance, and women regularly underestimate their abilities. Yet objective evidence points out the fallibility of these impressions. Women make up half of the global workforce, and studies demonstrate that companies who employ women in large numbers outperform their competitors on every level. Still, men get promoted faster and are paid more than women. So what's going on?

A tilted playing field is part of the equation. A 2015 study by the American Medical Association examined the nursing profession. Though women outnumber men by more than ten to one, male nurses still earn more. Even after controlling for age, race, marital status, and children in the home, salaries for males surpassed females by nearly $7,700 per year in outpatient settings and nearly $3,900 in hospitals.

What Kay and Shipman found at the heart of this disparity was that while women may be equally or even more competent than men, due to their lack of confidence they often fail to capitalize on their abilities.

Studies looking into this confidence difference in business found surprising statistics. Among business school students, for instance, men initiate salary negotiations four times as often as women. When women *do* negotiate, they ask for 30 percent less than their male coun-terparts. One researcher, Marilyn Davidson at the Manchester Busi-ness School in England, asks her students each year what they expect to earn five years after graduation. Every year she finds consistent differences between male and female students. Male students value their worth at $80,000 a year while female students expect $64,000.

Why this discrepancy? It's simple. On some deep level, we don't think we're worth it. We don't believe in our own abilities.

In particular, Kay and Shipman looked at a 2003 study by psy-chologists David Dunning from Cornell and Joyce Ehrlinger from Washington State University that measured the relationship between female confidence and competence. The psychologists were fol-lowing up on a previous finding, called the Dunning-Kruger effect, that demonstrated a tendency for some people to substantially over-estimate their abilities. In other words, less competent people are actually more likely to overestimate their abilities.

This is ironic for women, because even being fully competent, it turns out, does not mean a woman will *feel* more confident.

In the Ehrlinger-Dunning study, male and female college students were given a quiz on scientific reasoning. Before taking the quiz, they were asked to rate their own level of scientific skills. The psycholo-gists wanted to see if students' impressions of how they perform in science (a general perception) is shaped by a specific impression—did they get certain questions right? Getting a particular question wrong didn't affect their perception of their scientific skills—unless they were female.

Women rated themselves more negatively than men on their overall scientific ability (6.5 on a scale of 10, compared to 7.6 for the men). When it came to assessing how well they did in answering the scientific questions, the women thought they got 5.8 out of 10 questions right. Men, meanwhile, scored themselves at 7.1. Yet they posted almost identical results. Women scored 7.5, men 7.9.

Then the students, with no knowledge of how they'd performed on the test, were invited to participate in a science competition that offered prizes. Only 49 percent of the women chose to participate while 71 percent of the men signed up. Because women did not *feel* confident in their abilities—even though they scored on par with men—they backed off from the opportunity. Without that over-whelming sense of confidence, they didn't want to go further even when they presented comparable skills.

The reason this is important, Shipman and Kay argue, is what it shows us about this female-specific lack of confidence. When women don't believe they're going to be successful at something, they simply won't try, which forces me to recall my own retreat from the dance audition as a young woman.

This is not all just intellectual speculation of scientists. It's about the forces that shape our choices in the real world. Women, the sci-entists see, are frequently contained by a desire to be perfect and will not venture into pursuits at which they are not sufficiently sure they will succeed.

Several years ago, executives at Hewlett-Packard observed a similar phenomenon. The corporation launched an initiative to promote more women into top management. (Women like Carly Fiorina, I suppose, though she is not on record as being confidence-deficient.) Kay and Shipman explained that a review of personnel records found that women working at HP applied for promotions when they believed they met 100 percent of the prerequisites for the job. Men, on the other hand, felt qualified if they met just 60 percent of the qualifications. In "study after study, the data confirm what we instinc-tively know," state Kay and Shipman. "Underqualified and underpre-pared men don't think twice about leaning in. Overqualified and overprepared, too many women still hold back. Women feel confi-dent only when they are perfect. Or practically perfect."

So what can we do about this? Understanding the roots of this con-fidence deficit can go a long way toward creating solutions.

As children, boys are more socially conditioned to compete. When competition gets tough, the playing field turbulent, or the schoolyard rowdy, they're taught to accept those conditions. "Just rub dirt on it," is heard on playing fields after boys fall, a rallying cry to get up and try harder. This kind of programming makes them more resilient, teaches them to shrug off negative comments and to celebrate their victories while putting the losses aside. Girls, especially those who don't compete in sports, miss out on these lessons. Young women often nurture and support each other—wonderful traits—but they seldom encourage jumping back into a fray. This becomes a negative feedback loop. Kay and Shipman observe that girls lose confidence, so they quit competing, thereby depriving themselves of one of the best ways to regain that confidence. Because the bottom-line is this: Action is the key to confidence.

Taking a risk and finding out we can do whatever it is we endeavor, even if we fail on the first or third or sixth attempt, shows us that tenacity pays off. Eventually we will nail it. We must develop embodied wisdom in our own abilities; we must trust that even if we're not good at something right out of the gate, that we have the ability to learn and develop and grow. We must feel the muscle memory that can come only from hard-won experience. From that place of visceral understanding of our own potential and abilities, our confidence takes root and begins to bloom.

Any bookstore sells countless books on how to develop self-esteem, and women consume these tomes like Skittles. But confidence doesn't come from a book, any more than self-esteem, self-love, or any of the traits that make us into whole and strong people can be achieved with our intellect alone. We simply cannot think ourselves into that space. If we could, I would have mastered self-possession decades ago. Confidence develops organically out of our lived, embodied experience. We must act our way there.

If I want to gain self-esteem, I need to perform esteemable acts. If I want to feel brave, I must do things that scare me. If I want to develop confidence and I engage in an activity in which I have not yet developed self-assurance, I get to watch as my poise takes root and then begins to grow.

But I have to be prepared to wade through the fields of failure first. My wish for all of us, but for women in particular, is that we learn to let go of the perfectionism that teaches us to spell correctly, to always be on time and polite, to take care of the emotional needs of others, to avoid conflict and errors, to be "good girls" who get along with everyone. Enough! Those skills are not serving me, are not serving women.

Do you know women who reflexively apologize all the time? If you step on their feet, they apologize to *you?* They take on an overwhelming sense of responsibility and make it their business to make sure everyone is nurtured and cared for. I'm tired of being that woman. What about my own desires? My own unique self? When does the real me get to come out and play?

Never—unless I make time and room for play and lightness and begin to treasure my true self. And when I make that room, I learn to take myself less seriously. To laugh and make fun of my own failures. To embrace the flawed nature of my humanity. I still have trouble with appearing more conciliatory than I really am in order to not make waves, and with my excessive punctuality. My dad used to joke that I'd be early to my own funeral. But I don't want to be perfect like that anymore. I want to be fully alive.

And failure, I'm finding, is the path there.

But the side benefit of this aliveness, one I didn't even realize I was pursuing, is the ever-expanding well of confidence inside of me. Learning that I can handle this macho motorcycle machine gave me the courage to confront my spouse. Discovering I could backpack through days of rainfall and treacherous terrain emboldened me to ask for a raise. "Taking action bolsters one's belief in one's ability to succeed," Kay and Shipman write. "So confidence accumulates—through hard work, through success, and even through failure."

You don't have to backpack or scuba or rock-climb to learn these lessons. You don't have to be a woman either, as men struggle under similar crises of confidence at different times in their lives. You have only to act.

• • •

Before our rendezvous with the Uglies, we have breakfast and meet up with Donna, a friend from L.A. who flew to Chicago yesterday, then rented a bike so she could ride into Milwaukee and join us for the weekend. On first impression, Donna fits the prototype butch biker chick. She's a large woman by any definition—big personality, huge laugh, always accompanied by the throbbing sound system on her bike. She favors a leather vest with chains, baggy jeans, a bandana wound around her forehead. Tattoos wrap almost any exposed bit of skin, a cigarette never far away. *Large* also describes the size of her heart. When Rebecca and I decided to undertake this trek, Donna stepped up as our leather-clad godmother. She accompanied us to the Laughlin River Run, suggesting that we take turns leading the ride while Donna hung back to assess our road-handling skills. She reminded us to keep a steady pace, to watch out for our sister rider, to ride whenever possible in the number-two lane and coached us on how to be a good partner when riding two by two. After Laughlin, she invited us one evening for dinner, rolled out maps, and reviewed every possible route to Milwaukee.

Now that Donna's arrived, the first stop will be the Harley-Davidson Museum. George and Edna join us, and with Donna, we point the bikes toward downtown Milwaukee. The syncopated roar of our five bikes seems a rude intrusion on this peaceful Thursday go-to-school-and-work morning. I want to get out of the tranquil neighborhood as soon as possible so as not to disturb the quiet people who make their lives here.

Though this kind of neighborhood would have been where I belonged when my kids were young, I'm not living such a retiring life any more. I have settled into my little guest cottage in Los Feliz and taken on outings like motorcycle journeys, backpacking treks, white-water rafting, and marathon runs. I wrote about many of them in essays that eventually showed up on Facebook. Friends in unhappy marriages contacted me in private messages. "I'm afraid I'm going to be exactly where you are in five years and I don't know how to change things." A cousin in Ireland wrote: "I *so* understand what happened with you. The same is happening with me. And I'm afraid. I don't want this path to unfold." Few of these conversations took place in person, or even by phone. They seemed safe only when mediated by a computer keyboard, kept in the realm of the hypothetical, kind of like Googling "deteriorating marriage" to see what shows up.

I never aspired to this position, the one people seek out when pondering a divorce or dealing with life difficulties. I'm also held at a distance because embracing my life somehow threatens others' peace and security. But here I am.

The feeling echoes my high school pregnancy and being ostracized by my peers. When my pregnancy became known, my older brother Frank was away at college and wrote me a deep and thoughtful letter. Frank is laconic. Getting him to say much more than hello sometimes requires a cattle prod. But in this letter, he told me of his own experience being adopted, how he loved our family and felt an integral part of it and believed that I could give that same opportunity to the child I was carrying. There was no pressure, just information. I could certainly have chosen to have an abortion, but this option made sense to me in a deep way. I was still burdened with the Catholic guilt/saint stigma, and believed that by having the child, I would somehow repay the gift that Frank had been to my parents, my siblings, and me. It made me feel that my difficulties were worthwhile, that my struggle mattered. Some thirty-two years later, I still think the choice to give my baby up for adoption was the best decision for me.

But it was a decision that antagonized my peers, my pregnancy all too visible and maybe causing others to question their own choices. Some friends told me I was brave, as if I were *choosing* to be brave and not just trying to survive.

Looking back on that experience now, I'm grateful. I learned from that social exile how to make my own life and that my decisions were mine alone and did not need to be vetted by my peers. And though I have spent the last twenty-five years making a stable, quiet, and in some ways falsely secure life, I know I can craft a new one. I am doing so at this very moment as I ride into Milwaukee, acknowledging signs welcoming home the adopted sons and daughters of the city by virtue of our Harleys.

This 110th Harley anniversary is a point of self-respect for this city, the name *Harley* woven into Milwaukee pride. People wave. A bed sheet, spray-painted into a banner reading welcome riders, hangs from a freeway overpass.

We weave through an unexpected maze of road construction and wading pool–size holes in the asphalt. The directions we'd gathered before leaving the house quickly become useless. We wind and wend our way as the streets fill with motorcycles. The bikers we pass signal greetings to us. Eventually, the density of bikes grows until we're in a sea of motorcycles. I'm fighting back my own nervousness. What if I stall the bike now or put it down? Make a wrong turn and lose my group? Then Donna signals a turn to the right. We follow onto a large grass lot filled handlebar-to-fender with bikes. Parking attendants hand us plastic guards to place under our kickstands to prevent them from sinking into the grass and setting off a domino effect of tipping motorcycles.

I think this must be the main fairgrounds, but no. It's the overflow parking for the museum. All these bikers have come to pay their respects to the evolution, artistry, and iconography that is Harley-Davidson.

"Good thing we got here so early on the first day," Donna says. "The line will be a block long soon." It already looks a block long to me. We tour the museum, taking in some 450 motorcycles, dating from the early 1900s to the present day. Stories about the history of motorcycles, the people who have ridden them, and Harley culture line the walls. The museum overlooks the Milwaukee riverfront, with views of the city. I find myself hanging out near the windows, escaping as best I can the crowds of people exhibiting contemporary biker culture. I've never been comfortable in large gatherings. Outside, there's a gift shop filled with Harley paraphernalia as well as temporary structures in which to buy 110th anniversary T-shirts at inflated prices. Yet bikers keep buying and buying. We stand in yet another line to get our HOG chapter pins saying we've made it to the 110th. This is another ritual of this world I don't quite get. Donna tells me I absolutely must claim my pin; it's valuable. Sitting on the lawn, we eat bratwurst and popcorn, mandatory Milwaukee nosh, though not exactly suited to one-hundred-degree heat.

Rebecca tells us that we need to go to Harley headquarters a few miles away to pick up our parade passes. I don't quite understand the logic involved with who does and does not get a parade pass allowing us to ride in the huge pageant Saturday morning. But from the numbers of bikers showing up at Harley corporate headquarters, it looks as though there will be more people riding in the procession than watching. We meet up with some other female bikers we know from home: Marie and her friend Liz. We're now a group of six women bikers, plus George, a good sport, even when Donna starts calling our group "George and the Pussy Posse." We take a photo outside of Harley headquarters to mark the occasion.

The day is more of the same—bikers in sporting their "colors," drinking beer, getting sunburnt, wandering the Summerfest grounds. Riding back to Sue's late that evening, we get completely lost, Donna and George taking turns leading us farther and farther astray. We're trying to find the Dairy Queen that Google tells us is near Sue's house, but we keep ending up going the wrong direction. Eventually, we settle in with ice cream cones, happy.

CHAPTER THIRTEEN

CHAPTER THIRTEEN
BENEDICTION

> "Every society honors its live conformists
> and its dead troublemakers."
> —MIGNON MCLAUGHLIN

Day Eight: Friday, August 30
Rural areas surrounding Milwaukee

Rather than join the Harley celebrations today, we decide to go off-script and explore, hoping to find Holy Hill, a basilica a short ride from Milwaukee. Later we will meet a group of Uglies out at a farm one of them owns.

The ride takes us out into the countryside and we ease our way—up and down and around—through the green lushness surrounded by farmland. At the lane that leads to Holy Hill, a sign welcomes us, but I fly by so fast I think it says the basilica is run by Disgraced Carmelites. I know that that can't be true, but it makes me smile. If this place is indeed run by the disgraced, maybe there's room for those of us who find ourselves in the realm of imperfection, the struggling, the all-too-human

The full name is the Basilica of the National Shrine of Mary, Help of Christians, at Holy Hill. Established in 1906, the handsome neo-Romanesque church was built in 1926 and sits amid 435 acres of pastoral and woodland exquisiteness. Holy Hill draws some five hundred thousand visitors each year. Once we enter the church, I find out that it's run by the *Discalced* Carmelites of Bavaria. I'm kind of disappointed that they're not disgraced and learn that *discalced* means without shoes.

The chapels, with their hushed bearing, are a reflective retreat from the thunder and fumes of the Harley stampede. I breathe in the quiet of the echoey spaces and the waxy perfume of votive candles. All the prayers that have ever been uttered here, some expressed in wordless groans and sighs, are present. Ecstasy and grief, all rolled together. Reverberations of the countless choristers who have lifted their voices in praise and lament over the ages are nearly audible. The wood of the pew backs has been polished by the hands that have rested here, that have gripped on for reassurance, for courage.

In recent years, my spiritual journey has taken me from the rigid Catholicism passed on from my parents into a more open-ended direction. Huston Smith, the religious studies scholar and author on comparative religions, once said that if you dig deep enough into the traditions of any particular faith, you'll hit the "water table of our common humanity." I love the idea of this water table, that aquatic reservoir within the earth that sustains life, burbling beneath the individualities we think separate us, superficial differences like gender, socioeconomic status, education, and race. At the water table level, we are all more human than sinner, united in our essential loneliness and our longing for community, connected by our flaws and faults more so than by our accomplishments, all of us searching for the transcendent meaning we feel *must* be part of human existence.

I soak up the dark softness of the quarter light, the muted colors of the stained glass, the beatitude of the statutes' faces. The sculpture of Saint Thérèse of Lisieux beckons. I find myself standing at her feet, talking to her, asking for a blessing.

When my father was dying, he asked me to buy multiple copies of Thérèse's autobiography, *Story of a Soul*. He gave them as gifts to the hospice nurses who cared for him. He wasn't trying to convert them as much as he wanted to share a source of comfort with those who were so generous in their care. It was his way of offering a blessing. Though Catholicism was never able to comfort me in the same way it soothed my father, I shared the sense of tranquility he found there. My mother, whose middle name was Theresa, also had a special devotion to the saint. Though my childhood, like my experience of Catholicism, came with difficulties and pain, as does everyone's, I have finally come to see the gifts I received from both experiences.

Rebecca and I climb the 178 stairs up the basilica's 192-foot scenic tower where we drink in the 360-degree vista of checkerboard farmlands with patches of forest interrupting the symmetry of tilled rows. The winds buffet us; the height is dizzying. But if I keep my eyes on the distance, watch a bird as it lofts on the currents, feel the sun warm my arms and let the air ruffle my hair, I am able to absorb the beauty without the panic I normally feel with heights.

Studying the orderly farmlands below and feeling the calm of the chapels, I think of my Auntie Betty, my father's youngest sister. Betty became a nun in Ireland, joining the Franciscan Sisters when she was nineteen, going against the vehement wishes of her family. My father came around by the time she took her vows, but her other brothers and mother remained opposed. She served more than sixty years in Africa: under Idi Amin's terror regime in Uganda, providing teacher training to the young women there; in South Africa just prior to the abolishment of Apartheid, caring for AIDS orphans; and most recently in Zimbabwe under the crushing dictatorship of Robert Mugabe, working to prevent HIV. Now in her eighties, she's recently retired and returned to Ireland. She has lived what appears, to outsiders, to be a calm and ordered life: that of a nun. But it's been an existence of adventure and service and boldness and great wells of courage. But I didn't know that about her for a long time.

I grew up saying evening prayers with my siblings and parents, kneeling before an altar created on a wainscoting ledge in the dining room of our California Craftsman house, reciting the rosary and other formal devotions. Every night, I joined in communal prayer for *Auntie Betty in Africa*. By the time I finally got to meet her on her first trip to California on leave from her work, it was at the most inopportune moment. My mother was institutionalized again, and I, praised in letters to Auntie Betty for my devotion to my family, was now a disgrace, pregnant at sixteen. What would this holy woman think of me? I prepared my bedroom to share with her and braced for the lectures that would certainly ensue.

I needn't have worried. Betty was full of light and joy and acceptance, never once questioning how I ended up in this predicament, just dispensing love and support. She didn't pressure me to make any decisions that would have pleased her or my father regarding the pregnancy. Instead, she let me come to the decisions I needed for myself.

Over the coming years, we spent hours together in California and Ireland discussing and debating tenets of Catholic theology and speculating on the origins of my mother's illness. I was terrified I'd become mentally ill like her, and while my father would dismiss my concerns, Betty took my fears seriously and filled in pieces of the puzzle that had long been missing. So many topics had been tacitly forbidden from conversation in my household, yet Betty described my father's young life in an orphanage and helped me to understand my own place in my family narrative.

When my second book came out, she was again in California on leave. She knew my father had stopped talking to me for two years after the publication of my first book. While my father and I had tentatively reconciled, it was predicated on not discussing the details of our détente and what had caused it. At a family gathering, Betty showed him my just-published second book, something I had been understandably reticent to do.

"Look, Eamon. Bernadette has a new book out. Aren't you proud?"

His response was gruff and dismissive.

This tiny nun in her late seventies, no more than five feet tall with her puff of white hair, morphed into a tiger. She got in his face and with a calm but braced voice spoke to her big brother whom she adored and brooked only when provoked. "Just because you have been unable or unwilling to examine your own past and the ways you were hurt does *not* give you the right to stop her from speaking out about her own truth. Don't you dare try to take away from her the joy of her work." She put the book in his lap and walked away.

My father never did come to appreciate or acknowledge my work. But that moment of hearing her speak to him in a way I could never garner the strength to myself was one of the most healing of my life. It was the first time I could remember someone standing up for me. I realize, as I stand on the top of this basilica tower in rural Wisconsin, that she modeled for me the kind of badass woman I'd like to be. That it's not about the motorcycle and the leathers, or looking tough, or taking chances that other people admire. It's about standing up for who I am and creating space for the people in their lives to do the same. I don't think she ever planned to be a patron saint for female motorcyclists. I wish I could mint a little medallion of Aunt Betty, like a Saint Christopher medal, that I could glue to the tank of my Harley.

• • •

Rebecca and I meet the others in the basilica parking lot and I'm about to strap on my helmet when Donna approaches.

"I got you a little gift." She hands Rebecca and I each a small brown bag. Inside is a devotional scapular—a small felt rectangle attached by cords to another felt rectangle, both imprinted with images of saints. The scapular, dating back to the eleventh century, is worn on the shoulders generally under clothing, one rectangle on the chest, the other on the back. It is meant to remind the wearer of a commitment to a holy life. My parents, siblings, and I wore these at points during my childhood. I haven't seen or held one in years. In find this a remarkable gesture by Donna, a nonobservant Jew. My feet sink deeper into the water table of humanity.

We ride on to the homestead and farm owned by Ugly Verne Holoubek and his wife, Terri. J's family ran dairy farms in Minnesota, but they were nothing like this. Those farms were dedicated to productivity, to smelly work, to perspiration, to unending effort. But this farm seems magical, a place devoted to curiosity, to learning, to exploration. Verne helped pioneer the craze for screen-printed art on T-shirts in the 1970s. He designed and printed thousands of T-shirt designs, including many for Harley. As a product of his success, he created this farm to pursue his passions: rebuilding old farm machinery, motorcycles, and cars. We sit down to lunch in the guesthouse where a number of Uglies and their wives are staying. We meet Ugly J. D., who toured with bands like the Eagles and Bruce Springsteen most of his life. Then there's Ugly Leroy Dwight who's traveling with his wife, Sharon.

Verne's wife, Terri, offers to show us her quilting space. I expect a small room, a few bolts of fabric, and a solitary sewing machine. She leads us, rather, to a barn that's been converted into a vast workshop, the walls stacked with shelves of quilting fabric arranged by color and pattern, a delight for the eyes. There's enough inventory here to stock a small factory. An antique bed is draped with quilts dating back to the Civil War. Not only has Terri made a number of state fair award–winning quilts, she also restores and collects museum-quality quilts dating back to the late 1700s. A lovely black-and-white border collie lies in the sun by the door to keep her company.

Verne then takes us to "his" barn, which is both workshop and museum space for restoration projects. Again, the space is massive. A refurbished antique jukebox sits to one side. There's a panel truck from the 1930s, a Duesenberg, an early '50s Studebaker, a '54 Mercury, a Ford Flatbed circa the early 1950s, a functioning mini Harley made for a child, along with combines and other refurbished farm equipment. When working on a project, he disassembles it completely, repairing or replacing worn parts, sandblasting each piece, then repainting it all before reassembling.

I marvel at how Verne and Terri have been able to craft lives aligned with their passions. Though I'm sure a tremendous amount of hard work has been involved, they've found a way to have fun and indulge their joys along the way. They are an example for me. I want to construct a life like this farm, one that includes industrious work, but work that gives pleasure and satisfaction, and to feel a sense of curiosity and exploration in all parts of my life. We tour the rest of the property, highlighted by Terri's superb vegetable garden that's half the size of a football field with tomatoes so big I can see them from two hundred feet away.

But the afternoon is wearing on, plus we plan to go to a birthday party for one of my former students living in Milwaukee, then on to the bash party at the Summerfest grounds to see one of my favorite bands, the Gaslight Anthem.

• • •

"Pull the bikes into the barn now!" Verne orders, sprinting from the house just as we're saddling up and saying good-bye to the Uglies. "Big storm. It's barreling towards us right now." He points at the northeast sky. "I just got it on the radar."

I look at Rebecca. We've ridden in rain before. What's the big deal? And even if we're not riding, why put the bikes inside?

But Verne is adamant. "You don't want to be out in what's on its way here," he warns, pushing my bike through the roll-up door. "The bikes will take a beating." We park the Harleys inside the barn and hunker down.

I'm still rather awed by the Uglies as a group and have found them to be quite reticent. I'm comfortable with Rebecca's father and am growing comfortable with Verne, but the others feel a bit standoffish.

As long as we're stuck here, I decide, it's time get to know these guys and nudge them out of their reserved posture. To do so, I find myself saying things to amaze them. Immediately I recognize an old pattern. I've spent my life trying to astonish aloof, hard-to-impress men. My father, who I know on some level completely adored me, was often distracted with his own worries and inner life. After failing to get his attention in the way I desired—to get him to see me as I actually am—I did what I call my "tap-dance for daddy" routine. I do the same to get influential men to notice me, to talk to and be impressed by me. I don't do it as a flirty come-on. It's more my style to appear smart and interesting, to offer tidbits of information, to give the impression of being intelligent and worthy of weighty discussion. I flavor the conversation with technical terms like *displacement* and *cubic centimeters* calculated to convince Leroy, Verne, Oliver, and J. D. that I actually know something about motorcycles. I hear myself doing it, falling back on old behavior, even as I hate myself for the pretention.

"You guys, come look," Edna calls from outside. The big roll-up doors are still open and we see massive black clouds stampeding toward us, rushing, all a-boil. The sky is sepia toned, drained of all color. Thunder booms over our heads and makes me jump, Rushes of lightning streak across the now murky sky, slashing brilliant Zorro strokes against the dimness. The air, humid and hot all day, suddenly cools but now feels charged with static. When the rain starts, it falls in fat droplets. Edna, Rebecca, and I in motorcycle gear rush out to dance in the downpour. We look ridiculous. But we're from Southern California, a land of drought, and by now, I've forgotten about my mission to impress the Uglies. The rain is a benediction.

We're laughing to the point of hiccups, putting on this pointedly unintelligent and non-grown-up display with the Uglies right behind us, probably shaking their heads. I don't turn to look; I'm enjoying myself too much. I'm done tap-dancing for daddy. And even if I still fall into this trap occasionally, at least today I have ceased the shuffle-ball-step routine before it went on too long. I'll settle for progress rather than perfection.

The plump raindrops turn sharp and daggerlike, turning to hail. Verne was right about bringing the bikes inside.

It's time to get under cover and Verne has shut the large roll-up doors to keep the water out of the barn.

Soaking wet, we collapse around the bistro table and Verne hands us towels. The Uglies are drinking beer and eating chips. Someone presses a selection on the vintage jukebox. Bob Dylan starts to play. Though the weather is ferocious outside, the mood inside becomes festive. The dancing begins, though it's mostly Edna, Rebecca, and me.

What we thought would be a passing storm turns into an afternoon downpour. The white clay road we drove in on has turned to navy bean soup. And still the rain batters. We're stranded. Yet the mood inside is celebratory. We're like people stranded on a lifeboat. We know deliverance is on its way and there's nothing to do now but enjoy our time together.

I call the former student whose birthday party we were planning to attend. "We're stuck on a farm in a downpour," I say, words I never thought I'd ever have reason to utter. "I'm not sure we'll be able to make it." Two hours later, just before dusk, the rain finally stops.

Outside, two inches of rain have left the road pockmarked, puddles everywhere. The air heats again almost immediately. Rebecca and I wander down to Terri's vegetable garden, tromping through ankle-deep puddles in our motorcycle boots. The nearly setting sun breaks through the gloom and lights up a tomato plant as if God is directing my attention to it. The sunlit tomato almost falls from its vine into my hand. It's as big as a grapefruit and still warm from the earlier heat of the day, but washed in a sparkle of rainwater. I bite into it as if it's an apple. Sunlight and sweetness made from rain and grace and goodness fills my mouth. Verne said to help ourselves to whatever we like from the garden, so as Rebecca collects chili peppers to bring home to California, I eat two more fat orbs of tomato. The pale red juice runs down my chin and stains my T-shirt. By the time we saddle up, we've abandoned all thoughts of attending either the birthday party or the concert tonight. We have been honored with a day far better than any we could have planned and we accept it as the gift it is.

We ride home, our bikes splatted with sludge, my lower legs painted in lumpy whitewash.

Day Nine: *Saturday, August 31*
Milwaukee

Though we picked up passes that would have let us ride in this morning's Harley parade through downtown Milwaukee, we opt to sleep in. Who needs the hoopla when life, as offered, is so good? Donna is leaving today to fly back to L.A., and George and Edna will start their return trip home by noon. We enjoy a leisurely farewell breakfast with our host family.

Rebecca and I, finally on our own, meet up early afternoon to ride with the Uglies to the Summerfest grounds. Rebecca's dad, Oliver, shows up with a woman he'd met earlier at Sturgis who flew in for the event. She's on the back of his bike, no helmet to mess her hair, younger even than Rebecca, in raggedy jeans and stiletto heels, smoking incessantly. J. D. is along for the ride, Leroy and Sharon, too. Verne and Terri will meet us at the fairgrounds.

Yesterday, the day we expected to going to be humdrum, turns out one of the best of the trip. And today, the day we're wandering among Harley zealots at the motorcycle equivalent of Comic-Con, is supposed to be the culmination of this entire journey.

Shirtless, sunburnt men are everywhere. And beer. The men display leather and tattoos. Their "colors" distinguish their affiliations. The women seem to rank as additional accessories, mostly in the mandatory auxiliary uniform of tight jeans and bursting cleavage. Commemorative T-shirts are on sale every five feet. And beer.

We are given VIP access to a raised platform where organizers host a party for Harley dealership owners, providing an elevated view of the moving mosh pit of leather, tats, and silicone. Rebecca talks with a woman from Alaska who, like her, has recently taken over her father's dealership. We make small talk and think about leaving our roost to join the main festivities, but frankly, there's not really that much to do besides fight the current of the crowds or listen to bands we've never heard of. (All the headliners play at night.) Less than two hours after we arrive, it's time to leave.

Oliver invites us to an art exhibit by Ugly Paul Smith, the American designer who created the iconic Harley bar-and-shield logo and the company's Screamin' Eagle. The gallery parking lot is peg-to-peg with Harleys. I'm pulling off my helmet when one of the Uglies comes over to inspect my Izzy Bella, seeming to appreciate her stark lines and minimalist frame.

"You're one of Oliver's friends?" he asks.

I nod.

"From L.A.?"

I nod again.

"You rode here? On this Sportster?" he gestures at my bike. "She's beautiful, no question. But, man: That would hurt."

"Hey guys," he calls over his posse. "This little thing rode all the way from L.A. on this fence rail!" He claps me on the back, directing his comments at his friends: "I don't want to hear any more belly-aching from any of you gomers about your sore asses. You're on big cushy bikes with all that padding on your backside and this little woman rode some three thousand miles on a goddamn Sportster."

The men high-five me, ask about our route, and generally accept me into the true biker community.

When I get back to L.A., I will be thrilled further to receive an official Uglies tank top in honor of my badass Sportster skills.

Inside the gallery, Paul Smith's art reels me back to the 1970s and '80s, recalling his 1976 bicentennial tribute. I would have been in junior high back then. I eat cheese cubes and drink sparkling water. It's not that different from any other art gallery, just a lot more art on the flesh than on the walls.

Rebecca and I will head home tomorrow. The point of our journey, the Harley celebration in Milwaukee itself, has proven to be a nonevent. But the ride to get here and the coming trek to get home: That's what it's been about. Being stranded on a highway unsure of how things would work out and yet finding our way. Being tired beyond the kind of exhaustion I've known previously and yet discovering a tiny pocket of drive buried beneath the fatigue. Being unconvinced I had the chutzpah to make it this far and finding out I do. That's what I left Los Angeles to discover. And now starting the ride home tomorrow, just Rebecca and me? I'm excited and also scared. But my well of self-confidence is bigger than before.

• • •

I climb into bed and though sleep seems like the best option, I don't take it. Rather, I continue to Google orgasms and motorcycles. I still haven't told Rebecca about my experience crossing the Mississippi, but my curiosity is heightened. I find an account from one woman claiming that the experience of riding a motorcycle with Ben Wa balls is the most delicious experience possible, causing waves of orgasms to keep you company. I can't get this idea out of my head.

I learn that Ben Wa Balls, also known as love balls, geisha balls, and smart balls, come in a variety of sizes and materials and were made infamous recently in the erotic novel *Fifty Shades of Grey*.

Some Ben Wa balls are metal and naturally weighted, I read, while others are plastic with metal ball bearings inside. I gather that the smaller ball, inside a larger outer ball, creates a gentle vibration. According to *Go Ask Alice!* at Columbia University, "given their size and bright or metallic coloring, Ben Wa balls would not look out of place in the cat toy aisle of a pet store." I laugh at the description but sit up in bed when the site continues: "Degree of enjoyment may depend upon such factors as the size of the balls, the strength of one's vaginal muscles, and whether or not the wearer happens to be on a motorcycle."

The site claims that Ben Wa balls create about as much sensation as a tampon, but even so, they provide fantasy value for many people, increasing their pleasure-inducing effects. "They are rumored to have two main functions: strengthening the Kegels (thus intensifying sexual pleasure and orgasm) and providing sexual stimulation themselves."

Do they really work or is it all just a lot of urban mythology? "The jury's still out," the site concludes. "But worst-case scenario, if they don't turn out to be loads of fun or a good source of vaginal vigor, the cat will likely get a big kick out of them."

At least they approach the subject with a sense of humor. I realize I have taken sex far too seriously my entire life. Previously, I had cautiously discussed sexual matters with my friend Tara and she pointed out that while most of my friends were busy exploring their young sexuality as twentysomethings, I was married and having kids. Maybe it's time for some exploration. And really, let's face it: I'm fifty years old. If not now, when?

• CHAPTER FOURTEEN •
COMING HOME

It's not because things are difficult that we dare not venture.
It's because we dare not venture that they are difficult.

—SENECA

Day Ten: *Sunday, September 1*
Brookfield, Wisconsin, to Atlantic, Iowa: 446 miles

Rebecca and I get away early, leaving the interstate for a route through miles and miles of cornfields and farmlands. The smell is terrible. Manure and fertilizer, I guess. Ugly Vern has given us a route into Iowa that leaves the interstate after Madison. "It's much prettier than the main highway," he'd assured us.

He was right. Corn and agriculture and corn and agriculture, but lovely rolling hills and lots of green.

I know it's unreasonable, but I have held a grudge against Iowa my entire life, and yet this is the first time I've visited the state. When I was a child, my friend from across the street, Denyse, used to visit her older sister in Iowa every summer. I learned later that Denyse was being sexually abused by her father, our neighborhood mailman. To escape her home situation, the summer she was eighteen, she abruptly married an AWOL marine and stayed in Iowa. Her life there did not improve. One pregnancy was immediately followed by a second. Her husband was an alcoholic who couldn't hold a job. Denyse ended up working the graveyard shift at a chicken-processing plant to support their family. One morning her husband picked her up after her shift, still drunk from the night before. He ran the car off the road, and Denyse was killed. But he lived. Misdirected anger, I know, but I have held a grudge ever since.

Now the state has a brief chance to change my opinion.

"Think we can make it to Nebraska?" I ask Rebecca when we stop at a gas station some five hours into the day's miles.

"Not likely," she replies. "Not if we want to stay alert."

Using my smartphone, I randomly pick Atlantic, Iowa, another two hours further on, and I book a motel.

We arrive at our motel and within minutes realize the mistake. The motel is indeed right off the highway as we'd hoped. But all the shops and restaurants that once flanked it are shuttered. The place is a ghost town with this one nearly abandoned motel still standing. We might be the only guests in the joint. But we've already paid for the room and are exhausted. We want to strip off our riding clothes, shower, and get something to eat before we crash. At the check-in desk, there's a small, refrigerated case. The sign tells us that we can buy Swanson frozen potpies for only $1.75 and that Hungry-Man frozen dinners are also available. A complimentary microwave sits on the counter for guest use.

"Is there a restaurant within walking distance?" I ask the clerk.

"No, ma'am."

"Nothing?"

"No, ma'am. That's why we offer these frozen entrées." *Entrées.* That's the actual word she used.

"Thank you. But where *is* the nearest place to get a cooked meal?"

"Ten miles," she points in the opposite direction of the highway. "In town."

Showering and changing will have to wait. Everything hurts when we again mount the bikes we thought we had parked for the night.

In "town" we find a Burger King. The only other option is Oinkers, and though the restaurant has closed its main dining room for the season, they offer to serve us in the bar. We opt to share an Iowan steak, touted as some of the best beef in the country. The steak is only fair and barely an improvement on the frozen entrées back at the motel.

But the joy we feel when we can finally peel off our riding gear and fall into bed is unspeakable. Though I'm sorry to say, my opinion of Iowa has not improved.

Day Eleven: Monday, September 2
Atlantic, Iowa, to Ft. Morgan, Colorado: 513 miles

Nebraska is a uniform plane of grassland, cornfields, and more of the smothering of late summer. When we stop for gas and cautiously ask for a restaurant suggestion, we are directed for the second time on this trip to a local airport, this one in North Platte. We order the lunch special: something like chicken noodle soup poured over mashed potatoes and a side of canned green beans. For two days we have been riding through cornfields. I ask for corn on the cob, a seemingly reasonable request.

"Sorry," the waitress tells me. "We don't have corn."

"What fresh vegetables *do* you have?"

"There's a nice salad bar," she says, gesturing to the counter with trays of iceberg lettuce, canned vegetables, and goopy blue cheese dressing. Here we are, in the agricultural epicenter of the continent, and it's impossible to find anything to eat that hasn't arrived by way of a processing plant.

Our plan is to stop at a hotel in Sterling, Colorado, which we are careful *not* to book in advance after our last motel experience. When we turn off the interstate at the motel exit, we don't like the look of it. Parked beneath a tree—the only shade as far as the eye can see—it's at least one hundred degrees. We guesstimate out how much further we think we can make it.

"Forty-five miles. Fort Morgan," Rebecca taps the map. I say we go for it.

Day Twelve: Tuesday, September 3
Ft. Morgan Colorado, to Rocky Mountain National Park
to Silverthorne, Colorado: 486 Miles

We opt for a proper breakfast and start the day later than normal. The news on the dining room TV reports on the latest attempt by long-distance swimmer Diana Nyad to swim the 110-mile distance between Cuba and Key West, Florida. I have been following for two years her repeated attempts to complete the marathon swim, a feat she'd initially attempted at age twenty-eight at her absolute physical prime. And now, the newscaster says, Diana has just completed the swim at age sixty-four on her fifth attempt, thirty-three years after her first attempt in 1978.

After thirty-three years.

On her fifth attempt.

At age sixty-four.

Over the course of fifty-three hours, without the protection of a shark cage, at times singing to herself, or counting numbers, remembering the books of Stephen Hawking, or experiencing vivid hallucinations of *The Wizard of Oz* and the yellow brick road. I am awed. How many people tried to talk her out of attempting yet again what she had failed to complete so many times? That's what stuns me the most—not so much the swimming, but the failure and then the fortitude to sustain belief in yourself even when others have begun to lose faith in you.

I have never undertaken an ordeal like that, but I do know what it's like to keep myself going, to quiet the brain when it begs the body to quit, to stifle the voices that remind me of earlier failures and imply they're indicators of pending disappointment. The task I've chosen is undoubtedly easier than the one Diana chose. But then I correct myself. At a core level, there is no hierarchy when it comes to risk. Every challenge requires the same persistence and faith. Climbing a mountain. Getting a divorce. Starting a business. Going back to school. Healing a trauma. Swimming an ocean.

I'm filled with possibility today, knowing Diana Nyad finally made it to Florida.

We wind into Estes Park, Colorado, and then enter Rocky Mountain National Park. We ride along Trail Ridge Road, the highest continuous paved road in the United States, reaching an elevation of 12,183 feet, and following a path used by Ute and other Native American peoples for thousands of years. Forty-eight miles long, the path gives us vistas of Wyoming to the north, the Great Plains to the east, and the Rockies to the south and west. After days of riding though the furnace of the plains states, it feels odd now to have to bundle up against the cool temperatures and strong winds.

From Rocky Mountains National Park, we descend to the Glory Hole Café in Hot Sulphur Springs. At lunch, we meet three county commissioners, men who seem to wield power and know it.

"Those your bikes?" they ask.

"Nice ride," one commissioner says.

"I bought one myself recently," another one adds. The third one keeps flirting with us. As they leave the café, we overhear the female cook heckle the flirty one: "What would your wife say, talking to two pretty girls like that?"

We smile. I'm fifty years old; Rebecca's in her early forties. We are most definitely not above being called pretty girls. A lot has been written about how women, after a certain age, become invisible. It's nice to see that's not altogether true.

Our plan is to make it to Silverthorne, Colorado, where, oddly enough, both Rebecca and I have friends who have invited us to visit. Our first stop is to see Susan and Tom, fellow writers who are building a house there. Then we cross town to visit Amy, like Sue in Milwaukee,

another of Rebecca's college roommates. We enjoy the savory, unpro-
cessed delight of homemade fish tacos with Amy, her husband Jim,
and daughters Abby and Hannah. After a brief rainstorm, the girls
take turns sitting on our bikes. We snap pictures of them, posing as
mini biker chicks, just as a double rainbow arcs across the twilight.

Day Thirteen: Wednesday, September 4
Silverthorne, Colorado, to Madrid, New Mexico: 336 miles

When I wake early the next morning and can't fall back to sleep, I'm
again in thrall to my new obsession with Ben Wa balls. I Google for
sex shops along our route. I know this much about myself: If I don't
fully pursue this idea now, while I'm away from home and the usual
inhibitions, I may never play out this hand. Besides, this also feels like
a form of risk taking. By now I should be brave enough to broach the
topic with Rebecca.

I find a website for a store in Albuquerque characterized as "a guilt-
free, shame-free environment for women and men to learn about
enhancing relationships and sexual happiness." The *sexual happiness*
part sounds right.

Before we leave the area, we visit with Susan and Tom again to visit
their adorable café, Inxpot, in the nearby ski resort town of Keystone.
We eat our second breakfast of the day together. By the time we pack
the bikes and finally hit the road, it's past one in the afternoon, the
latest we've ever started. But we're traveling only three hundred or so
miles today. It should be easy.

When we stop for gas, I finally screw up my courage.

"So, there's this place in Albuquerque," I say. " I'd like to stop if
we have time."

"Of course. What is it?"

I lay out the whole story: the orgasm on the Mississippi (which,
disappointingly, has not occurred since), plus what I've learned on
the Internet.

She laughs. "This could be interesting."

An hour further down the road, we hit a rainstorm. Soon every layer is soaked down to the skin. Each time we consider stopping to put on rainsuits, the storm looks as if it's about to clear, so we keep riding. Then another downpour begins.

Darkness is coming on long before we're close to Santa Fe. We should never have socialized and stayed so late when we had such a distance to go. My right turn signal has burned out but I don't know it. I'm leading and Rebecca is trying to follow but she's confused by my lane changes and at one point we almost collide.

By the time we approach Santa Fe, it's seriously dark and we still have to cover the final twenty-nine miles to Madrid along a rugged two-lane highway. I lead but worry I won't see the signs for the turnoff to my friend Emily's home. Ever since that night when I hit the old man, I've been worried about my night vision. My optometrist assured me my vision is fine, but still I fear I can't see well enough to find the street I'm looking for.

Little rocks strike my knees. I open my face shield to see better. I wish I wasn't so tired. I wish we'd left earlier. Why is it taking so long? Why do I think I'm indestructible? When will we ever arrive?

We eventually find the street, but it's a dirt road corrugated with potholes and rocks—great for a dirt bike but a nightmare for a street cruiser. We inch our way down. There are no streetlights and I can see only the narrow cone illuminated by my headlamp. Emily lives with Kent in an old church he's converted into their home. I stop but can't tell which vague shape in the darkness is a house and which is a church. Every crevice and bump we ride over jolts me. I feel as if I'm going to drop the bike at any moment.

But Emily has heard our bikes and comes outside to meet us. She gestures to where we should park: up a slight gravel hill, just inside the property's gate. I try to crest the hill repeatedly, but roll back down again and again. My tires spin. I'm too tired. I'm going to put the bike down. I give up and park my bike in the dirt street. When Rebecca tries to park her own bike, the exhaustion and lateness of the night take over. The motorcycle's weight pulls to the right and she crashes to the ground. Kent comes out and helps right the motorcycle.

We get to the restaurant just minutes before the kitchen closes.

I first met Emily when we taught together at Antioch University in Los Angeles. We quickly became friends. When she went on maternity leave in March of 2010, the university hired me to take over her position full-time during her leave. She found another job, though, right after her son Ronan was born, and relocated to Santa Fe. Ronan was diagnosed at nine months of age with Tay-Sachs disease, a rare disorder that progressively destroys nerve cells, usually resulting in early childhood death. Her essays and book about this experience have comforted parents, family, and caregivers dealing with fatally ill children. She wrote with such mettle, facing the worst possible narrative, and did not sugarcoat a thing. She inspired and emboldened me to begin to take the first steps to live the life I truly wanted. During the first few months after my separation, I was trying to write with the kind of boldness and courage that Emily brought to the page. But almost every night I had nightmares about her. That's how dangerous it all felt to me. And yet she inspired me to go deeper, to write more, to dig in.

Ronan was a child I knit for, a child I loved to hold and carry and sing to. I loved him. And though in many ways Emily was devastated by that loss, she was not destroyed by it. She gave me new courage in the way she was rebuilding her life. During Ronan's last days, after the ordeal had shattered her marriage, she met Kent. He stepped up at the worst moment of her life and stood by her throughout. He was with her when Ronan passed and invited her to live with him in the church he'd converted into a home.

"Kent wants to get married," she confides to me, "but I don't think I will. Not unless we end up having a child together."

"Are you thinking of that?"

Emily is in her late thirties and, like many, feeling the mainspring of her biological clock winding down, fears the opportunity for motherhood will slip past. "Everyone tells me it's too soon, that I need to finish mourning Ronan. But I will mourn him the rest of my life. If I'm going to ever get pregnant again, it will have to be pretty soon."

She asks about my life and tells me how proud she is of me for following my heart.

"Yeah," I agree, "but being fifty and divorced kind of sucks."

"I know. But lots of things suck. What are we going to do: Go back to a life that no longer fits? We can't go backward."

I marvel at her tenacity and optimism. She knows the cost of love. She's paid it. Yet she's willing to try again.

If she can start again, I know I can, too.

Day Fourteen: Thursday, September 5
Madrid, New Mexico, to Tempe, AZ: 457 miles

We're ready to ride out of Madrid early, before eight, when Emily and Kent's neighbor, out walking a dog, admires our bikes. "Where you headed?" he asks.

"Arizona for today. Eventually Los Angeles."

"There's a wonderful small highway that runs along the New Mexico–Arizona border. It's a bit longer than the main interstate, but worth the miles."

We write down the directions and thank him. First stop, though, is Albuquerque.

• • •

We find the sex shop midday, a florid storefront in a sketchy neighborhood. I had been hoping it might be more inviting. Once inside, though, the young woman working there is friendly and helpful. I explain my mission: to experience Ben Wa balls on a motorcycle. She goes through the various options and convinces me that the best approach is a single silicone ball the size of a jawbreaker. She says it's a good introductory option. "If nothing else, you'll improve your pelvic floor muscles by doing Kegel contractions." Gynecologists and obstetricians recommend Ben-Wa balls in conjunction with Kegel exercises and vaginal weights to improve the elasticity of the vagina and to increase bladder control. So really, she rationalizes, this is an exercise in improved female health.

When she puts it that way, I feel less weird about the whole experience.

I step into the bathroom at the shop and put the ball inside. At my insistence, Rebecca also buys one but decides to wait to try hers out.

We head west on the interstate—homeward. In about an hour, we'll stop for gas and start on the smaller roads Kent's neighbor told us about. As I ride, I keep waiting to feel the first vibrations of that distinctive tingle. Nothing. This is a complete letdown. Eventually, I figure I may as well do some Kegel exercises. At least *some* good will come of all this.

When we stop for gas, Rebecca is curious. "Well?" she asks.

"Utterly underwhelming," I report.

The next leg of the journey becomes exceptionally memorable for two reasons. The first is the remarkable scenery as we parallel the New Mexico–Arizona border. It's desertlike, but rolling hills approach and recede, filling my eyes with subtle desert hues against a brilliant sky. The second is that all those Kegels perhaps jump-started the Ben-Wa ball because something amazing starts to happen. Over a distance of about one hundred miles, I experience a dozen gentle, rolling orgasms and am kept in a state of heightened arousal. They're not the slam-bang magnitude of orgasm that leaves you limp and speechless, but subtle and delicious and send shivers up my back.

We eventually stop for gas and I grab Rebecca by the arm. "You. Must. Try. This."

She laughs. "I knew something must have been going on!" she says. "You kept speeding up, then for no reason, slowing way down. It's a good thing we're out here in the boonies. I don't think trying that in L.A. would be such a great idea."

"But really, Rebecca, you've got to try this!"

"Not this time," she says. "One of us needs to be the designated driver."

Day Fifteen: *Friday, September 6*
Shelter in place, Tempe, AZ

We sleep in and, still in pajamas, lounge the morning away. My friend Tara pleads for more specifics about the Ben Wa ball. We'll be back in L.A. tomorrow, so we proclaim today Recuperation Day. Massage. Manicure and pedicure. Rebecca talks me into a bikini wax, which I've never done. Out of our leathers, armored pants, and smelly T-shirts, we enjoy the sheer and gauzy freedom of girly-girl clothing. When I return to L.A. tomorrow, I have no idea what my life will hold. Will I ever meet someone who might be a companion like Kent and Emily found in each other? Will the Kegels ever translate into a shared sexual experience again? Where will my life head next? I do know one thing, though. Whatever's next, I'm ready for it. Undertaking this motorcycle journey has given me more courage than I ever knew I possessed.

We have plans to go out to dinner tonight as a final hurrah. But a haboob dust storm is threatening and from what I hear, best practice is to shelter in place. We cancel the reservations and settle for home cooking and some Netflix. Later, Laura, a mutual friend from L.A., calls Tara.

"I'm here with Bernadette and Rebecca. They're on their way back home after riding their motorcycles to Milwaukee," I overhear Tara say. "I've got two big-ole Harleys in my driveway."

There's laughter and conversation, but I'm mostly watching the movie. I don't know what's said on the phone next, but Tara's face drops and she hangs up abruptly.

I look at her, eyebrows raised. "What happened?"

"I don't know how to say this," Tara starts. "But, ah, Laura asked if you were gang-raped on your trip."

"She was kidding, right?"

"I'm not so sure."

"I hope you told her we were fine."

"Yes. It's just that she said it so casually. As if it was the kind of thing that was expected when you take off on a Harley."

I think back to what I learned earlier about the dearth of female road trips. If we've created a culture in which it's sensible to assume that two women crossing the country on motorcycles are setting themselves up to get gang-raped, wow. It's more than just television and film portrayals that will have to change.

CHAPTER FIFTEEN

CARDIOLOGY

I am always doing that which I cannot do, in order
that I may learn how to do it.
—PABLO PICASSO

I'm back in L.A., settled into the "new normal." When I stop moving long enough to center myself, I feel it: my heart throbbing through my skin and bones, pushing and pulsing in a movement so subtle I spend most of my hours unaware it's there. The beat is syncopated and oh-so vulnerable.

Is this all that's keeping me alive?

• • •

When I allow myself to feel my heartbeat, I am filled with longing. I want to feel another's heartbeat. I wish to put my hand against another's chest and feel its distinct, rhythm, to lay my head against a sternum and hear the subtle thumps.

I want to hear it: blood pulsing. I want to feel it: life.

Dating. Romance. Sex. Previously, these human elements were always inextricably tied to the future. A teenager dates to find out who she wants as a boyfriend. During college days, who to sleep with. And then maybe we start looking ahead for prospective life partners. Always, the focus is on something yet to come: With whom to set up house? To marry? To have kids?

But now, all those life stages are behind me. There's no clearly defined future to look toward. So what now? What does it mean to be interested in someone? How do I navigate these unfamiliar waters?

I know the possible pitfalls. Sex brings a thrill, a kind of high. I could use that high to distract me from what's really going on in my life. Plus, sex has a not-to-be-underestimated chemical component: oxytocin.

Recently, watching *The Sessions*, a movie about a paraplegic who hires a sex surrogate, I am deeply moved with its explication of the human need for intimate touch. The look on the man's face, the way the two people communicate via their bodies. Watching that film, sex becomes more sacred to me than all the Catholic indoctrination I've received. The female sex surrogate is being pulled into something with this man. Sex is only part of it and yet is paving the way. The oxytocin response is doing exactly what it is meant to do by bonding these two human people together.

I consider the hormone oxytocin, known as the "bonding chemical." It evokes feelings of contentment, reduces anxiety, and produces calmness and security when in the company of one's mate. It is a small molecule, or peptide, that serves as both a neurotransmitter, sending signals within the brain, and a hormone, carrying messages in the bloodstream. When scientists have inhibited oxytocin in the lab mammals, mothers are known to shun their offspring. But when oxytocin is induced in these animals, the peptide causes the mothers to nurture not only their own offspring but also the offspring of other animals, even of other species. The levels of oxytocin in our system tell us when it's safe to relax and cuddle and also stimulates feeling of trust. Oxytocin is produced when we kiss, have sex, experience orgasm, hug, and nurse a baby.

Looking further into this question, I contact Paul J. Zak, author of *The Moral Molecule: How Trust Works*, a study of the role oxytocin and our personal biochemistry play in the development of sympathy, love, and trust. Zak is a professor at Claremont Graduate University and directs the Center for Neuroeconomic Studies there. I first became aware of Zak through his TED lecture. After reading his book I ask him for some insight into the changes I'm experiencing since my breakup and my father's death. I tell him I'm puzzled about what is happening biochemically, and what role oxytocin might be playing in this transformation.

His immediate assessment is that I'm experiencing the effects of lower estrogen and more testosterone. "You're probably experiencing increased libido as well," he suggests, though I've told him absolutely nothing that would lead him to that spot-on conclusion. I'm glad we're talking by phone so he cannot see my color rise, and I decide not to mention Ben Wa balls.

"You are doing things that are midlife crisis-ish. Your father's death probably had something to do with that." Since I was the primary caretaker in my family of origin, and then again in my marriage, I would have created over the decades a feedback loop that supplied me with ample amounts of oxytocin. "Those were all the factors that kept you in that oxytocin loop: the children, having a regular sex partner."

Oxytocin not only bonds us to others, but also triggers dopamine and serotonin, the feel-good chemicals that help us enjoy life and feel alive. Zak speculates that as a recovered drug addict/alcoholic, I'm likely driven by a craving for dopamine that's stronger than the average person's, what is sometimes called a "dopamine-seeking brain." Thus, I have an increased need for oxytocin and the dopamine it triggers.

But then, from a biological perspective, I moved into a new phase of life sparked by major life changes. The kids, whose hugging and cuddling when younger kept the oxytocin flowing, were now either gone or leaving, supplying less of the magical O drug. I also found myself without any meaningful connection with my spouse, at the same time realizing I probably had another thirty-five or forty years of life expectancy. With the drop in dopamine and serotonin brought on via oxytocin withdrawal, I still craved and needed those feel-good chemicals.

"Once those hooks were gone, your underling physiology changed," Zak speculates. "Unconsciously, you had to reconsider what it is in life you value and how you might want to live out the rest of your days."

He believes that from a chemical perspective, there was probably a change in my testosterone-to-estrogen ratio, adding to the equation. With a decline in testosterone, a person becomes less interested in exploring and more risk averse. This explains how I had been more content during the years I was raising children. The low testosterone helped fuel my contentment. And *that* became the feedback loop that perpetuated itself. The quieter my life became, the quieter I wanted it.

But now the opposite is true. Since I am no longer getting that chemical high from my kids and family life, I am creating it myself through the motorcycle. That stimulation, he speculates, creates a higher testosterone level, which helps to raise dopamine levels and causes me to pursue even more risks.

"Once you get a taste, then you want more."

Zak tells me about his own experience with risk, wanting to skydive and having to deal with his fear and reticence. "At first I was terrified," he says, as he considered the pros and cons. If he died skydiving, his kids would be okay, biologically at least. They were eleven and fourteen at the time. But he also knew that if at age fifty-two he didn't do it now, he might not have either the time or physical capacity to explore it later. "I have a limited window of opportunity. I recently started skiing again for the first time in twenty years. I wouldn't want to be doing that at age sixty-two, but I can do it now."

With these neurochemicals that seem to drive behavior, he explains, an acclimation process occurs. We adapt to our environment and the cycle continues to feed the cycle. More risk taking perpetuates more risk taking. "But once you get out of the system, the feedback loop starts to weaken."

Examinations of brain development in young boys and girls show that boys tend to have underactive dopamine systems, he tell me. "So we see lot of risk taking among young men. They're doing that to spike dopamine."

But while these boys continue their risk-taking behavior, other things happen that reinforce the cycle. They start gaining dominance over other boys who don't want to take the same risks. They also become more attractive to girls. Until the brain starts inhibiting these behaviors, which for young men is around age thirty, this is the feedback loop, resulting in more and more risk taking.

The same thing, he speculates, is happening with me. "You're a youngish middle-aged woman who's now seen as a cool lady. You get caught up in this persona, you like the new perspective. And so you have that feedback loop. You're living closer to edge and it's invigorating."

Just like his own experience skydiving. "Skydiving is the most life-affirming thing I've ever done," he says. "I have a friend whose wife suddenly left him after seventeen years and four kids. I'm trying to get him to go skydiving so he can remember what feeling alive is like."

Likewise, a newly wakened sexuality can have a similar effect, he tells me.

But I protest. Women at midlife are seen in our society as lacking sexually, as having lost interest. Why this disconnect?

"Maybe it's the whole angel-whore dichotomy," Zak explains. "We want women to be sexy and good girls at the same time. Then we have the whole 'cougar' thing going on these days, Demi Moore and all that." But one thing is clear: From an endocrinology perspective, we see that while some perimenopausal women become uninterested in sex, others become more interested.

And does the motorcycle itself play a role in these changes?

He thinks it does. Plus, it's likely my dopamine-hunting system would not have rested until I found something that fed it. But unlike those who turn to drugs, alcohol, unsafe sex, or gambling, he believes that I discovered a productive way to get the dopamine.

Perhaps, I suggest, the motorcycle helps supply me with dopamine by way of oxytocin?

He thinks about this for a bit. He's not convinced. "Nonsocial stimuli do *not* cause oxytocin," he explains. "It's always produced for social reasons. However, vehicles are very interesting in this context . . ." After Zak ponders a bit more, he instructs me to look up the YouTube video on Fritz Heider and Marianne Simmel's experimental study of apparent behavior conducted in 1944 (https://www.youtube.com/watch?v=n9TWwG4SFWQ).

The minute-long animated video features shapes interacting with each other soundlessly. Healthy people always say that the larger triangle in this film is beating up the smaller shapes, Zak explains. This is because the shapes are moving. Once they are moving, we assign intention to them. We assign emotion. We believe they're moving for a reason. Thus, they're easy to anthropomorphize.

Similarly, a motorcycle is moving and can create a very intimate experience. "There it sits, between your legs, almost a part of you." And the motorcycle is more than just the bike itself. A rider is also connected to a larger community of other bikers, meaning it's not inconceivable that a person might have a bonding (therefore oxytocin-spiking, dopamine-enriching) experience with a motorcycle.

"Wouldn't it be fun to see if your oxytocin level increases as a result of riding the bike?" he proposes. "If so, this would be the first evidence I know of that motorcycling causes oxytocin to rise."

How can we prove this theory? Zak and I decide to arrange a time to take blood samples, both before and after riding the motorcycle, to see what's happening biochemically when I ride. With a date for the blood tests set, I have to wonder if I'm bonded with a bike, literally having an affair with steel and leather.

• • •

In the meantime, though, there's still the question of real-life human bonding. I'm on a first date, having dinner with a man in my Los Feliz neighborhood. It's the only date I've had in the year since my marriage ended that feels like it might lead to a second date. He suggests a walk after dinner but doesn't try to hold my hand or make any moves.

"You know," he says, "whoever you have sex with for the first time after a twenty-five-year marriage will have quite a challenge on his hands. Some men might be intimidated."

I agree.

"It might be awkward and weird," he continues. "That's a long time to have been with only one man."

The date ends with a peck on the cheek. Perhaps my situation is too daunting. I drive home depressed.

But half an hour later, my phone buzzes with a text. "I like you. You're age appropriate, attractive, and single. How would you feel about being playmates?"

As he sees it, entering a marriage is like buying a house, while a friends-with-benefits situation is like staying in a hotel for a night or two. But being a playmate? "That's more like leasing," he explains.

"We can take things on a day-by-day, month-by-month basis and see how it goes. But at the very minimum, we might have fun with each other."

I'm not sure I'm ready to be a playmate, but I *am* ready to find out.

A few nights later he comes to my place to pick me up. It's late. We meet in the darkened Hollywood street dressed casually in T-shirts and jeans. This is purposefully not a date. We are road-testing companionship/playmate compatibility. There is no *will he or won't he?* No *does he like me? Am I cute enough?* Just: *How do we feel together?*

He takes my hand and I lean my head against his chest. My skin flushes where he touches me. He inches my face toward his and kisses me. I see myself for exactly what I am: a stack of dry tinder just waiting for a spark. Suddenly, I don't need violins to serenade me. His mouth is enough.

Before the night is over, the tinder burns away. The awkwardness he predicted fails to materialize. He takes a photo of our clothes clumped together on his bedroom floor. "My favorite picture," he says.

The next day, I wait for the panic to set in. *What have I done?* But it doesn't arrive. Then I wait for my imagination to dress up this little excursion in fancy dreams of romance. That doesn't happen, either. There is nothing manic and grasping about how I feel toward him, and that alone is unusual. I am calm. And feel appreciated.

We make plans to see each other in a day or two, and then again. And again. It's nice to be partnered, however casually, with a man again.

Three months later, I try to hold my expression neutral as he tells me that, from his perspective, playtime is over. My life has become too complicated for him. We've already discussed my plans to go to French Polynesia for three months on sabbatical and he's not pleased. He's decided he's not into the long-distance thing. Plus I'm in the midst of moving farther away from Hollywood, where he lives, making me geographically less desirable. And my risk taking is pulling me in directions he doesn't care for. While I'm fine with this kind of upheaval in my life, he's not.

I'm not completely surprised. He has been pulling away in the weeks leading up to this night. I say good-bye and make it all the way to my place, front door shut and bolted, before I allow myself to feel the stings. One by one, the little dreams I'd conjured to share with him—whale-watching excursions, tours of the old downtown Broadway movie theaters, camping trips, meeting my kids—disintegrate like partially emerged butterflies, dead before they've extracted themselves from their cocoon. Maybe that's the course of these things, I console myself as I destroy a box of tissues. If you're not moving toward a deeper intimacy, you're moving away from it.

I haven't been dumped in thirty years.

Still, I regret not one moment. During those months with him, I exorcised the young-girl mentality that held me hostage for decades, convinced me that to be with a man is to plan a concrete future. I learned to appreciate the experience-by-experience nature of the time we shared. I learned to be fully present with another person—body, spirit, mind—and yet to hold no huge expectations of what things mean and where they are going.

I also learned that I am an attractive woman who heartily enjoys sex, that I can navigate a grown-up world in which male-female relations do not revolve around marriage and the future. I no longer feel as if I'm withering away for lack of human touch. The more desperate feelings of desire have substantially eased, as have my fears of being left by a man. I have learned to be alone and to value my own company.

Now that the supposed "worst" has happened and I'm on my own again, I know from tangible experience that being alone can be a good and rich thing.

And I have figured out to some degree what I want.

Which, it turns out, is decidedly more than a playmate. Some of my favorite moments with him were far from sexual. The joy of texting someone to see how his day is unfolding. Making plans. Inviting a person inside my life. Sex is great, but those other moments are key.

Plus my favorite: listening to another's heart next to my cheek, my head on a welcoming chest, knowing that when he snuggles close enough he can hear my pulse, too.

It may be a while before I experience this closeness again. I am leaving for three months in Tahiti to visit family and will probably be alone for the foreseeable future. But now, I feel my own heart doing its thing. The pulse and beat, the whoosh and release. It's magnetic and draws me. I still wish to reach out and feel another's heart thump, but for now, my own is enough.

This heartbeat. My heartbeat.

This is what is keeping me alive.

CHAPTER SIXTEEN

THE HUMAN RACE

Do one thing every day that scares you.

—ELEANOR ROOSEVELT

I crouch at the starting line at 4:30 AM, stretching tentatively, my palms indented with loose bits of asphalt, feeling twitchy. It's still dark, the stars hidden beneath cloud cover. Already eighty-four degrees. With humidity running well above 80 percent, it feels like the midnineties, though the sun has not even begun to rise. Not an ideal day to run the 21 kilometers (13.1 miles) of a semimarathon, as it's called here in French Polynesia, especially for someone used to running in the arid climate of Southern California.

Half an hour ago I watched as participants in the full marathon took off with the blast of the air horn. Many of them looked like the runners back in Los Angeles: iPods strapped to upper arms, waists garlanded with energy packs and electrolyte goo, legs striated with sinewy muscle, singlets sporting competitor numbers hanging slack on slender torsos. Most were wearing regular-looking running shoes; more than a few ran barefoot.

Now the rest of us cluster together waiting our turn. I'm nervous. This will be the first race I've run without Rebecca. (*Trot* is actually a more accurate description for what we do, *run* being a little too ambitious.) I'm in a foreign country where I don't speak the language, about to run a race I haven't trained for, amid weather conditions that are utterly unfamiliar and punishing.

Why, dear God, did I sign up to this? The feedback loop of risk taking is clearly at work.

Three weeks ago, I moved to the village of Pao Pao on the island of Mo'orea in the South Pacific. (Look at a globe. Put your finger on Hawaii and then draw a line directly south. Those microscopic dots between South America and Australia? I'm on one of those.) I'll be here three months, living with my brother Frank and his Tahitian family of six. The languages spoken are French and Tahitian. I know only English and some rusty Spanish. Most people here are dark haired and bronze skinned. With red hair and freckles, I don't quite fit in. But I'm hoping there's a place for me somewhere here on the island of Mo'orea, and that in finding it I might also find my place in the larger world.

The question of what I'm doing in French Polynesia in the first place is hard to answer. Here's the pat response: I'm on sabbatical from the university. Sounds ideal. But the truth is stickier. I'm here in many ways to lick my wounds. I feel as if I've run at least twenty marathons since my marriage ended, just surviving the challenges and upsets, learning how to hang in no matter what. Back in L.A., my life used to fill two thousand suburban square feet shared with three kids, a dog, and husband. It has now been pared back, stripped away one shred at a time, until it's just me, tender at the bone, fitting into four hundred city square feet.

When my daughter, Hope, left for university this past fall, the all-consuming child-rearing portion of my life came to a bittersweet end, leaving me to figure out who I was and where I was going. So I'm staying on a tropical island many people call paradise, trying to make sense of it all. J would tell you I'm having a midlife crisis. But it's more than that. And though friends and colleagues think I'm indulging in an extended vacation highlighted by fruit-rich drinks served in coconut shells by handsome cabana boys in the languid postswim/postyoga afternoon, the truth is different. And I knew it would be when I bought the plane ticket.

Many days I take in my surroundings as if I'm inside some kind of tropical snow globe. Lagoons and bays of transparent blue-green water, sandy beaches, coral reefs, and lushness surround me. Yet my life is also a shambles. I stare at the bay as bits of snow-like debris from the self-inflicted agitation settle. I am lonely. I feel disconnected from all I've known. I'm hoping I'll recognize a path forward when I can finally see objectively again.

I had no idea, for example, that a semimarathon would be part of the deal.

In the three weeks I've been here, the challenges have been considerable. I live in a house open to the elements—think *The Swiss Family Robinson* treehouse, minus the tree. The house has a roof and low walls that rise from the foundation to waist level. Everything else is open to the great outdoors. Vegetation creeps its way in. Geckos scale my bedroom walls and click at me during the night. Insects are at home here, as is the occasional wild chicken that flies into the house, causing me to screech while my nieces and nephews laugh. Feral dogs congregate outside my bedroom hoping for scraps, and a 150-piece rooster orchestra breaks into song every morning at 3:00 AM. It's hard to shower without being bitten by mosquitoes or stepping on insects.

My second week here, the rains came. Eight days of nonstop torrents, sometimes so loud that normal conversation was impossible. The turquoise bay filled with runoff from the pineapple plantations until Cook's Bay looked as if it were filled with chocolate milk. This was not the tropical paradise I had been promised. Meanwhile, everything in the open-air house—sheets, towels, clothing, pillows—became dank and smelled of mildew. Clothes could not be washed because there was no way to dry them. My leather belt grew a mildew fur coat one day that, when washed off, came back the next. I climbed into damp sheets at night, put my head on a damp pillow, and wished for Vicks VapoRub to put under my nose to overpower the clammy, mildew stink. Those were the nights I wanted to cry myself to sleep, but I dared not for fear of insulting my brother and his family. I know they're doing all they can to make my time here pleasant; it's just so foreign.

And some days I feel so broken.

Meanwhile, my legs have taken on a leprous look, thanks to the toxic reaction I'm having to the mosquito, no-see-um, and other insect bites. My sister-in-law Hinano sewed me a mosquito net that is both gorgeous and functional. There are no Target stores here, no Internet to order what you need and have it sent to you by express FedEx. You go to the market each afternoon to see what's available, and whatever's there, that's dinner. If there's no fish, you pick something else. No tomato sauce, no spaghetti tonight. You need something like a mosquito net, you make it. And as long as you're going to the effort, you might as well make it beautiful. Even the light poles are festooned with flowers and coconut palms woven by anyone in the mood. The desire for beauty seems deeply entwined in the DNA of all Tahitians.

Little by little I am grasping new ways of being. One night, Frank asked if I knew how to make pizza. Aware their kitchen had limitations, I first queried him: "You have measuring cups, a rolling pin, a board to roll out dough, pizza pans?"

"Yeah, yeah. Let's just get the ingredients," he said. But when we got home, the truth came out. "I lied," he said, "but I'm sure you can figure it out."

Substituting glasses for measuring cups, an old wine bottle for a rolling pin, the dinner table as a rolling surface, and large pans never intended for pizza, I improvised. Whatever I created was sure to be a disappointment. But the dough rose miraculously, then rolled out to just the right size for the three extra-large pizzas I was constructing.

The first one came from the oven to *oohs* and *ahhs* of my impressed nieces and nephews. Everyone sat around the dinner table, expectant. Maybe my efforts would pay off, after all.

But then the oven, which doesn't seem to have any temperature settings, started to cool. Perhaps the propane had run out? The second two pizzas drooped in the oven, the dough gummy and failing to crisp. We ate the first pizza—not nearly enough for seven people—and fed the second two to the wild dogs.

What I haven't learned yet is how to fully belong.

I feel at times like an intruder in my brother's family, as if, in giving up mine I've also surrendered the right to belong to any family. Plus there's all the history. Frank is older by nearly five years. Growing up, we both struggled to help raise our younger three siblings in the shadow of our mother's mental illness. He adopted a stance of impenetrable self-sustainability, a can-do attitude that I tried to emulate, but often failed. At university, when he couldn't afford the dorm fees, he set up a tent in the redwood forest surrounding the school, showered in the gym, and studied in the library. He has little patience for the rest of us who are not quite as capable as he is. When the rains started here, he gave me the keys for a small, five-speed truck. The vehicle had no power steering, reverse gear was located in a different place than I was used to, and the two-wheel drive was wholly inadequate when the road to the house had become a muddy, boulder-strewn river. After I drove home one night in the downpour, terrified I'd get stuck, I told him I'd prefer to wait for the rains to let up to continue driving.

"Oh, come on!" Aggravation made his voice sharp. "We grew up in the same house. If I can figure out this stuff, so can you." I sulked, until twenty minutes later when Terava, his adult stepdaughter, got stuck in the same stretch of rapids where I had nearly swamped. With Frank's four-wheel-drive truck and a lot of cursing, we extracted her car. I was sorry she got stuck but was glad I'd held my ground.

Still, the old impulses remain. This is the brother I looked up to as a child. He was a star on the high school swim and water polo teams. I floundered in that same pool, trying and failing to make my mark.

In college, he pursued marine biology. I tried to follow suit until I failed chemistry. It's painful to admit that I'm often unable to live up to his ambitions for me, or even the targets I set for myself. And yet, the discomfort is easing. I'm learning to tease him, the lion whom, as a child, I would never dare taunt. We're getting comfortable with each other.

He gave me a hard time the other night when, serving as his sous chef, I asked how he wanted the broccoli and carrots chopped.

"For God's sake: Make a decision. Chop the damn things!"

Instead of moping, I shot back at him, brandishing my chef's knife in his direction. "Be nice to me or you can chop the vegetable yourself."

"You tell him, Auntie!" his family rallied to my side.

"Hey, it's been decades since we lived with each other," he said, defending himself from the sudden onslaught of support they gave me, his arms raised in surrender. "I have a lot of shit giving to make up for." We all laughed. Something is healing.

In packing to come here, I brought my running gear with the thought that I'd go for the occasional trot. The heat and humidity have forced me to scale back my normal 10K training runs, so when I first heard about the Mo'orea marathon, I knew I couldn't be ready in time. Then I reconsidered. If I lowered my expectations, did only the half marathon and gave myself permission to walk as much as needed, perhaps I could complete the distance. A doctor's physical was required, so I navigated the medical system with assistance from my niece, conversing stiltedly with a French doctor. After that, I registered to run. The night before the race, I walked down the dirt-and-rock road from the house alone in the dark, a headlamp lighting my way, to attend the runner's Pre-Race Pasta Party.

My heart banged as I checked in without a family member to translate. I showed my bib number and the woman welcomed me. Eating my pasta alone, I watched the Polynesian dancers and fire-eaters do their thing. All around me, people spoke French and Tahitian. I felt like an outsider, reinforcing my primary fear that I will never belong.

Race day, I woke at three thirty, dressed in the dark, and followed the beam of my headlamp to the starting line. A man in a pickup truck passed and shouted *"Bon marathon!"* My smile lit the darkness as bright as my headlamp.

At the starting line, the officials give out information about the race and I have no idea what they're saying. But I get the general idea and follow the rest of the runners as we bunch up closer to where they want us to start. Huddled together, I see a man wearing a shirt from A Runner's Circle, the little running shop in my Los Feliz neighborhood in L.A. This flimsy connection to home suddenly makes him seem like a long-lost relative and I want to hug him. Instead, I touch him gingerly on the shoulder. "Do you speak English?" He shakes his head. I point first at his shirt and then at me, trying to pantomime the significance. He nods, smiles. But I don't think he gets it.

Eventually the air horn blasts and we take off in a pack. Less than a mile into the race, we pass the intersection of the little dirt road that leads to my brother's house. I'm surprised to the point of tears to see Frank, Hinano, and my nephew Tangaroa standing on the roadside at 5:00 AM cheering me on. The path I've been on these past two years has felt so lonely, so void of familial support. To have family, especially my older, revered brother, standing in the predawn light to cheer for me is energizing. And humbling.

I find my stride and settle in. Water stations appear every 2.5 kilometers, but instead of offering simply drinking water, they also provide gloriously wet sponges to squeeze over head and body to cool off. There's no Gatorade or hydrating drinks, but occasionally fruit juice is offered or slices of pineapple and papaya. The sun begins to rise, painting the bay nectarine and rose. The route runs parallel to the shore, so we're always within arm's length of the ocean. The view is stunning. More families have come to the roadside to cheer. Some yells "Go! Go!" in French: *"Allez, madame!"* Others shout encouragement in Tahitian: *"Faitoito."* By 7K, I'm feeling weak, but I remind myself that I came to join my sweat with others, to be part of something bigger than myself. I'm not here to set any personal best. The day heats up and the sponges are not nearly as frequent as I'd like. But my legs keep moving.

When I hit the 11-kilometer mark and stop for a sponge, I'm almost knocked on my ass by the leader of the full marathon as he laps me and grabs for a sponge. *"Pardon! Pardon!"* he shouts, trying to right me as he runs on.

Soon, the elite marathoners are lapping me. I don't care. Small groups of Tahitian musicians set the beat, singing the runners forward. A battery of drummers on a flatbed truck drives up and down the road and thrums out a beat to keep us moving. Onward! I'm in the swim of humanity now. Just a runner among runners. Not American. Not English-speaking, just another human.

Journalist George Monbiot recently termed our era "The Age of Loneliness." He cites how those societal structures that used to hold us together and make us community are now no longer operative. Our aspiration for the wealth and prestige we think we're owed drives us further away from those with whom might develop bonds and, instead, puts us in competition with each other. This is the illness of modern man, Monbiot writes, an infection I've been struggling to heal in the wake of my marriage's demise. Without the nuclear family I crafted, how am I to belong in the larger world?

In his report in *The Guardian*, Monbiot argues that "as humans, we are shaped, to a greater extent than almost any other species, by contact with others. The age we are entering, in which we exist apart, is unlike any that has gone before." He decries loneliness as the epidemic it's become among young adults and as the affliction of older people. This tide of loneliness, he contends, is rising with astonishing speed.

"Yes, factories have closed, people travel by car instead of buses, use YouTube rather than the cinema. But these shifts alone fail to explain the speed of our social collapse. These structural changes have been accompanied by a life-denying ideology, which enforces and celebrates our social isolation." He describes the war of every man against every man as "the religion of our time, justified by a mythology of lone rangers, sole traders, self-starters, self-made men and women, going it alone." For us humans, we who are the most social of creatures, we who cannot prosper without love, there is now "no such thing as society, only heroic individualism. What counts is to win. The rest is collateral damage."

Has my drive to become fully myself created my own loneliness? I don't wish to live in a world apart from others. But in separating from my husband, I think I separated myself from the entire human race, stanchly determined to prove to myself my own strength and resilience. Even with the motorcycle, I made sure I had only a solo seat, so resolute was I to be responsible only for myself. And now, perhaps, that's shifting. Maybe I'm ready to invite others into my life, to risk being authentic and in communion with others?

As I finally approach the finish line, a marathoner comes up from behind me. How he knows I speak only English, I have no idea. "Come on. You and me," he says in English barbed with a strong French accent. "We'll finish together." I rally and try to match his stride, but lose him a hundred feet before the finish. Still, I did it. I finished the race. Frank and Tangaroa are at the finish line, cheering. The volunteers garland my neck with leis of fresh flowers and sea-shells. I am given my finisher's T-shirt.

Back home after the race, I fall deeply, satisfyingly asleep. I have done something profoundly important. I have tried, literally, to join the human race, to add a few calories of exertion to those of the people with whom I find myself sharing a house and an island. Terava will show me two days later that I finished 350th out of a field of 358. It doesn't matter where I finished. Only that I was part of it.

In the months to come, living in Polynesia, I will learn a few things: I will learn that a *pareu*, a rectangular piece of colorful fabric, can be made to function as a dress, a skirt, a shawl to shade the sun, and a towel to roll out at the beach or dry off with after a swim. I will learn how to wield a squash-size racket that electrocutes mosquitoes while simultaneously carrying on a dinner conversation. I will learn that stale bread gets chucked from the dinner table out into the yard for the wild chickens and dogs to appreciate. (And though it's called a yard, the land is much wilder than that suburban image elicits, more like a rain forest that's trying to take over the house.) I will learn how to eat rambutan, a spiny red fruit that's similar to lychee, how to buy fruit and roast chicken and whole raw fish from vendors set up on folding tables along the main road, how to know which food scraps to add to the worms in the compost bin, which go in the trash, and which are put out for the feral animals. I will learn to say hello, good-bye, please, and thank you in both Tahitian and French. How to go to the store early each morning for the freshly baked baguettes that are a breakfast staple. How to make *poisson cru*, similar to ceviche with the raw fish "cooked" in lime juice, then mixed with tomatoes, onion, cucumber, and freshly squeezed coconut milk. I will learn through painful experience how to treat the fungus that grows on the bottom of the foot, splitting the skin between the toes, and how to squeeze fresh lime onto a wound when you cut yourself on the coral reef.

I will learn that my older brother loves me and likes having me as part of his family. And that I can start the process of belonging any time I choose.

CHAPTER SEVENTEEN

YES

Do not fear mistakes. There are none.

—MILES DAVIS

"You free next Saturday to help me with a project?" Frank asks one lazy Tuesday evening.

Other than write at the UC Berkeley Field Station, walk to get a coco from Snack Rotui (pierced-open-before-your-eyes, chilled coconuts, just waiting for your straw to drink the delicious coconut water), or stream a movie, there isn't much else to do on this quiet island. There's zero nightlife, no coffeehouse in which to hang out and chat with people, and everyone's in bed, the island pitch-dark by eight thirty each night. Of course I'm free.

"What do you have in mind?"

"There's a film crew coming. A TV show out of Canada about stand-up paddleboarding."

"Yeah?" I don't quiet see where I fit in. I don't know how to paddleboard and I know nothing about television production. I sure hope he's not expecting me to make pizza for the crew.

The production company apparently wants to film some local paddling and will plug Frank's ecotourism side business, Tahiti Expeditions.

"I need a touristy-looking person to paddle in the canoe."

"And I've got the look, right?"

"Yup."

The following Saturday we meet up with the crew. The cameraman, Zach, will film segments featuring two on-camera personalities, a pretty young blonde woman, Nikki Gregg, and Jimmy Blakeney, a tightly muscled slightly older guy. Both of them are Bic Stand-Up Paddleboard team members. (Bic, the lighter company, has made it big in the watersports realm.) Apparently, they're minor celebrities in that world and are going to learn to paddle an outrigger canoe for their audience back home. Frank has arranged for his two adult step-sons, Tahiri and Tangaroa, to paddle as well. Tahiri will serve as the steersman, guiding the canoe and setting the paddling pace. Tahiri and Tangaroa know what they're doing, and the TV folk at least have a basic understanding of paddling.

Me, not so much.

The sport of *va'a*, as it's called here, is huge. Kids learn to paddle from young ages and compete through their school careers. When local elementary school children were invited last month to an event at the Berkeley Field Station, I marveled when the local kids didn't arrive by car or bus or foot. Rather, a flotilla of outrigger canoes came through the early-morning mists, appearing as if by magic, with singing and music played on Tahitian guitars. Paddling is one of the primary venues for young men and women to set themselves apart from their peers. The larger seagoing canoes still traverse the Pacific across countless miles, from Hawaii, or to Easter Island.

Va'a is completely ingrained in the culture. Originated by the Austronesian peoples of the islands of Southeast Asia for sea travel, outrigger canoes were used for the original migrations of the Austronesians eastward to Polynesia and New Zealand and west across the

Indian Ocean as far as Madagascar. In other words, outrigger canoe is how the people of Polynesia came to be the people of Polynesia, the method of transport used to settle these islands. The history is rich and the respect the sport garners is well deserved.

We will be paddling a six-person canoe. Tahiri gives us instructions on how to hold our paddles (which I have been positioning wrong until this moment), and we climb in. The TV people are affable. Nikki sits behind me and we make small talk. Jimmy is intense and sits in the front of the canoe and helps set the pace. We cruise around the lagoon while Zach, in a Zodiac that Frank pilots, films us. Every time we stop, Zach asks the on-air folks to describe the experience. They talk about the similarities between outrigger canoeing and stand-up paddleboarding, compare the difference in paddles, marvel at the clarity and warmth of the water. Frank comments on camera about the regal history of the sport. I just paddle and try to keep below the radar. The sun feels lovely on my shoulders, not too hot and paired with a light sea breeze to keep us comfortable. I'm wearing tons of sunblock because, like Nikki, I've stripped down to my bikini.

We continue paddling around the lagoon for most of the day while Zach gets shots. So far, I'm managing fine. The hardest part is switching the paddle from one hand to the other when Tahiri gives the command. Every six or eight or ten strokes, Tahiri barks an order that means "take one more stroke and then change hands." Ideally, all five of our paddles should hit the water at the same time once that shift has occurred. But I end up fumbling, coming in late, or hitting the water so that a spray of saltwater shoots up my nose. Still, we're not out to set any record and no one seems to care that I interrupt the cadence. It's a leisurely kind of day and we enjoy it. My arms grow weary but I keep up. When Zach wants to film the canoe from a distance traveling fast, he tells us to go all out. We do and the bow leaps forward. We move at such an amazing speed circling the lagoon I wait for us to lift off the water. We're elegant and swift. It's wild how, working together, we're so much more than the sum of our parts. Discovering how fast we can paddle bonds us as teammates. I'm glad I agreed to this adventure.

Glad, that is, until I learn about part two of the film assignment. Frank had mentioned something previously but either I hadn't fully caught on or didn't realize his plans involved me. Before dawn tomorrow morning, we'll get into Frank's Zodiac and tow the outrigger canoe from Mo'orea over to the island of Tahiti. There, we'll meet one of the top U.S. paddlers, a Hawaiian athlete just arriving in Polynesia, along with his girlfriend who is also a serious paddler. Then, with Tahiri in the steersman position, the two TV paddleboard celebrities, the two Hawaiian paddling pros and (gulp) me, we'll paddle the fourten-mile crossing from Puna'auia, Tahiti, to Mo'orea. That means crossing a section of open ocean called the Sea of the Moon, and finishing at Temae, a scenic blue-green lagoon on Mo'orea, all under the lens of the camera. I wish I'd known this tiny detail before I paddled so vigorously today. My arms will be like lead tomorrow.

But this is what my life is becoming about finally, or is becoming once again. I was more like this as a kid, always ready to raise my hand and say, "Yes, I'll try." "Sure, let me have a go at that."

One of the reasons I'm so open to the idea of *yes* these days is a side effect of midlife crisis. For as much as we make fun of this idea, and I've spent enough energy this past year and half trying to prove I'm not having one, the truth remains: I'm going through some kind of transformation I hadn't anticipated. In 2014, *The Atlantic* published an essay by Jonathan Rauch, "The Real Roots of the Midlife Crisis," where I find some of the basis for the life changes I'm experiencing.

In looking at levels of human happiness around the globe and how those levels change with age, researchers have identified what's called the Happiness U-curve: Levels of happiness drop precipitously for almost all cultures in the mid to late forties. But then, after a few years of lowered levels, the happiness index starts to rise again, eventually reaching higher than in younger years. The resulting graph looks like a smile.

The article cited other studies that confirm this finding, basically that though it's possible to have life satisfaction in middle age, it's simply *harder* during that time than at other points in a person's life. Statistically speaking, going from age twenty to forty-five entails a loss of happiness equivalent to one-third the effect of involuntary unemployment, Rauch reports. A big part of this midlife dissatisfaction, it seems, has to do with our expectations. A German study supported this finding by demonstrating that younger people consistently overestimate how much satisfaction they expect they will enjoy five years forward. On the other hand, older people tend to *underestimate* their future satisfaction. "So youth is a period of perpetual disappointment, and older adulthood is a period of pleasant surprise," Rauch writes. Between those two age milestones is when the U-curve serves up the one-two punch that knocks many of us off our game. Not only does satisfaction with life decline at that age, but expectations also wane, *and* at an even faster rate. People at middle age tend to be both disappointed and doubtful that anything better is coming. No wonder our generation feels so cranky and desperate.

But there's good news. At some point, expectations stop declining. They may settle at levels lower than in youth, but reality, meanwhile, begins exceeding those low expectations. "Surprises turn predominantly positive, and life satisfaction swings up," Rauch writes.

And when does this typically happen? Right where I am today, Rauch says, at age fifty.

Now that I've finally stopped expecting my life to be perfect, expecting all my goals to come to fruition, now that I've made peace with some of my more glaring character defects, I'm so much easier to please. When life hands me a delightful surprise, like being asked to paddle across the Sea of the Moon, I'm thrilled by it and not looking at it as an indicator of what other goodies might be next. At another point in my life, I'd want to prove myself as a "real" paddler and make plans to work on my paddling when I return to L.A. You know, to show *them* what I'm worth.

Amazing *them* is exactly what I've spent too much of my life trying to do.

Because, guess what? There is no *them*. There's only me. My worth is based solely on what I think of myself. When I act in a worthy way, I feel self-worth. Not because someone else anointed me with it. Simply because I know myself and what I've done. Likewise, I have a new ability to show up in this moment and to paddle for the sheer joy of it. My merits as a paddler have nothing to do with my worthiness. This is grace. I need not prove myself as valuable, but simply believe that I am.

• • •

The next morning, I get up at three, and Frank, Tahiri, Tangaroa, and I drive to the field station to load the Zodiac. Nikki, Jimmy, and Zach are already there. The inky black morning is thick with moisture, with the possibility of rain in the forecast. We bounce across the sea in the Zodiac, with Tangaroa in the outrigger canoe towed behind us, steering with his paddle to keep the canoe aligned with our rubber skiff. The sun starts showing itself, painting the eastern horizon in pale ginger and blue black, the hues of a bruised nectarine. In the three months I've lived here, it's the most stunning sunrise I've witnessed.

It takes two hours in the Zodiac to make the crossing. I wonder how long it will take us to do it by paddle power. According to the plan, Tangaroa will ride in the Zodiac with Frank and Zach. We all know I'm the weak link. If my strength fails or if I just need a break, I can signal for Tangaroa to take my place. I'm hoping not do that, but I give myself permission to fail in order to have the courage to start.

We meet the two Hawaiians at the dock in Ta'apuna, find a beachside hotel to use the bathroom, eat some snacks, and get ready to go.

Maneuvering through the harbor area we pass surfers and swing wide past party boats moored just off the coast to give young adults a place to stay up all night imbibing. Then, before we know it, we're on the open ocean. The water is not typical gorgeous Tahiti blue, but steel gray with clouds threatening, the air hot and humid.

We paddle. I am not adding much forward momentum to the canoe, but I'm pulling my own weight. With the Hawaiians onboard, we're going at a faster clip than yesterday. We settle into a rhythm. Thanks to my long-distance motorcycling, marathon running, and backpacking, I may not know how to paddle with the smoothest stroke or steer a straight course, but I do know how to do one particular thing: hang in there.

After about an hour, we stop for a drink of water and a granola bar. A thick clamor of seabirds has been circling and then dives right next to us, attacking a school of fish. Both islands are far in the distance and we are truly at sea. In many ways, being here, feeling the swells lightly rock us, aware that we're far away from everything we depend on, like electricity or phones, is like being on a motorcycle on a freeway in the middle of rush-hour traffic. I have the sense of being somewhere I'm not supposed to be, of being one of a small percentage of people who gets to know what this feels like. I also know that my strength, such as it is, will be needed to get us home again.

But then the birds are gone and it's time to get back to paddling. Zach jumps out of the Zodiac and into the water to film us as we paddle. Frank maneuvers the Zodiac for aft, oncoming, and tracking shots. We paddle. Blisters start to bubble on my hands and fingers. My shorts are soaked, my hair and face drip salt water from the spray of clumsy paddle changes. We paddle. The little island in the distance, Mo'orea, grows as the island of Tahiti behind us shrinks away. We paddle. I think of asking Tangaroa to take over for me, but I don't. We paddle.

As we enter the bay near Temae, I keep missing the paddle changes, too depleted and body-fried to sustain focus. The Hawaiian in the seat behind tries to cue me when to change. But I'm off. I don't care. I'm still paddling. We glide over the blue-green waters that make Tamae one of the most gorgeous beaches in the world. And still, we paddle. By the time we come ashore on the sandy lagoon, we have paddled for four hours and covered some fourteen miles. My head aches from the steady concentration, my shoulders are searing in pain, my palms are raw, and the joints of my legs, I'm certain, are permanently fused. But we did it. I did it.

Crossing the Sea of the Moon via outrigger canoe had never been on my bucket list. But neither was learning to ride a motorcycle and riding from L.A. to Milwaukee. Nor climbing Mount Whitney. Nor surviving a divorce at age forty-nine.

• • •

My sojourn in Tahiti is running out and Frank is distressed that we haven't done more. A few weeks ago, we took a group of high school students visiting from New York City to Tetiaroa, Marlon Brando's private atoll, and camped there a few days. The Brando, an all-inclusive, super-green hotel, is preparing to open soon and we lived among the construction workers and learned about the delicate ecology of the atoll. Brando's son, Teihotu, took us to Bird Island, one of the smaller motu (or "islets") of Tetiaroa, to see where some of the most rare and beautiful pelagic and shorebirds nest. While there, we were caught in a tropical downpour and had to seek warmth by stripping down to our bathing suits and submerging in the lagoon water until the storm passed. Then a "cyclonic event" diverted all air and nautical travel with its battering winds. Those of us sheltered in tents had to join the students and teachers in the dorms.

When the storms passed, we learned about the novel system for cooling the luxury hotel that pumped cool, deep water from the ocean and transferred its coolness to fresh water that is then circulated through the buildings. In downtime, I watched lemon and whitetip sharks circle in front of the communal cantina, awaiting scraps. They show up daily after mealtime, just beyond a sign: INTERDICTION DE NOURRIR LES REQUINS / DO NOT FEED THE SHARKS.

Tetiaroa and the paddling adventure, Frank decided, weren't quite enough. Next, Frank and I should make plans to go to an outlying atoll, Rangiroa, 225 miles away, where we'll dive the atoll's celebrated coral reef. It's logical that Frank, with his background in marine biology, has been scuba diving most of his life. As a kid, he used to dream about breathing underwater just fine. Anytime he dives now, he tells me, it's that same experience again: Breathing underwater feels totally natural to him, like returning to a normal state he doesn't get to experience in his land-based life. I, on the other hand, took classes to become scuba-certified when I was twenty. I panicked the first time I was asked to stay at the bottom of a swimming pool and breathe with a tank on, certain I was going to run out of air and die. I finally completed the two required dives to earn my certification but never dived again. Thirty years later, can I remember how to do this? Do I even want to?

I sign up for a refresher dive on Mo'orea while Frank makes plane reservations. The dive master is a retired Frenchman who is patient when we make our outing into Opunohu Bay. We start to descend and the panic grips me again. *I can't stay down here! I'll drown!* I give the thumbs-up gesture for us to return to the surface. "Something wrong?" he asks when we surface.

Okay, this is it. Either I decide I can and will dive, knowing that I'll be okay, or I decide this is too much for me. Which will it be?

"I just needed to calm myself," I tell him. "Let's try again." I try to slow my breathing and we descend. Five feet, ten feet, twenty feet. We swim along the bottom of the bay, looking at coral, tropical fish, sea cucumbers. I work to keep my breathing even and calm. After forty minutes, he gives me the thumbs-up. I can't lie: I'm relieved it's over. When I climb aboard the boat, though, I'm swelled with a feeling of accomplishment.

A few days later Frank and I take a ferry from Mo'orea to Papeete, then fly to Rangiroa, one of the largest atolls in the world. The lagoon's exceptionally clear water and the diverse marine fauna make this a major diving destination. We're staying with Frank's friend and fellow ecotour guide Ugo in a little cottage. Ugo recommends a local dive company and we make arrangements to do a drift dive through Tiputu Pass, one of two places where the larger ocean flows into and out of the Rangiroa lagoon. We will dive as the tide is changing and be carried by the current, viewing coral, sharks, barracuda, and amazing fish.

We are a group of six divers, one dive master, and a videographer to capture it all. I pair up with Frank as my buddy. The dive master warns us to be alert to the ascending current we'll hit about two-thirds of the way through the dive. We need to make sure we don't accidentally ascend with the current. Ascending too quickly causes decompression sickness, also known as the bends, which can lead to severe joint pain, unconsciousness, and even death. As we descend I stay focused on the magnificent coral and sea life. Frank, on the other hand, dives as though he's moving through his natural habitat, and I try to emulate him. The shifting tide carries us gently; it's like being on a ride in Disneyland with beautiful plants and creatures gliding past. I keep checking over my shoulder to make sure Frank's with me.

I'm pleased with how the dive is going, and the panic is just background noise. The dive master takes my hand. He guides me to a large rock and presses my hands on it, gesturing for me to stay put. Next, he brings another woman from our group over to the same rock and puts her in place as well. I don't know what's going on, but I'm sure it'll all make sense in a minute.

But a minute stretches into two. The girl looks equally puzzled and raises her shoulders. *Why are we here like this?* I glance around to locate my dive buddy. I don't see him.

I can't find the dive master either, nor the rest of the group. Just this girl next to me. I look up at the surface above. It's a long way up but I can still see the light streaming down through the layers of water. My depth gauge reads twenty-six meters. Eighty-eight feet. I've never been this deep.

What if the dive master doesn't come back for us? Maybe something happened to Frank and that's why I can't see him. Maybe I should make a break for the surface. But I breathe deep and try to rationalize. The dive master is a professional. He knows what he's doing. Frank has done this a million times. He's fine. I'm fine. I have enough air. Look at that coral over there. See how that fish has asymmetrical stripes. I focus on my meditation breathing. All is well. All is well.

It feels as though hours pass, though it's maybe only three or four minutes. Finally, the dive master returns and motions for us to follow him. I'm flooded with relief. I won't have to decide about making a break for the surface. We follow and before I know it, our group is reassembled and moving into a trench-like area where the current is moving much faster. We blend with the flow and are swiftly carried along. I am still struggling with surges of panic but also learning to relax. There are more sharks and barracuda and some of the weirdest fish I've ever seen. A Napoleon, also known as a humphead wrasse, swims by. A prehistoric cartoon fish, he's as big as three men, sports massive lips and looks like he belongs on *The Flintstones*. I'm so caught up with the strange creature I don't notice I'm ascending. The dive master catches my hand. He gestures for me to go back down. He points to the ocean's surface, awfully close.

Eventually, we ascend, stopping a few meters below the surface to acclimate for five minutes before heading all the way up and finding our boat. When I break the surface, I'm buffeted by waves and wind, but I'm excited. Yes, I was scared and nearly panicked, but I did it.

Back on the island, walking to town for lunch, Frank is harsh. "You need to pay more attention to your depth," he scolds. "If the dive master hadn't come and got you when you hit that ascending current, you would have been toast. That was a major fuckup."

I shrink an inch with each word. At lunch, I learn that during the period when I thought I'd lost Frank, he was right behind me, a few feet away. I couldn't see him because my tank obscured my vision. He had an eye on me every moment of the dive. And his scolding, I finally realize, is rooted in concern. If something happened to me, if I had ascended fully, I could have been seriously injured, maybe even killed. And he felt responsible. Still, I am deflated from our conversation and we have another dive scheduled for this afternoon.

We dive again after lunch and I agree to keep closer tabs on my depth. For once, I don't panic on the descent. I stay level with Frank and the dive master and pay closer attention to what's taking place all around me.

The next day, on our third dive, I'm really getting it. The day is stormy with showers. We are dropped off from the boat in the middle of massive waves and pelting rain. I descend without a problem and find the undersea world calm and disconnected from all the ruckus going on above.

- CHAPTER EIGHTEEN -
EVOLVE OR DIE

One does not discover new lands without consenting to
lose sight of the shore for a very long time.

—ANDRE GIDE

My time in French Polynesia has continued my "coming out" as a risk taker. I've determined, for instance, that I'm a dopamine fiend, willing to do almost anything to get that brain chemical that's fired up these new and novel experiences. For me, that highly satisfying risky-business neurotransmitter keeps me perpetually on the lookout for a new way to attain it. At the same time, though, as a result of a quarter century spent care-giving and nurturing, I am uncomfortable indulging this drive, as if it's something to be ashamed of.

While here on Mo'orea, I hang out at the UC Berkeley Gump Field Station, sharing space with students from universities around the world and their professors studying coral-reef ecology. I love the research vibe as teams of marine biologists study the effect of aggressive damselfish on the coral reef, and whether ocean sediment on algae makes a difference to the herbivorous fish that eat it. Others study the amazing coral regeneration currently taking place right before our eyes.

Prior to 2008, the coral reef surrounding this small triangular island had been subject to relatively few natural disturbances. The well-developed reef and lagoon were almost undisturbed. Then a pair of events changed everything. First, the migratory crown-of-thorns sea star, *Acanthaster planci* (many people know sea stars as starfish), moved into the area wholesale and ate all the coral it could get its greedy little teeth around. As a result, the sea star population swelled. When all the coral was gone, the crown-of-thorns population crashed with no remaining food source. Then in 2010 Tropical Cyclone Oli veered close to the tiny island, churning up the bay and destroying what few coral holdouts might have escaped the sea star invasion. The researchers were in a panic. Was this the end of the coral reef?

These two events radically changed the fragile ecosystem that supported not only the reef fish and mollusks that lived in the coral, but also the countless people who fed on the sea life and the fishermen who made their living catching them. A coral reef is basically the nursery of the ocean. Doom here foretells a much bigger problem.

But as the researchers came up with increasingly radical plans to try to change events, the elders on the island knew better and tried to tell the researchers that the story doesn't stop here. Don't fish in the lagoon, the elders said, and wait.

As a result of the devastated coral, the algae began to take over, thriving in sudden abundance where the coral had once been. Because of the massive, new surge of algae, the population of herbivorous fish who eat the algae was the next species to explode. Those same fish that the elders said to stop fishing in the lagoon then ate the algae back, thereby clearing the surface for a new generation of coral to take root in the fertile beds now free of the crown-of-thorns sea star hordes.

Sure enough, biodiversity began to reassert itself. The coral was coming back.

The scientists here set out every day with questions in mind and a plan of observation and experimentation to see if they can answer them. During the rainy season, work is suspended with the torrential downpours. But when the downpours calm and the silt settles and the waters clear, it's back to business studying life on and around the coral reef.

I love watching and talking with the scientists. I'm thrilled by the questions they ask, and the fact that they keep going out into the bay, time and again, until they either prove or disprove their theories, hoping, more than anything, to understand something new about the coral ecosystem. What I love most is the way they value their own curiosity and consider their explorations part and parcel of what they do. I want to adopt that attitude more in my own life, to not be so hesitant to step out of what I *do* know to explore what I don't.

I spend evenings in the open-to-the-elements house, draped in mosquito netting, watching TED lectures on my iPad. One night I happen on one by George Monbiot, the same journalist who wrote about the "era of loneliness" for *The Guardian.* His lecture focuses on the rewilding of Yellowstone National Park. This takes me immediately back to that stunning visit Rebecca and I shared last summer on our motorcycles, the grasslands and mountains and elk and bison we saw, the magnificence of the place.

Rewilding, like the natural regeneration taking place on the coral reef, speaks to me of rebirth and my own personal evolution. I start to see my risk-taking adventures as more than just crazy dopamine fixes I crave. Perhaps I am rewilding my own ecosphere.

Humans, Monbiot points out, evolved during times a lot more threatening than now. "We still possess the fear and the courage and the aggression to navigate those times," he says. But in our safe and comfortable lives, we don't get to experience that wilder side of ourselves. The dominant aim of industrialized societies has been to conquer uncertainty, to know what comes next. "We've privileged safety over experience and we've gained a lot in doing so, but I think we've lost something too."

He considers Yellowstone. During the seventy-year absence of wolves in the region, the elk population took over the park and ate almost all vegetation despite human intervention to control them.

Then, the wolves were reintroduced in 1995 with a pack of fourteen wolves at first, then seventeen more the following year. That was it. Thirty-one wolves added to the mix of this iconic park encompassing nearly thirty-five hundred square miles.

When the wolves were reintroduced, they hunted the elk, exactly as scientists had predicted. What wasn't expected was how the wolves' presence changed elk behavior. The elk now avoided parts of the park where they might be easily trapped, like valleys and gorges. Those places, in turn, started to regenerate. The valley sides, previously razed by elk, now sprouted forests. Songbirds and migratory birds returned, great flocks of them. The renewal didn't stop with the trees and the birds. The new abundance of trees meant more beavers, who in turn built dams that then provided a habitat for other creatures: otters, muskrats, fish, ducks, reptiles, amphibians.

In addition to culling elk, the wolves also stalked coyotes. The animals that are naturally prey to coyotes, like rabbits and mice, experienced population growth. In turn, they attracted hawks and weasels, foxes and badgers. The birds of prey were not far behind, happy to feed on the carrion created by the wolves. Bears, too, increased in number, also drawn by the carrion and new berries produced by the regenerating shrubs.

As a result of this handful of wolves, even the waterways changed because the regenerating forests stabilized the banks so that they collapsed less often. That meant that the rivers became more fixed in their course. "So the wolves, small in number, transformed not just the ecosystem of Yellowstone National Park, this huge area of land, but also its physical geography."

Hearing this, I can't help but wonder about the changes in my own life that have occurred in the past two years, allowing similar regeneration. By leaving my comfortable life and striking out on my own, I opened my life to predators against which I had set up barriers, barriers that I had in place my entire adult life. Now I would have to confront those predators. How would I pay the bills as a single mother with kids in college? What was I going to do about that rat under the sink? How would I deal with a broken-down car? Who was I going to talk to at 3:00 AM in the wake of a nightmare? How was I going to navigate my sexual behavior as a newly single woman?

Even to get to this place of questioning took wholesale destruction. But then again, the coral was all but destroyed by the sea star. The elk were culled by the hungry wolves. I left behind the family structure I'd spent twenty-five years building. Everything, decimated.

Looking out on the bay today takes me back to being a kid in Sequoia National Park. We camped there every year and trailed national park rangers as they taught us to distinguish between sugar, Jeffrey, and podgepole pines, identify the various birds, and understand the complex web that made up the coniferous forest. My favorites, of course, were the giant sequoias, the world's most massive trees. Even as a child, I felt a great affinity with them; something about my red hair seemed to connect us. I learned that tannin in the sequoia's bark gave it its distinctive red hue and protected it from insects and fire. The effects of past fires can be seen whenever you walk in a sequoia grove. Black scars, in some cases centuries old, mark every one of the larger trees, though I picture them as a badge of honor. I've seen several with the entire heart of the tree burned out, a cavity large enough to stand inside and look up through the shell, like a giant chimney, and view the sky. And yet, those burnt and disfigured trees continue to live. A ranger once told me that as long as one centimeter of the cambium layer running up the side of the tree remained unharmed, the tree could still regenerate. These trees are massive, the largest living things on Earth, and it takes only one unharmed centimeter for recovery.

Yet it has been man's misplaced efforts to enforce an unnatural degree of security that harmed the sequoia groves more than anything. Going back to the 1900s, the National Park Service mandated fire suppression. It was assumed that fire is a bad thing, a source of death and destruction. But life and nature are much more nuanced. It's hard to find things that are simply good or bad. We accept that water is the source of all life. Without it we die. And yet, through rain, ice, snow, and erosion, it's probably the most destructive natural force on the planet. The key role fire plays in the survival of sequoias (like the key role risk and sensation seeking play in my own life) was not apparent for a long time. But the truth is this: Without fire, sequoias cannot survive.

First, fire clears out excess underbrush, allowing sunlight to reach tiny sequoia seedlings. Then, in order to release their seeds, sequoia cones need to dry and open. Fire is the most effective agent for this process. Finally, the remaining ash makes a perfect natural fertilizer, creating the ideal soil bed for the newly released sequoia seeds.

Here on Mo'orea I experience wonderful write-the-folks-back-home kind of moments: swimming with sharks and stingrays, snorkeling the coral reef, drinking coconut water straight from the nut. There are also challenges, like the rains that wash the road away, requiring my help to rebuild it, mosquitos that swarm with their irritation and potential for Zika virus, the persistent stink of mildew. Fun in the sun and challenges in the rain come together, as happens in all of life. If I had come here as a tourist, I could have stayed in a deluxe hotel and insulated myself from much of the havoc. But I didn't ask for a tourist's experience of Mo'orea.

And I don't want a tourist experience of my life.

To partake in a rich life, I need biodiversity. I need both the respites of security and the moments of risk. The times I say "fuck it" and the times I buckle down and get to work. The times I sacrifice for my children, my job, my loved ones, and the times I claim my own moment in the sun. One side without the other is not balanced. My life, until now, has been one long surrender. That isn't good for me, for my children, my family, my friends. I have been only half alive. The only way to be truly present, I am learning, is first to be truly present to myself. To experience my wildness fully. To reintroduce risk and biodiversity. To ask question like the researchers. To not know. To risk the wolves, the fire, the sea stars. To be willing to evolve or die.

Any motorcyclist knows one truth as a fact of physics. When trying to make a tight turn, you cannot pull back and you cannot go halfway. If you fail to lean your full body weight into the turn, you will not make it. To survive, we have to take the counterintuitive approach. Lean into what scares you with all your might. Throw your body into that turn even when it feels like it will kill you.

CHAPTER NINETEEN

EIGHT DAYS IN PARADISE

> To dare is to lose one's footing momentarily.
> To not dare is to lose oneself.
> —SOREN KIERKEGAARD

The air temperature on the island of Mo'orea is eighty-four degrees at this very moment. There's a slight breeze. The water, not a thirty-second stroll from where I sit, is eighty degrees and the most crystalline turquoise I have ever seen, visibility measured in the tens of meters. I watch paddlers glide by in outrigger canoes. The occasional sailboat crosses the lagoon. Palm fronds shiver in the wind. A flying fish breaks the surface. The day is nearly silent. A coconut bobs on the water.

Be. Here. Now.

I look at my feet—where am I on this planet?— and repeat that three-word mantra. Because if I don't, I will ruin the eight days I have left here in paradise, thinking about, waiting for what has not yet, and may not ever, come to pass.

In the three months I've been here, getting the closest approximation of a suntan I'm ever likely to experience, I swim daily in Cook's Bay, visit sparsely populated atolls, wear a *pareu* around my hips and a flower in my hair, drink mango juice, and eat papayas from the tree outside my bedroom. This is the first time in nearly thirty years I've been away from the pressures of daily life.

Yet I want to go home.

And I want to kick myself for even having the thought.

Next week, when I return to my apartment in Los Angeles, I will go back to regular working hours and commuting through traffic. I have to schedule a dental appointment, deal with the contentious details of divorce and the sale of our family home, issues I've shelved by my absence. Who wants to go back to that?

Why then am I counting down the days until I climb aboard a jumbo airliner and fly back across the Pacific Ocean?

What's next? That seems to be the question I've been asking my entire life, unable, unwilling to stay with what *is*, expecting whatever's next to be better somehow than what's happening now. The grass is always greener. Except that it isn't. And I'm old enough to know better.

I remember being pregnant with Hope, my third child, and impatient at the end of the pregnancy. Can't we just get this over with already? Can't we move on to meeting this child and starting a relationship with her? There are times now when I wish I could go back there, to the exasperated, tetchy woman I had been and sit with her, experience fully the last time she'd ever feel a child move within her. Or the last time she'd nurse a child. Or the last time the family she'd created would live together under the same roof. But she can't.

I can't. I wished every one of those moments away, looking for what was next, and they are gone forever.

So why do I want to leave so badly now?

Part of the problem is a man.

• • •

I was doing research from Mo'orea into the neurotransmitter dopamine, a chemical I know plays a deep and abiding role in my yearning for adventure and risk. I was curious about the entire dopaminergic system and how it varies by individual in hopes of better under-standing what is driving me. Much of the research I found was difficult to digest without formal training in neuroscience. Then I happened upon the work of a biological anthropologist, Helen Fisher of Rutgers University. She is a human behavior researcher and has studied romantic interpersonal attraction for more than thirty years. I wasn't so much interested in the romantic part of her work, but her books gave succinct descriptions on how differing brain chemicals motivate us and our desires. Finally able to understand on a basic but cogent level how and why these chemicals do what they do, I was intrigued.

Fisher considers four brain chemicals key in determining personality traits. According to her model, dopamine is the chemical that drives "explorers" like me, those who seek novelty, who are willing to take risks, who thrive on curiosity, creativity, and spontaneity. Serotonin rules the roost with "builders," those who are conventional, calm, moral, respectful of authority, and rule-based. Those driven by testosterone tend to be "directors." Their traits are to be analytical, self-controlled, independent, competitive, and decisive. Estrogen, meanwhile, makes for "negotiators" who are social, intuitive, sympathetic, idealistic, tolerant, and agreeable. Though we all have both primary and secondary chemicals of these four that drive us, the primary chemical is the one she most closely focuses on.

Each of these four brain chemicals, she argues, can be traced back to their evolutionary roots across the eons. As our forebears became established in ancient Africa five million years ago, people with these different dispositions took on different roles in their communal groups. "The ancestors of contemporary Explorers roamed far into the dangerous grass, returning with meat, nuts, and information. The antecedents of today's cautious Builders guarded the group and gradually built the rituals of tribal life. The predecessors of our modern mechanically minded Directors invented better spears and traps and calculated the coming of the rains and waning of the moon. And the forebears of today's imaginative and intuitive Negotiators held the group together with their social skills," she explains.

Fisher then extrapolates who matches up with whom best romantically based on these chemicals, positing that explorers generally do best with other explorers (they become playmates together), as builders likewise thrive when paired with others like them. In these pairings, the *birds of a feather* concept is at work. On the other hand, directors generally do best with negotiators and vice versa, demonstrating the other adage, *opposites attract.*

She's careful to note two additional brain chemicals that should also be factored in: norepinephrine, a chemical closely related to dopamine, which undoubtedly contributes to some of the explorers' traits, especially their energy and impulsivity. And oxytocin, a chemical synthesized, stored and triggered (in large part) by estrogen. This is the same chemical Paul J. Zak will attempt to measure in me, both before and after riding the motorcycle. Oxytocin most likely plays a role in the negotiator's compassion, trust, and intuition. But none of these chemicals acts alone. Rather, families of chemicals produce the traits Fisher labels as explorer, builder, director, and negotiator, and the specific activities of any one chemical are not as significant as the ratios and interactions among all of them.

Nevertheless, only dopamine, serotonin, testosterone, and estrogen have been directly associated with a wide range of personality traits. The cocktail of these four chemicals most likely forms the foundation of these basic styles of thinking and belonging.

Fisher's research attracted the attention of an online dating service startup. They hired her to develop a questionnaire based on her theories of compatibility. The result was Chemistry.com, an online sister service of Match.com that operates similarly, but with pairings based on brain chemistry as its organizing principle. According to the Chemistry.com website, as of June 2013, more than eight million people have taken the Chemistry.com personality test. (You can, too: http://www.chemistry.com/lovemap/questionnaire.aspx).

Of course, being the curious explorer I am, I had no choice but to take the test. I signed up to see if what Fisher posited could be seen as true in my life. Keep in mind that during the time I've been single, I've set up numerous online dating profiles only to pull them down the moment emails started coming in. Being contacted by strange men was too odd and out of my frame of reference. I couldn't respond to a single one. But as long as I looked at Chemistry.com as a form of research, I figured I could explore this online dating world from the distance of four thousand miles with no real skin in the game, so to speak. Maybe I could develop some flirting chops after twenty-five years atrophying without having to actually *meet* anyone. The perfect training-wheels situation.

Except that I met someone. Another explorer, like me.

Only we haven't met.

R suggested we become "pen pals." Since I'd be out of the country for the next six weeks, I said yes. We've been writing and texting and emailing, exchanging photos, talking via a smartphone app. Every few days he talks about getting on a plane and flying to French Polynesia so we can finally meet. It's been so very long since someone has shown a deep interest and since I've been ready to get to know someone else.

I worry, though, in quiet times. If I wasn't so far away, I might not be as forthcoming. It's easy to fess up to all kinds of things when you're separated by this many miles and have no way to meet in person anytime soon. I tell him not to fly here; I'll be back in L.A. soon. He asks me to come home early and I'm considering it. Maybe the anonymity of the Internet is allowing a deeper intimacy to develop because it's not really real. And yet, I don't care. I'm having fun.

Still, from my research into Fisher's work, I learn more about explorers like me and this man with whom I'm in communication. It's like crack cocaine, the incessant flood of messages we're sending each other, inciting the need for more, more, more. I don't think I've ever dated an explorer before. That must be what has been missing in my life. If I'd known this magical stuff earlier, maybe I would have married a fellow explorer and my life would have been different.

I learn from Fischer that my sensation-seeking disposition is largely inherited. The gene labeled D4DR I mentioned earlier controls much of the dopaminergic system in the brain regions used for thinking, feeling, and motivation, and a specific allele of this gene is associated with several types of novelty seeking. "Old or young; male or female; rich or poor; educated in the ivory tower or in the mean streets: people who have inherited this gene in the dopamine system have an appetite for variety."

Contrary to popular belief, women in their teens and twenties are just as eager as men to chase new experiences, though they tend to prefer exploring nontraditional music, visual art, drugs, the intellectual fringes, and spiritual practices rather than physical challenges.

While, as we've seen, this hunger for adventure generally declines with age in both men and women as levels of dopamine decrease, older sensation seekers continue their exploration throughout their lifetimes by reading, traveling, going to the theater and movies, listening to music, attending arts events, and pursuing creativity in myriad ways. "Moreover," Fisher explains, "middle-aged women begin to score higher than men in overall sensation seeking. They buy more books. And they support the travel and leisure industry—cajoling their partners to accompany them to the Great Wall of China, Victoria Falls, Patagonia, or myriad local cultures."

She got that one right. And my interaction with this man is probably just another form of sensation seeking. Still, here I am, having this exchange and enjoying it all immensely. Our discussions are wide-ranging and interesting. He's smart and funny. I want to meet him, which will require ending my paradise hiatus, and risking the potential destruction of this innocent, just-getting-to-know-you phase.

How angry will I be if I return home early to find out this vacation romance was nothing of substance and that I squandered my last few days in paradise thinking about something that was only an illusion? And yet, from this perspective, it's all so alluring.

Be. Here. Now.

I know the truth: If it weren't for this romantic prospect, I would have found something else, some other "next" to draw me away from what's here and now. This is one of the downsides to being an explorer. We can be so optimistic that whatever's coming is going to be better than we have now that we fail to appreciate what *is* happening now.

Either way, things change. What was great at first becomes less great over time. What was skull-crushingly painful in the moment eventually heals. Nothing remains static. There will never be a day in my life with every detail lining up in perfect harmony so that I may capture that moment and press it in a book for posterity.

Besides, thinking about home is another channel to distraction. Being fully present, even in paradise, is not always easy. The three months I've been away have given me time to put things into perspective, to come to see who I am as a human in this world and to step away from that imagined mother I had created for the past twenty-six years. Being alone and mostly unable to converse with people for much of this time has been good for me. I have cried a lagoon worth of tears over the end of my marriage and how I should have known better, intervened sooner, been smarter, sexier, somehow changed the course of events. I have also missed my three grown children in a way that will be, I must remind myself, the new normal.

Be. Here. Now.

I tell R I need to stay until the end of my scheduled time away. I have few plans for the next eight days. Some writing. An afternoon swim. A walk or two. Everything seems to be winding down and that's the hardest time for me. I'm good at the planning stage. I'm less good at seeing things through. But that's what I'm hoping to do now. To feel the water as it's on my skin, smell the fruity air near the pineapple plantation, enjoy the warmth of the breeze and try not to wish I were somewhere else. Because we all know the truth: The moment I get home, I'll start wishing I was back here again.

So I keep reminding myself of today's reality. The air temperature on the island of Mo'orea in French Polynesia is eighty-four degrees right at this moment. There's a slight breeze blowing. The water is eighty degrees . . .

Be. Here. Now.

• • •

He walks into the neighborhood coffee shop and introduces himself. There's an awkward hug and kiss and the medicine ball slam of truth slams my solar plexus. I have been so misguided. How could I think I might know someone I'd never met? The clumsy reality is like a bad smell, filling the space between us. There's nothing here. No spark, no frisson. *Nada.* I spent that last six weeks in paradise obsessing over this person who is not at all whom I'd made him out to be.

It's a good lesson. If I have a strong enough desire, I can make anything over into what I want it to be. I made R into someone he's not in order to match my own desires and needs, and he did the same with me. I constructed and assembled him from the smallest of details: photos, the sound of his voice, a few of his stories. But I didn't *know* him. I created him whole cloth, the perfect man. Only he isn't. And it's taking this unpleasant shock of recognition to see that. We both see it.

I'm back in smoggy L.A. with no wonderful man after all, having left behind paradise in a rush. Be. Here. Now. I'm no longer on Mo'orea with its crystal-clear water, but my life is about to unfold in a new and bigger way. I will put this man behind me. Reclaim my little rental space. Light a candle. Dance around in the dark. Relish being single. Become aware of my intrinsic wholeness. Feel the pulse of my being.

CHAPTER TWENTY

FAILING (AND FALLING) BETTER

○

And the day came when the risk to remain tight in a bud
was more painful than the risk it took to blossom.

—ANAIS NIN

It's 9:00 AM on a frigid January morning in the town of Ouray, Colorado, population one thousand. Located ten miles northeast of Telluride (but a fifty-mile drive due to the severity of the landscape), Ouray is known as the "Switzerland of America" because of its setting at the narrow head of a valley, enclosed on three sides by steep, granite peaks. Dramatic mountains lurch up all around me, rising so fast from the valley floor I feel dizzy looking at them. The vistas seem even more intense through the spectral air. It's like Mo'orea, but for those who prefer snow. The cottages, shops, and steepled church are postcard-worthy, as are the people and dogs that briskly pass. Everyone has that burnished skin that comes from living in the cool clean air. I feel like I'm in a Patagonia catalog.

I should be drinking in this striking locale and all it has to offer. I should be soaking up its natural gorgeousness, breathing in the rugged magnificence of this planet and be filled with gratitude to be alive today.

But I'm not.

I'm sitting in a Subaru, trying to talk myself off a ledge. I have come to join in the Ouray Ice Festival, where participants take clinics in the finer points of ice-climbing, a sport that involves chopping and bashing up vertical frozen waterfalls. For the past half hour, a continuous stream of climbers has been walking past the car, anxious to get to the pitches to try out or improve their skills. They're all cinched into sturdy climbing harnesses, carabineers clanging from gear loops, helmets to protect precious brain matter. They carry their ice tools like gunslingers and clomp about in heavy boots fit with twelve-point crampons that sound like crushing pottery on the hard-pack snow.

Forty minutes ago, E, the man I've been dating, the very real man who is not a figment of my imagination nor made up from a rich tapestry of my wants and desires but a hands-on, *let's be in this together* kind of man, took off with a friend and their guide for an all-day backcountry climb. I am signed up for a novice ice-climbing class that starts at nine thirty and am trying to rally the nerve to put on my gear and step out of the car.

But it's warm inside the Subaru and cold and scary out there. The guys will be gone at least eight hours. There's no one to audit whether I go to the class or not. I could simply imply that I went and spend the next few hours scouring the adorable little town, drinking hot chocolate, petting the friendly dogs that seem everywhere, and try to stay warm.

Or I can gear up and go see what's what.

You would think that I've done enough crazy-ass stuff in the past few years that nothing I might undertake would really surprise me. That said, I'm still terrified of heights and until a few months ago would have sworn I'd never embrace any sport that involves heights and massive gravity consequences. Summits of any kind make me vertiginous, producing enough sweat to penetrate even multiple layers of clothing. My daughter, Hope, has been trying to lure me into skydiving with her for two years. But so far, no go. I can't get over the fright.

And yet, I am here.

E's unlike the other men I've dated in the two and a half years I've been single: the cop who lived on a sailboat, the surfer who built hotels, the college professor who was into photography. We clicked in a way that was new for me. Thus far, everything has been amazingly easy between us. I don't know if that's a good or bad thing, but I like the fact we share a love of outdoor sports and what others might term "extreme" activities. When I told a friend about him and how well things were going, explaining the backpacking, hiking, and trekking plans we were throwing around, she laughed. "He's just like you," she said, "only on steroids."

Two months ago he got me to try rock-climbing. We went to Point Dume in Malibu where a ninety-foot cliff rises vertically from the beach. We'd climbed its sloping backside to its top and there clipped in fat locking carabineers that created bomb-poof anchors for the climbing rope. As part of standard safety practice, he tied me into the anchor bolts as he worked. The air was barely warm and the ocean breeze took a bite, but the day was gorgeous. The afternoon sun was starting to lower over the ocean and a wedding party was setting up on the beach below. A photographer snapped pictures of the bride against the rugged rocks and ocean. Peeking over the edge, I hoped I wouldn't become a wedding crasher. I purposefully didn't think about the climbing I was going to attempt once the anchors were locked off and the rope was played out. There was no sense wasting all that energy on anxiety when I was going to need whatever strength I might rally to actually climb.

But as I sat there watching seagulls and pelicans sail on the air currents, I made up my mind about a few things. First, I decided that unless necessary, I was simply not going to look down when I climbed. Whenever I look down from a height and see how far I could fall or catalog all the ways I might hurt myself, that's when I freak out. I would just concentrate on moving up the rock face, one step at a time. Kind of like the way I've been navigating this relationship with E: not questioning what's happening, not thinking about what I stand to lose or how badly I might get my heart broken. I'm just trying to enjoy the minute-by-minute experience as it unfolds, knowing that everything has its season and nothing lasts forever. Learning, as I have, to just take things one moment at a time.

Second, if the rock-climbing becomes too scary or if I decide it's something I'm not comfortable with, I am going to speak up and stop. I no longer wish to participate in the "tap-dance for daddy" I've been doing all my life to impress men. No more. This will be *my* climb, if I do it at all, and E will have to accept me either way on my terms.

Back on the beach, I pull on a climbing harness for the first time in my life. Each leg goes through a loop of webbing that connects to the waist belt and the belay loop, the point at which a fist-size knot connects the rope to E, who will stay on the beach, maintaining tension on the rope to make sure I'm safe. If I take a fall or slip, his job will be to arrest the fall. He will do this by a technique called belaying—playing out the rope through a friction device on his harness as he watches me climb, prepared to brake my fall if I come off the rock.

My life will literally be in his hands.

I tighten my helmet and E has me repeat the set of verbal commands we'll use to make sure we are always on the same page. I quickly realize that the rope is not just a safety apparatus but an organic thing that transmits subtle messages between climber and belayer.

Behind me, the wedding guests have begun to seat themselves, the ceremony about to start. My feet are squeezed into climbing "slippers," soled with sticky rubber that, I assume, will cling to even the smallest nub or pocket in the rock. It's a matter of trust. The shoes will adhere to the rock and hold me, but only if I believe they will.

I place my first foot and stand up, pawing the rock for a handhold. Then I panic and grab for the rope, grateful for this tiny grasp of security. But the rope is there only to catch me if I fall, E reminds me, not for me to climb. I need to let it go and keep my hands and feet on the rock face itself.

I find an edge to place my foot and push upward again. The tiniest bit at a time, I'm doing it. One foot, then the other. An arm reaches, fingers feel for a thin crack. My foot searches the surface for an indent, finds one. I rise.

I'm so busy focusing on what I'm doing, I don't feel scared. E calls out directions: "To your left. Move your foot to your left." I do as instructed, and like a magic door opening, a placement appears. I move up farther and feel a thunderbolt of excitement. For this moment, I am strong and capable. I'm doing something I never dreamed I could do.

I step up to a thin slab and reach. The ascent is far from effortless, still there's no fear involved. But then, about thirty feet off the ground, my arms start to tire and my quads shake. I can't find the next foot placement. I'm stuck and I don't know what to do. I'm certain there's no way I can go farther.

"Just a couple of inches to either side," E calls. "Just move and you'll see a way."

I don't want to let go of this thin grip I've already got. Though it's tenuous, I can't let go even if it means I move up to something more secure. He keeps urging me to take a step. Tentatively, my fingers begin to scour the granite. The ocean is beating right below me but it's nothing compared to the pounding of my heart.

Don't. Look. Down.

When I don't find anything of substance to grab hold of, I reach out with one foot feeling for a flake or a grainy pocket. I keep replaying in my head the first rule of climbing, to keep three points of contact with the rock at all times. But I'm ready to give up. I believe I've reached my limit.

And then it appears, a tiny notch for my right foot. I push forward, moving up, and up some more.

Don't. Look. Down.

Like motorcycling. Like scuba diving. Like outrigger canoeing. Like entering a new relationship. Like learning a new language or writing a book or painting a landscape or writing some music. Don't. Look. Down. Keep climbing. Hold tight to that wonderful rock that beckons.

I keep ascending, continuing to amazing myself. My arms and legs shudder from the exertion and the surges of adrenaline. But this is how we learn. We can't be an expert the first time out. By the time I've climbed to our agreed high point, I'm spent. Instead of pretending I'm stronger than I am, I claim my limits, calling out to E. "That's it for today. I'm ready to come down."

He acknowledges and tells me to sit back in the harness so he can lower me, something I've never done and have never even seen someone else do. "Keep your feet wide and out in front of you," he calls. I try to do as instructed, but clearly I have not understood. Because I have climbed diagonally to the right, when I sit back, I have no idea the rope will pull me back to the left. I try to get my feet out in front of me, but fail. I get a harsh introduction to a new climbing term: *pendulum.*

Basically, I tumble and swing across the face of the rock. E immediately brakes my fall, but I'm free-swinging across the rock, slamming into the face, flipping nearly upside down, dangling. Fortunately my helmet absorbs the impact and I finally stop swinging some thirty above the beach. E directs me to right myself and spread my feet against the rock as he slowly lowers me to the sand.

My heart is pounding, my hands are sweaty. If I had known E longer than just a few weeks at that point, I may have burst into tears. I've had the wind knocked out of me, but mostly, I'm embarrassed.

He comes rushing to my side once I'm safely on the beach. "I am so sorry," E apologizes over and over. "I should have kept you on course. I should have prepared you better for coming down. I would never endanger you." He wraps me in a hug.

Other climbers come over to see if I'm okay. It's quickly clear that I'm only a bit shaken and then the timbre of the conversation shifts.

"Wow. That was spectacular!"

"Are you trying out for Peter Pan?"

"The whole wedding stopped to watch," someone mentions, gesturing to the wedding party where the nuptials have since resumed. He high-fives me.

Once the adrenaline passes, though, I realize that though I'm a bit bruised, I'm not genuinely injured. I tried something scary and survived the worst I could imagine—falling.

And I am okay.

In the following months, E takes me climbing at Red Rock outside of Las Vegas. Now that I've visualized that I can do this, I climb more fluidly and top out at a one-hundred-foot wall on the first attempt. A group of hikers pass below, stopping to watch and comment. I tune them out and keep my attention on where it needs to be: on the rock in front of me, finding a thin edge to support my shoe, then crimping an eroded knob with my fingertips.

Of course, knowing I have been safe in the past and able to do something scary doesn't mean that I am ready to do what's next. That's what I'm thinking as I now put on my harness and crampons in the cold Ouray air, adjust my helmet to go meet my ice-climbing class.

Ouray is the winter ice-climbing capital of the United States, home to the world's first dedicated ice-climbing park. Dozens of frozen waterfalls, refreshed nightly by sprinkler nozzles, create eighty- to two-hundred-foot-high climbing tests, winding through more than a mile of the Uncompahgre Gorge. The annual Ice Festival is a weekend extravaganza of competitions, exhibitions, and instruction with many of the world's top ice-climbers. It's basically a geeky Mardi Gras, just with frostbite.

I am obviously not among the elite climbers, only the rankest of beginners. Still, I know a few things. I know, for example, that vertical ice-climbing is accomplished with the use of crampons, pointy bear traps that clamp to the bottom of your boots, and ice axes, also known as ice tools. To ascend, climbers kick the front points of their crampons to create a platform on the vertical ice. They swing ice axes overhead to establish an anchor to step higher on the crampons. The strength of the ice is often surprising. Even if the axe pierces only a centimeter or so, that's enough to support a climber's weight. Again, the concept of trust is critical. It seems impossible that my ice tool, barely embedded into the ice, is enough to hold me—but it does. I'm learning to believe.

A young climbing pro, Anna Pfaff, teaches my class. Like most of the instructors, Anna has established a reputation as an ice-, rock-, and alpine-climber who spends months each year trekking and climbing in Nepal, Patagonia, and throughout the Rockies. My fellow students include another middle-aged woman who recently moved to the Ouray area to work on her ice-climbing skills, and three men, two of whom are surgeons. There's a connection, I see again, between those who like to take risks. I shouldn't be surprised when I learn that our teacher is also an ER trauma nurse.

Anna is patient and gentle as she explains the "syllabus." First, we'll climb just a small way using only our crampons without the benefit of ice tools at all. She demonstrates how, when the points of her crampons are securely planted, she can stand and rest comfortably along the face of a frozen waterfall. No hands necessary. She wants us to learn to trust our legs, to see how vital their strength is.

The next exercise is to climb with only one ice tool, to learn how to securely place the pick and to realize we can get by with less security than we think we need. That one centimeter of penetration is all it takes to hold me. I recall the massive sequoia trees and how one undamaged centimeter of bark running up the tree's trunk is enough for it to survive and thrive. Soon, after we've worked on the one-handed technique, Anna says we now can use both tools.

She notes that men tend to overrely on brute arm strength. "Women, on the other hand, learn early on to trust their legs because they know they're never going to have the same kind of upper-body strength." Women tend to excel at ice-climbing because many have studied dance or possess excellent balance, poise, and flexibility. They can do moves that men will never be able to do. The only way a man can execute the same maneuvers is to compensate with brawn. But for newbies, that can be a mistake. Anna sees it all the time: Men start climbing and relying on their arms to pull them up. So much work! So much wasted energy! While at the same time, a much smaller woman will pass all the guys. "Don't be one of those guys who think he can power his way up," she calls out. "Use your legs."

We pair off and belay each other. I work on my tripod position: two legs firmly planted, supporting me, one ice tool reaching up. Two feet, one arm. Two feet, next arm. When I sustain this rhythm, I move smoothly. However, I do not look down. The ice routes surrounding us are filled with other classes; about 40 percent of the students are women. This is one sport where men do not have much of an advantage. I am getting higher and higher. Punching the points of the crampons, it feels as if my feet have superpowers, holding me in place on the vertical ice wall. Little spurts of exhilaration keep me company as I climb.

The thing I have to monitor with ice-climbing (like motorcycling, parenting, dating, and life as a whole) is how anxiety can make things much harder than they need to be. When I get scared, I tend to hold on too tightly and deplete precious energy. The solution, many propose, is to relax, simply loosen my grip.

A climbing magazine article by Brian Rigby observes that stress itself is usually the culprit. I know from my own life that when I'm uncomfortable with anything (and this goes beyond ice-climbing), I experience a stress response, which in turn creates physiological changes. My heart rate and breathing increase. I switch from the slow-burning aerobic system, which runs primarily off stored fat, to the faster anaerobic system, which is primarily fueled by carbohydrates. My core body temperature rises and I sweat. Adrenaline provides sudden bursts of energy and mediates these changes.

If the only time I experience this stress response is at the height of exertion, then the adrenaline burst is productive and necessary. But my anxiety and fear elicit these changes long before I ever leave the ground.

Anxiety is the enemy. Increased mental stress causes this whole adrenaline-boost package to get to work. Novice climbers (novices at anything) begin a task with their systems already stressed, experiencing the same physiological state that more advanced athletes encounter only during difficult passages. Instead of moving smoothly through the easier parts of a climb and reserving my stamina for the tougher pitch, I waste precious energy.

This premature release of adrenaline causes my body to rely on carbohydrates for fuel, which in turn creates an increase in blood lactate that causes muscle burn. My endurance evaporates, my resolve to continue dies, I feel fatigued when, in reality, I haven't yet done anything *that* demanding.

This is normal, I have to remind myself. It does not mean I shouldn't continue, only that I'm spending a lot of energy on anxiety. And this anxiety sends my body faulty signals about how hard I'm working and creates the sensation of premature fatigue. Though my actual strength might be unaffected, the increase in body temperature signals me to slow down so that my core temperature can decrease. Everything in my chemical makeup tells me I need to stop.

The lesson applies beyond the waterfall of ice. If I focus on lessening my anxiety, then I will reduce all the negatives associated with it. My metabolism will edge back toward burning fat, my core temperature will cool, and I will experience the climb (or whatever else I might attempt) as a realistic interpretation of its actual difficulty and my abilities. I will live my life more fully.

So what are we to do about this? As newcomers to whatever activity we select, we cannot just will ourselves to have zero anxiety. But we can learn to recognize that anxiousness and try to manage and understand it. As I continue to face new challenges that scare me and gain confidence in one pursuit, that emboldens me in other realms. Nothing is wasted.

Plus, there are ways to manage the terror. First, I can identify the source of my anxiety. Am I afraid I'll fall? Okay, I can practice falling on the route to assure myself that I'll be all right. Does it freak me out that others are watching? Then I can climb when fewer people are around. Am I doing something I know I'm not yet prepared to do? If that's the case, I can stay within my limits until I feel ready to move forward.

Next, I need to give myself permission to fail. The more pressure I put on myself to perform, the greater my anxiety. When I give myself permission to fail and remove my own self-imposed goals, I'm more likely to succeed. *Lessen your expectations* has become my new mantra.

Third, I can practice. According to a 2007 applied physiology study, simply repeating a climbing route just one time decreased anxiety by 16 percent. Repeating it numerous times reduces anxiety further. (I liken this to making pancakes. You know how the first one is always kind of thin and pathetic and not as yummy as later ones? My early efforts on any given day are early pancakes. As I get increasingly comfortable with what I'm doing, my ability to relax and let go of anxiety will increase.)

For some people, creating rituals before and/or after difficult activities can help. My son, when dealing with a severe anxiety disorder in high school, would reward himself with Skittles for making it through each class. I sometimes light a candle before sitting down to write a difficult passage. We may laugh at such superstitions, but they often work.

Finally, it's helpful to keep in mind that the stress I'm experiencing is an adaptive response. We experience these physiological changes because they're intended to increase our strength, focus, and drive, giving us the energy we need to succeed. If I'm anxious, I can concentrate on how the stress response is going to help. It focuses me, energizes me, keeps me on my toes.

Brian Rigby, the author of the climbing magazine article, cites his own experience as a rock-climber. Over time, as his level of anxiousness eased, he says he rarely gets stressed. He is also able to see when his ego is pushing him to do something he's not ready to do, or when peer pressure nudges him beyond his skill level. He reminds himself that the experience is not about the outcome of a climb and that failure just means he's pushing his limits and learning new things. "I am still in a battle with my ego which drives me to perfection, but the good thing is that now I have tools to work with my inner chatter," which means that he's able to focus on progression instead of perfection.

Though I was not so thrilled about falling at Point Dume on the beach, as I climb now on the ice in Ouray and find my rhythm, I discover reasons to be grateful for that experience. I know that if I fall, my belay partner will catch me. I know that if I ride my motorcycle five thousand miles across the country and back, the road will bring me home. If I paddle an outrigger canoe across the Sea of the Moon, scuba-dive off a remote Pacific atoll, or leave the security of marriage, I will land on my feet. If I try to build a relationship with a new man, not knowing how or if things are going to work out, I believe I can recover from whatever heartbreak might be in store. And I can open my heart to whatever joy might be lurking in the possibility of couplehood. I need never again stay in an unhappy relationship simply because I'm too afraid to strike out on my own.

As a result of these passages, I have come to envision the entire universe as a benevolent system that has me in a kind of climbing harness and continues to tether me on a safety line. I can make poor choices, reaching too far, not getting my crampon in deep enough, misjudging the ice's stability. Yet I know that the harness is there and the rope will catch me.

I consider all the tough lessons that have made this fact evident to me. I add them up. The still-unfolding divorce, the death of my father, the suicide of my friend's teenage son just days before little Ronan died from Tay-Sachs, the car accident with the ninety-one-year-old man, the tears I've shared with my children as we've navigated a new family structure. And before those challenges, there was the mental illness and then death of my mother, a teen pregnancy, my son's near drowning, J's pulmonary embolism that almost killed him, the foreclosure that cost us our house, my son's anxiety disorder.

The list goes on. Because this is life. We're here to learn and expand and grow. The only way that happens is when life challenges us. Unlike what many of us think, life isn't about finding a safe place, getting all our details nailed down, and then holding it all, like a tableau stuck in time.

It's about chance and risk and failing better.

And yet, for the first time, I finally feel the tug of the rope that keeps me anchored, the sense that some kind of higher power, some God, the universe, whatever you want to call it, some compassionate and generous force is belaying me, keeping an eye, and is there to catch me when—not *if*—I fall. And that allows me to fly.

Security is mostly a superstition. Life is either
a daring adventure or nothing.
—HELEN KELLER

Rebecca rides my motorcycle while I drive my car the thirty-six miles
east of Los Angeles to Claremont to meet up with neuroeconomist
Paul J. Zak. I'm driving so as not to "contaminate" my blood before
he can take a baseline reading. He's going to test my blood, before
and after riding, for three hormones: oxytocin, testosterone, and
ACTH (adrenocorticotropic hormone, a fast-acting stress hormone
that's a precursor to cortisol).

I follow Rebecca eastbound on the Foothill Freeway and get a
chance to admire my elegant dame, Izzy Bella. As she moves poetically
through traffic, I realize I am not the same person I was three years
ago when I first cautiously lowered my weight onto a motorcycle. I
approach life with a new kind of zest and enthusiasm. I feel emotions
more keenly than before, even the tender and excruciating ones.
According to researchers at Stanford University, the human body
replaces itself with a largely new set of cells every seven to ten years, and
some of our most important parts are revamped even more rapidly.

Whether it's replenishing lung cells, shedding skin, or sprouting new hair, the human body is in a state of constant flux and change.

If my recent experiences are any indication, my psyche is going through a rejuvenation, too.

Change of some sort would have been inevitable. The fact that I have transformed in ways that please and make me feel more whole as a human, though, is due unequivocally to this grand venture into risk taking.

Risk, as a concept, has a hard time of it in our thoroughly pre-planned society. Yet taking risks is central to who we are as humans. If you're like me, though, you may have bought into the philosophy that settling your life and planning to the utmost what your future holds is what we should strive for. Most regard this as the ultimate badge that we are grown-ups.

It's time to reconsider that myth.

• • •

When I meet Zak, the first thing he does is apologize for not hugging me. He's a well-known hugging advocate and claims he can prove that embracing a person for twenty seconds can increase oxytocin levels and make both parties feel better and more predisposed to trust. Since we don't want to spike my oxytocin level, then, no hugs until the blood work is done.

He sends me into a quiet room where I sit alone for ten minutes. This is to "quarantine" me from any social interaction I might have with Zak, Rebecca, or Zak's research assistant that could influence the results. He then takes the "before" blood sample and sends me out into the parking lot to ride my motorcycle for about twenty minutes.

I ride along a portion of historic Route 66. Compared to Los Angeles traffic, it's a quiet stretch of road along the foothills, and as I zip along, I enjoy the scented oils from the eucalyptus trees and a feeling of being in command of my bike. I encounter only a few cars and the ride passes without incident.

When I return to the little Craftsman house that's been converted into the Center for Neuroeconomic Studies, Zak takes another blood specimen. Before we say good-bye, he feels it's okay to indulge a big bear hug.

• • •

Months pass and the results finally come in. According to Zak, they make an amazing amount of sense.

My oxytocin level is up 18 percent after riding the bike. I remember from Zak's book that he took blood samples before and after the vows at a wedding. While my oxytocin didn't elevate quite as high as the bride or the bride's mother, I'm on par with the groom. Either way, it's a sizable increase.

ACTH, the fast-acting stress hormone, is up only 8.3 percent, which means I'm a very relaxed rider. Zak is amazed I had such a nominal increase while on the bike. He'd expected to see a 30 to 50 percent increase from such a focused, strenuous activity. "This is evidence that you are 'one with the bike,'" he says, "like it's an extension of your body and you feel natural using it."

The testosterone numbers are equally interesting. My pre-ride test established a baseline of 18.5 nanograms per deciliter (ng/dl), what would be expected in the midrange for women my age. But after riding the motorcycle, my testosterone actually dipped to 15 ng/dl. We are both surprised.

"Why did it fall?" he asks rhetorically. "We know you weren't stressed, which can reduce testosterone levels." He thinks that one possible interpretation is that I was so relaxed that I didn't need to show off or preen.

So, I ask him, what's the major takeaway?

"As you hypothesized, it seems like riding your cycle is a social activity from the brain's perspective. We don't know about others, but for you, for that particular ride, your brain was receiving positive social information from those around you, which is the only way your brain makes oxytocin, other than birth, breastfeeding, or sex—all of which I'm pretty sure you didn't do during your ride!"

"But wait," I interrupt. That doesn't seem right. I didn't feel social or aware of other people on the ride at all. I bring up the hypothesis we'd discussed a year earlier, about the moving shapes in the You-Tube video and having a relationship with the bike. Does he think that theory no longer holds?

"Did I really say that?" he laughs. "It's either brilliant or stupid, I'm not sure which." He's going to have to think about it.

If that's not the reason, I speculate, maybe my level jumped because I'm having a relationship with myself. Maybe oxytocin increases when one is authentic and present with one's self.

While that's a supposition he's heard before, Zak says it's difficult to test experimentally. Scientists in the last twelve to fifteen years have seen that the only way to cause the brain to make oxytocin is to have a positive *social* interaction, something that requires the participation of others.

Still, it's possible, he says. "We can't rule it out."

He's quiet for a bit. I can almost hear the gears turning in his mind. "What I said last year, about the moving shapes? It sounds sort of smart." His voice begins to rise as he puts the pieces together. "If it's the relationship with the bike, it makes total sense. You're relaxed. Your stress level's dropped. The drop in testosterone is small, but yes, you're one with this machine. It's as if you're having a relationship with it, a bonding experience."

All the markers are there, he tells me. It's like you are sitting on the couch holding hands and watching TV with this machine.

The human brain, he tells me, is in a very real sense, a lazy organ. It gives us systems meant for one purpose that can be used for others. We evolved this oxytocin-based care and nurturing system to raise our young. But it also manifests with animals in that pained feeling we get when we see a bird fall out of its nest, or the way we feel calmed when we pet a cat or play with a dog. There's no reason this same brain system couldn't develop a relationship with a dynamic machine that moves, takes us places, that we have experiences with.

When the results first came in, I tell him, I posted them on my Facebook page. A number of people wrote to tell me how confirming the information was. One said he'd been trying for years to explain to people the feeling he gets while riding and no one got it.

"Holy crap: That's cool!" Now Zak's really animated. "It gives us a little more confidence that's the right interpretation."

He thinks it through out loud. "A motorcycle is moving and can create a very intimate experience. There it sits, between your legs, an intimate a part of you. It responds to your commands. And the motorcycle is more than just the bike itself. A rider is connected to a community of riders."

As such, he decides, it's not inconceivable that a person might have a bonding (therefore oxytocin-spiking, dopamine-enriching) experience with a motorcycle.

But there are caveats. We did this experiment on only one rider on one particular day. As the rider in question, I was aware of the results I was hoping to see. It's far from a scientific trial that can prove anything, but it hints at an explanation. Despite the lack of methodical validity, it's enough evidence for me.

Oxytocin is an amazing molecule that helps humans in a multitude of positive ways: increasing generosity, putting us at ease, reducing social fears, decreasing pain, and acting as an antidepressant. Oxytocin naturally enhances a sense of optimism, trust, mastery, and self-esteem.

But here's the cool part: I get to create it in my own brain. Thanks to cooperative brain chemicals and the wonders of neuroplasticity, and thanks especially to my motorcycle, I have become a new person.

But risk itself gets the true credit. Without the risk that got me on the bike in the first place, I would likely be deficient in oxytocin, in all kinds of positive brain chemicals, deficient in my full response to this life I've been graced with.

Perhaps it's time we redefine risk to include its upside. We know that risk is not just the possibility that something bad or unpleasant will happen, but the certainty that something new and unexpected will occur. Our brains and bodies are biochemically programmed to thrive on change. Challenge will open up and show us a new side of ourselves. If, as science has demonstrated, all the cells in our bodies are made new every seven to ten years, it make sense that our brains, our psyches, our self-images might undergo a similar transformation. In my own case, I feel like I'm almost halfway through that complete transformation.

ACKNOWLEDGMENTS

Like every challenging journey in life, writing a book takes the support and love of countless people. I am blessed in having many sources of light and love in my life.

For teaching me about fearlessness and risk taking at the most core level, my three stellar children, Jarrod, Neil, and Hope, are unparalleled.

I am grateful for all in my literary community who hold me close and keep me sane, especially Tara Ison, who has to convince me regularly to keep going; agent Bonnie Nadell, who keeps pointing me in the right direction; and editor Dan Smetanka, who helps me find home. Counterpoint Press was stellar in its support of this book. I especially thank publicist Megan Fishmann, copyeditor Mikayla Butchart, and publisher Rolph Blythe for their loving attention to my work. Literary sojourners who carried me on this path include Emily Rapp Black, Nina Revoyr, Felicia Luna Lemas, Charles Flowers, Rob Roberge, Jillian Lauren, Lynell George, Victoria Patterson, Gayle Brandeis, Christine Hale, Brad Kessler, Patrick O'Neil, Craig Clevinger, Rae Dubow, Patrick McGowan, Kitty Nard, and Edmond Stevens.

Doctors Edward and Leah Schneider gave me a gorgeous above-a-garage abode when I needed it. Thank you for your hospitality and generosity.

My brother Frank and his wife, Hinano, lured me to Mo'orea, French Polynesia, during the writing of this book, a gift I treasure greatly, while the staff of the UC Berkeley Gump Field Station and the Atitia Cultural Center on Mo'orea welcomed me with great hospitality on that beautiful island.

Many friends held my hand when I felt shaky, including Joseph Argazzi, Tom Haskins, Brad Griffith, Juliana Jones-Munson, and all the folks at Hollywood and Gardner.

I owe an eternal debt of gratitude to Emily Shokouh and everyone at Harley-Davidson of Glendale, in particular Oliver Shokouh, Ernie Snair, Maddeson Kline, Lee Hanes, Mario Vindeni, and Kiersten Cherry. Thanks to Edna and George Clingerman and Donna Kaminsky for riding to and around Milwaukee with me, and to Roger and Crystal Graves, Amy and Jim Anderson, and Sue and Russ Kahler, who gave me a place to stay as I traveled.

I am grateful to the students, faculty, and administration of Antioch University Los Angeles for supporting my efforts and being a beacon of hope.

And finally, for my father, who said I could be anything I wanted. I don't think you had motorcyclist and *divorcée* in mind, but I hope this book might please you all the same.

BIBLIOGRAPHY / REFERENCES

BOOKS

Apter, Michael J. *The Dangerous Edge: The Psychology of Excitement.* New York: Free Press, 1992.

Barger, Sonny. *Let's Ride: Sonny Barger's Guide to Motorcycling.* New York: William Morrow, 2011.

Books-Dalton, Lily. *Motorcycles I've Loved.* New York: Riverhead Books, 2015.

Brizendine, Louann. *The Female Brain.* New York: Random House, 2007.

Cloninger, C. Robert. *Feeling Good: The Science of Well-Being.* New York: Oxford University Press, 2005.

Csikszentmihalyi, Mihaly. *Flow: The Psychology of Optimal Experience.* New York: Harper & Row, 1990.

Fisher, Helen. *Why Him? Why Her?: Finding Real Love by Understanding Your Personality Type.* New York: Henry Holt, 2009.

Gallagher, Winifred. *New: Understanding Our Need for Novelty and Change.* New York: Penguin, 2010.

Holbrook Pierson, Melissa. *The Perfect Vehicle: What Is It About Motorcycles.* New York: W. W. Norton & Co., 1998.

Ison, Tara. *Reeling Through Life: How I Learned to Live, Love and Die at the Movies.* Berkeley: Soft Skull Press, 2015.

Joans, Barbara. *Bike Lust: Harleys, Women and American Society.* Madison: University of Wisconsin Press, 2001.

Kay, Katty, and Shipman, Claire. *The Confidence Code: The Science and Art of Self-Assurance—What Women Should Know.* New York: HarperBusiness, 2014.

Lyng, Stephen. *Edgework: The Sociology of Risk-Taking.* London: Routledge, 2004.

McBee, Randy D. *Born to Be Wild: The Rise of the American Motorcyclist.* Chapel Hill: The University of North Carolina Press, 2015.

Northrup, Christiane. *The Wisdom of Menopause: Creating Physical and Emotional Heath During the Change.* New York: Bantam, 2012.

Rapp, Emily. *Poster Child: A Memoir.* New York: Bloomsbury USA, 2006.

———. *The Still Point of the Turning World.* New York: Penguin Press, 2013.

Strayed, Cheryl. *Wild: From Lost to Found on the Pacific Crest Trail.* New York: Vintage, 2013.

Thompson, Hunter S. *Hell's Angels: A Strange and Terrible Saga.* New York: Ballantine Books, 1996.

Tsing Loh, Sandra. *The Madwoman in the Volvo: My Year of Raging Hormones.* New York: W. W. Norton & Co., 2004.

Zak, Paul J. *The Moral Molecule: How Trust Works.* New York: Plume, 2013.

Zukerman, Marvin. *Sensation Seeking and Risky Behavior.* Washington, DC: American Psychological Association, 2007.

SCHOLARLY ARTICLES

Brown, Susan L., and I-Fen Lin. "The Gray Divorce Revolution: Rising Divorce Among Middle-Aged and Older Adults 1990–2010." Working Paper Series, WP-13-03, National Center for Family & Marriage Research, Bowling Green State University, March 2013. https://www.bgsu.edu/content/dam/BGSU/college-of-arts-and-sciences/NCFMR/documents/Lin/The-Gray-Divorce.pdf.

Dreber, Ann, and David G. Rand, et al. "Dopamine and Risk Preferences in Different Domains: Faculty Research Working Paper Series." Faculty Research Working Paper Series, RWP10-012, Harvard Kennedy School, April 2010. https://research.hks.harvard.edu/publications/getFile.aspx?Id=529.

Frias, Araceli, and Philip C. Watkins, et al. "Death and Gratitude: Death Reflection Enhances Gratitude." *The Journal of Positive Psychology* 6, no. 2 (March 2011): 154–62.

Grucza, Richard A., and C. Robert Cloninger, et al. "Novelty Seeking as a Moderator of Familial Risk for Alcohol Dependence." *Alcoholism: Clinical and Experimental Research* 30, no. 7 (July 2006): 1176–83.

Josefesson, Kim, Markus Jokela, and C. Robert Cloninger; et al. "Maturity and Change in Personality: Development Trends of Temperament and Character in Adulthood." *Development and Psychopathology* 25, no. 3 (2013): 713–27.

Kajtna, Tanja, and Matej Tušak, et al. "Personality in High-Risk Sports Athletes." *Kinesiology* 36, no. 1 (May 2004): 24–34.

Keltikangas-Järvinen, Liisa, and Markus Jokela. "Nature and Nurture in Personality." *Focus: The Journal of Lifelong Learning in Psychiatry* 8, no. 2 (spring 2010): 180–86.

Meyer, Patricia. "'We're Just Women Who Like to Ride': An Ethnographic Journey on a Woman's Motorcycle." PhD diss., Department of Speech Communication, Southern Illinois University Carbondale, August 2009.

Thomas, William E. "Don't Call Me 'Biker Chick': Women Motorcyclists Redefining Deviant Identity." *Deviant Behavior* 33, no. 1 (2012): 8–71.

Vail, Kenneth E. III, et al. "When Death Is Good for Life: Considering the Positive Trajectories of Terror Management." *Personality and Social Psychology Review* 16, no. 4 (November 2012): 303–29.

Zuckerman, Marvin, Sybil Eysenck, and H. J. Eysenck. "Sensation Seeking in England and America: Cross-Cultural, Age, and Sex Comparisons." *Journal of Consulting and Clinical Psychology* 46, no. 1 (1978): 139–49.

MAINSTREAM ARTICLES

Firestone, Robert. "Life-Affirming Death Awareness." *The Human Experience* (blog), *Psychology Today*, March 26, 2010, https://www.psychologytoday.com/blog/the-human-experience/201003/life-affirming-death-awareness.

Halterman, Todd. "This is Your Brain on a Motorcycle." *Sometimes Nothing . . .* (blog). February 15, 2012. http://www.sometimesnothingisarealcoolhand.com/2012/02/this-is-your-brain-on-a-motorcycle/.

Harley-Davidson Motor Company. "Study: Women Have a Powerful Option to Find Happiness in 2014." December 27, 2013. http://www.harley-davidson.com/en_US/home/events/press-release/general/2013/news126.html.

Kay, Katty, and Shipman, Claire. "The Confidence Gap." *The Atlantic*, May 2014. http://www.theatlantic.com/magazine/archive/2014/05/the-confidence-gap/359815/.

LeVan, A. J. "Happiness Is Risky Business: 5 Best Practices of Happy Risk-Takers." *Flourish!* October 22, 2012.

McGill University. "Alcoholism Could Be Linked to Hyper-Active Brain Dopamine System." *ScienceDaily*. August 2, 2013. http://www.sciencedaily.com/releases/2013/08/130802131843.htm.

Monbiot, George. "The Age of Loneliness Is Killing Us." *The Guardian.* October 14, 2014. http://www.theguardian.com/commentisfree/2014/oct/14/age-of-loneliness-killing-us.

Park, Alice. "Why We Take Risks—It's the Dopamine." *Time.* December 30, 2008. http://content.time.com/time/health/article/0,8599,1869106,00.html.

Patoine, Brenda. "Desperately Seeking Sensation: Fear, Reward, and the Human Need for Novelty." The Dana Foundation. October 13, 2009. http://www.dana.org/News/Details.aspx?id=43484.

Rauch, Jonathan. "The Real Roots of Midlife Crisis." *The Atlantic.* December 2014. http://www.theatlantic.com/magazine/archive/2014/12/the-real-roots-of-midlife-crisis/382235/.

Roberts, Paul. "Risk." *Psychology Today.* November 1, 1994; November 20, 2015. https://www.psychologytoday.com/articles/199411/risk.

Thomas, Susan Gregory. "The Gray Divorcés." *Wall Street Journal.* March 3, 2012. http://www.wsj.com/articles/SB10001424052970203753704577255230471480276.

Tsing Loh, Sandra. "The Bitch Is Back." *The Atlantic.* October 2011. http://www.theatlantic.com/magazine/archive/2011/10/the-bitch-is-back/308642/.

University of Missouri–Columbia. "The Bright Side of Death: Awareness of Mortality Can Result in Positive Behaviors." *ScienceDaily,* April 30, 2012. http://www.sciencedaily.com/releases/2012/04/120430164359.htm.

Veselka, Vanessa. "Green Screen: The Lack of Female Road Narratives and Why it Matters." *The American Reader* 1, no. 4 (February/March 2013). http://theamericanreader.com/green-screen-the-lack-of-female-road-narratives-and-why-it-matters/.

Williams, Florence. "This Is Your Brain on Adventure." *Outside.* March 19, 2009. http://www.outsideonline.com/1896581/your-brain-adventure.

Young, Larry, and Brian Alexander. "Chemistry Makes Us Cheat." *Salon.* September 11, 2012. http://www.salon.com/2012/09/11/chemistry_makes_us_cheat/.

Zuckerman, Marvin. "Are You A Risk Taker?" *Psychology Today.* November 1, 2000; July 17, 2012. https://www.psychologytoday.com/articles/200011/are-you-risk-taker.

TED TALKS

Brown, Brené. "Listening to Shame." Filmed March 2012. TED video, 20:38. http://www.ted.com/talks/brene_brown_listening_to_shame.

————. "The Power of Vulnerability." Filmed June 2010. TED video, 20:19. http://www.ted.com/talks/brene_brown_on_vulnerability.

Fisher, Helen. "The Brain in Love." Filmed February 2008. TED video, 15:56. http://www.ted.com/talks/helen_fisher_studies_the_brain_in_love.

————. "Why We Love, Why We Cheat." Filmed February 2006. TED video, 23:27. http://www.ted.com/talks/helen_fisher_tells_us_why_we_love_cheat.

Jobs, Steve. "How to Live Before You Die." Filmed June 2005. TED video, 15:04. http://www.ted.com/talks/steve_jobs_how_to_live_before_you_die.

Monbiot, George. "For More Wonder, Rewild the World." Filmed July 2013. TED video, 15:10. http://www.ted.com/talks/george_monbiot_for_more_wonder_rewild_the_world.

Nyad, Diana. "Extreme Swimming with the World's Most Dangerous Jellyfish." Filmed October 2011. TED video, 16:57. http://www.ted.com/talks/diana_nyad_extreme_swimming_with_the_world_s_most_dangerous_jellyfish.

————. "Never, Ever Give Up." Filmed December 2013. TED video, 15:35. http://www.ted.com/talks/diana_nyad_never_ever_give_up.

Zak, Paul. "Trust, Morality—and Oxytocin?" Filmed July 2011. TED video, 16:34. http://www.ted.com/talks/paul_zak_trust_morality_and_oxytocin.